MW01631009

Tattooed Walls

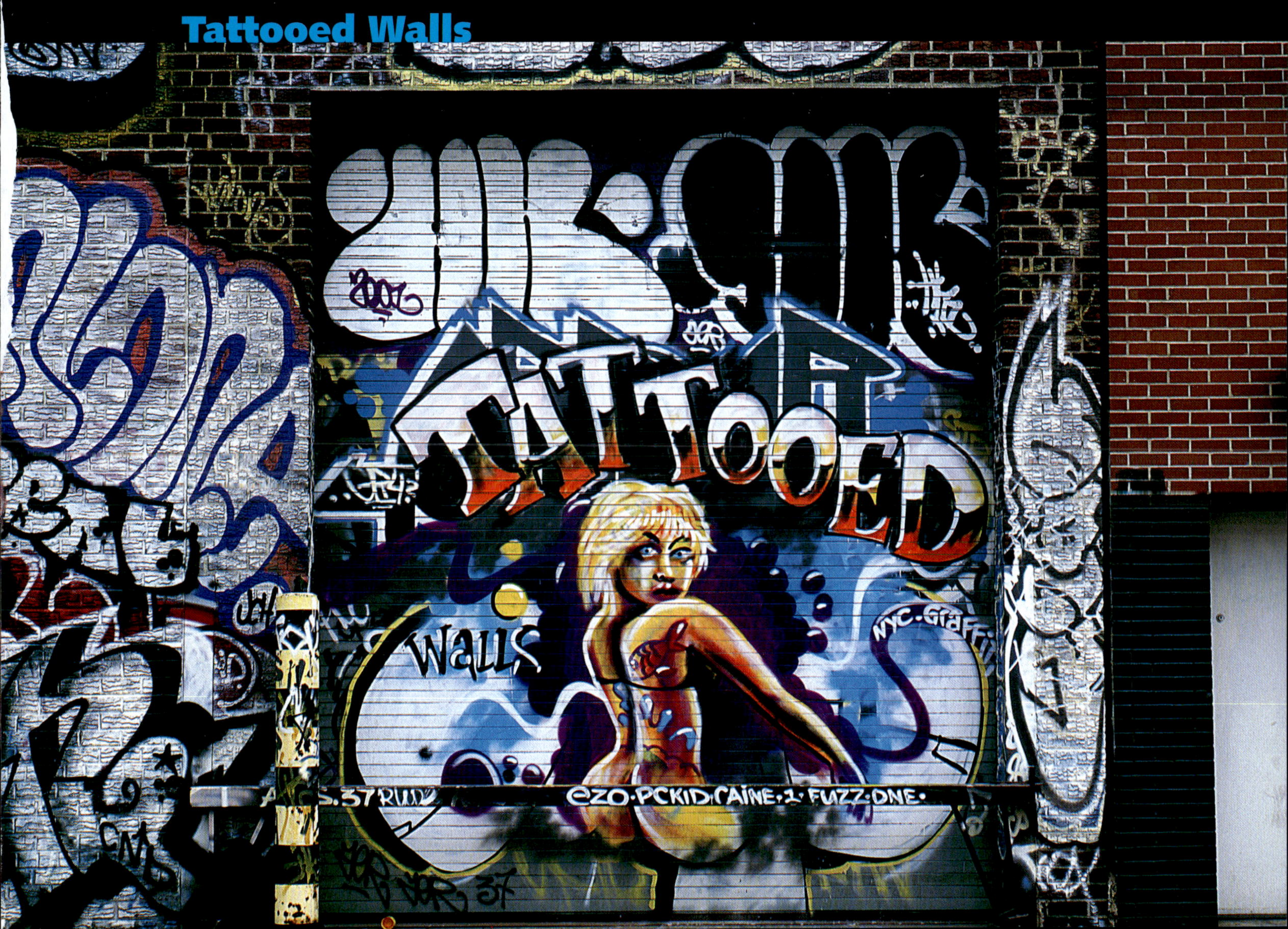

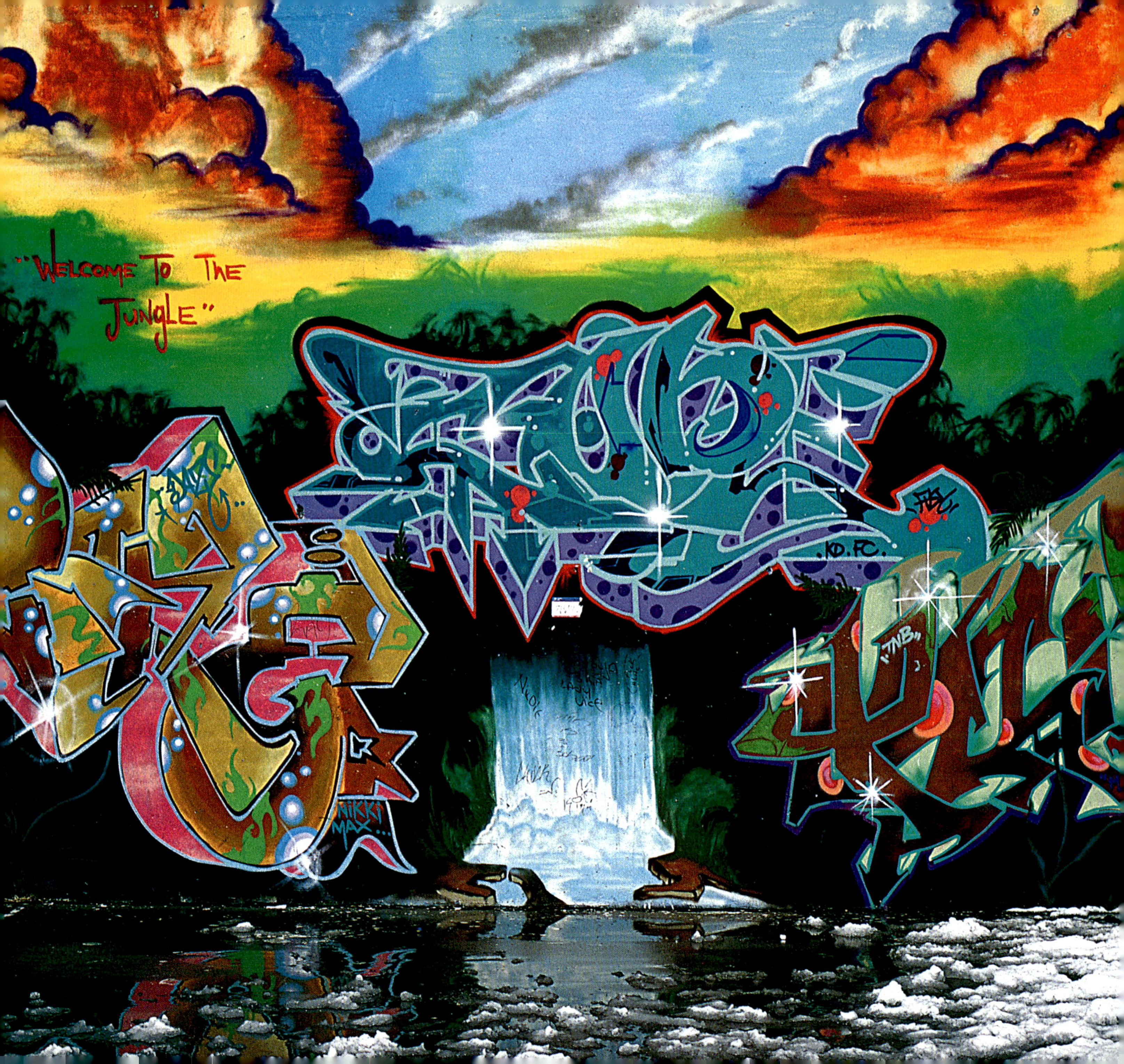
"WELCOME TO THE JUNGLE"

Tattooed Walls

Photographs by Peter Rosenstein with text by Isabel Bau Madden

Foreword by Stefan Eins

Interview with James de la Vega

University Press of Mississippi   Jackson

www.upress.state.ms.us

The University Press of Mississippi is a member of the Association of American University Presses.

Manufactured in China

First edition 2006

Page 1: Greg Sessoms's interpretation of "Tattooed Walls" on a Queens wall which he signed PCKIDONE

Page 2: Decorative wall in a handball court in the Bronx painted by DAZE, COPE, and TKID.

Library of Congress Cataloging-in-Publication Data

Rosenstein, Peter.
Tattooed walls / photographs by Peter Rosenstein with Isabel Bau Madden.— 1st ed.
p. cm.
ISBN 1-57806-869-X (cloth : alk. paper) 1. Street art—New York (State)—New York. 2. Mural painting and decoration, American—New York (State)—New York. 3. New York (N.Y.)—Pictorial works. I. Madden, Isabel Bau. II. Title.
ND2638.N4R67 2006
751.7'3097471—dc22
2005026274

British Library Cataloging-in-Publication Data available

To my son, Tommy,
and in memory of my father, Herbert Rosenstein,
and Velcro, my cat.

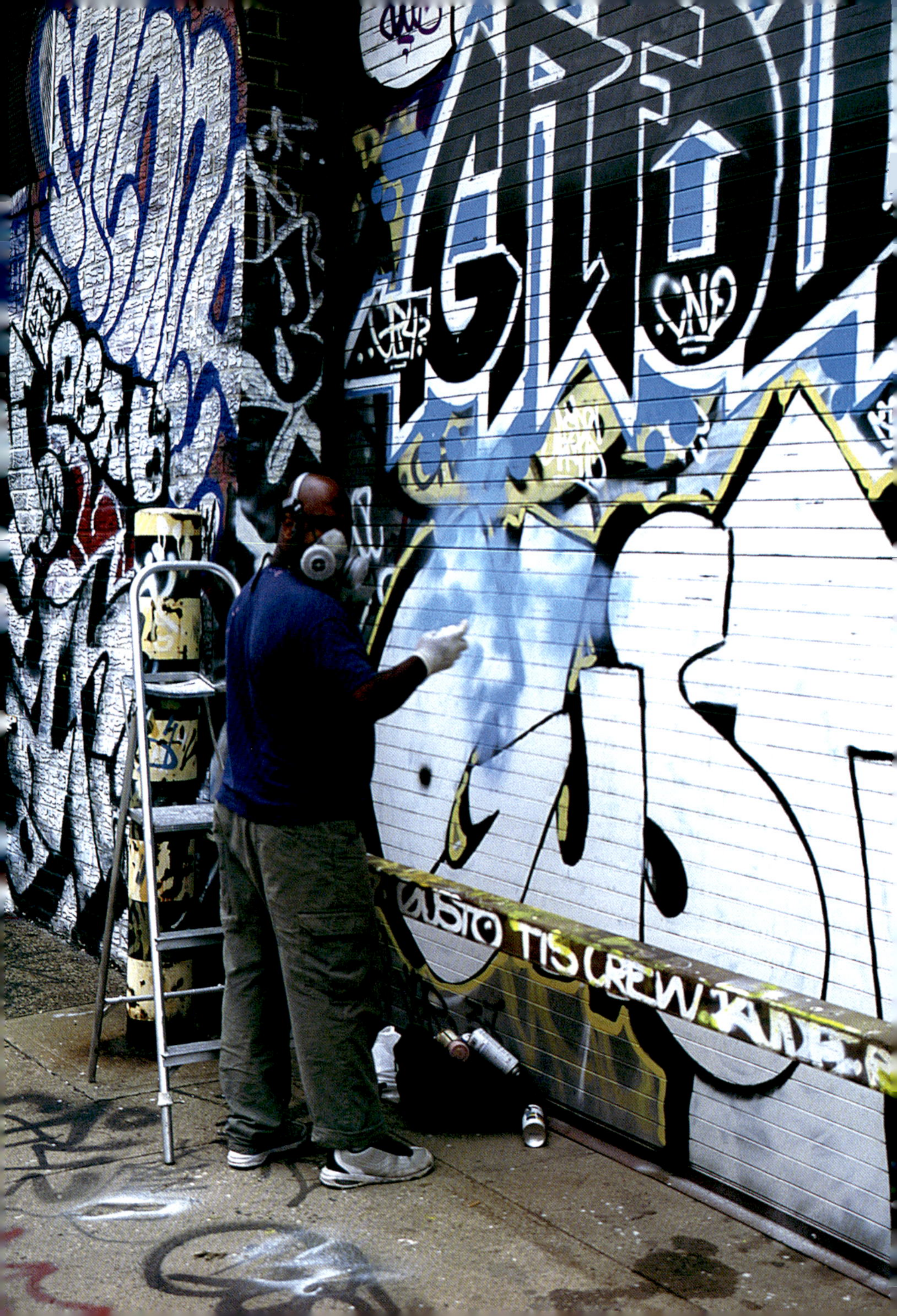
TIS CREW

IN MEMORIAM

November 29, 1963–October 19, 2005

Gregory Sessoms, 42, aka PCKID and PCKIDONE, died suddenly in his sleep on October 19, 2005.

A self-described "artist making a difference," he was a graffitist extraordinaire who also left his mark as an accomplished illustrator, painter, and designer.

He was a walking encyclopedia about New York City graffiti history, and we are grateful for his invaluable contributions to *Tattooed Walls.*

The Art of Graffiti Writing

A Historical Evaluation

Stefan Eins

> "Street Art is the foundation of the 21st Century"
>
> —Graffiti, East 4th Street, New York City, N.Y., 1985

The art and writing in the tradition of the New York Subway Graffitists—as it has been practiced since the late 1960s—has become an international phenomenon and is presently practiced globally. Typical examples of such practice in New York in recent history are included in this book,[1] although not all public art in this book is in the tradition of the art and writing on subways.

The foremost basic intent of the artist creating in the tradition of the New York Subway Graffitists is to write, represent, and sign, or tag, his or her name. This is why this art is importantly called writing. At times representational imagery—characters—such as faces, figures, and whatever else the writer might choose are added. Aerosol spray cans are the preferred tools of the Subway Graffiti writer. Felt-tip markers like Magic Markers are also commonly used in this field of practice. Writing and art in the subway tradition can be found worldwide on walls in public locations, highways, and railroad cars, but graffiti writing does not appear in the subways of New York much anymore. Graffiti is the general term; there is much graffiti—some of it excellent and exciting—that has nothing to do with the subway writing tradition.

Graffiti in the tradition of the subway writers has been and is presently practiced in the following forms or expressions:

- Tags: The signatures of writers, applied virtually anywhere and everywhere
- Throw ups: Bigger, more elaborate tags in more than one color on public surfaces (walls, handball courts, trucks, cars, etc.)
- Burners: Whole sides of a subway or a railroad car, or big pieces on public walls
- Whole trains (one whole side of a train, all cars)
- Paintings
- On leather and denim jackets, T-shirts, and other items of clothing
- The writer's books (original drawings, sketches, outlines for burners and throw ups, tags, collected tags from other writers, collaborations, etc.)

Unique to this art form are the following characteristics:

- Its various styles and their development
- Its origins (comics, calligraphy, popular culture, etc.)
- Art made on moving surfaces, which changes the traditions in visual arts (comparisons to film are possible)
- The fact that the creator addresses the public directly, without the selection processes imposed by the courts earlier in history, the salon, the curator, the gallery owner, the art critic, or the collector, and without art market considerations
- The random tagging by many different writers on public surfaces

The resulting accumulation of individual tags mentioned above introduces a novel modus of presentation as to individual identity in relation to others. When an individual's tag is done, a new whole emerges—a whole that is altered by any such new tag.

I consider the visual aspect of good Subway Graffiti and works in the tradition of the subway writers in all its forms among the most powerful, vibrant, strong, free, independent, and interesting in their color combinations in the arts in recent art history. Maybe in all of art history. Someone with peripheral knowledge is in no position to disregard or disagree with this statement. Only someone well-informed about Subway Graffiti practice can challenge this view. Uninformed positions, statements, and assumptions—not necessarily conscious—can be found frequently in the art world. Lack of knowledge also can lead to decisions not to exhibit the writing and art of Subway Graffitists.

Creative expressions that address the public directly, as in Subway Graffiti, do so without the involvement of the collector, the gallery owner, the critic, and the curator. For this type of art, the modus of communicating is dramatically different. Such a difference makes it a freer and more independent art. The case could be made that all public surfaces are available to the public for individual creative expressions. On the issue of legality and good art: One has nothing to do with the other.

Graff in the tradition of the subway writers is a political art and activity because it challenges the established norms of property rights and because it represents a novel mode to express oneself creatively. It is an act of rebellion, as expressed by the graffitist FUTURA 2000: "Art Terrorism" (ca. 1980). I see a connection between Islamic laws not allowing visual representations other than writing and the art and traditions of Subway Graffiti writing. It is also a form of calligraphy—maybe the most developed form of calligraphy ever.

Artist Jenny Holzer states: "Abuse of power comes as no surprise." In connection with graffiti art, the abuses occur in the power of the railroad and subway authorities, of the government in general, of one race over another, of one culture/subculture over another, of the educated, and of the ones with money. Difficulties in communication can probably also be attributed to the cultural differences between the practitioners of Subway Graffiti, mostly African American and Hispanic with some notable exceptions, on one side, and mostly white, European American representatives on the other side. Imagine a museum curator with a Ph.D. in art history dealing with a teenager who grew up in a ghetto and does not have a high school diploma. Elements of cultural and racial alienation on both sides can affect their communication.

Fashion Moda's Role

Fashion Moda showed the writing and the art of Subway Graffiti first in 1980 and in numerous exhibitions afterward—locally in New York, nationally, and internationally. Fashion Moda is a catalyst for creativity, invention, beauty, and realization. From a timeless concept (*Artforum*: "Fashion Moda has been around forever"[2]), a museum of science, art, invention, technology, and fantasy developed in the South Bronx from 1978 to 1993.

"Fashion Moda was visionary in its ambition to celebrate the convergence of different cultures. . . . In all of its signage and publicity material, the name Fashion Moda was printed in English and then repeated in Chinese, Russian, and Spanish versions. . . . Eins was the first to recognize the brilliance of graffiti art and introduced many of the most talented 'writers' to the art world and the public."[3]

The first graffiti show at Fashion Moda, Graffiti Art Success of America, in 1980 was curated by CRASH and NOC167. Participants included ALI, CRASH, DAZE, DISCO, JOHN FEKNER, FUTURA 2000, KEL, MITCH, NOC167, LADY PINK, TRAMP, ZEPHYR, and others. This show and the subsequent Fashion Moda exhibition at the New Museum of Contemporary Art in New York in 1980–81 received much media attention, and Subway Graffiti became a movement in the art world.

Diego Cortez included works from both shows in New Work/New York (1981) at PS 1, which is now part of the Museum of Modern Art in New York. Subsequently, the Subway Graffitists were showing in art galleries and museums. Among them were the galleries of Sidney Janis and Barbara Gladstone in New York, the Bologna Museum, which presented a show organized by Francesca Alinovi called Arte di Frontiera (1984), and the Groningen Museum, which showed Coming from the Subway: New York Graffiti (1992).

Fashion Moda's premise is that art/creativity can happen anywhere and that art can be appreciated and made by people who are known and unknown, trained and untrained, rich and poor. Regular art world traditions focus mostly, though not exclusively, on the saleable object. That's why painting has dominated the art world and the recent history of Western art. Fashion Moda's more open, non-exclusive approach to present art relates to random events in life's formation, to the chaos theory, and to the laws of the creative process.

It was inspiring to set up shop in the South Bronx and find the evolving culture of HIP-HOP (rap, graffiti, break dance, etc.). HIP-HOP is unique for many reasons, one reason being that it is the first time in history that teenagers and youths have created their own culture. HIP-HOP has become a global phenomenon. Contrary to certain beliefs, HIP-HOP (graffiti included) never dominated Fashion Moda's exhibitions program, although it has been a vital part of it.

Fashion Moda seemed particularly suited for Subway Graffiti shows because its South Bronx location made it culturally close to graffiti's roots. Being located on the street level means providing direct connection to the street and the anonymous public. Also, writers could tag and in the backroom the tags were not removed. Fashion Moda has a tradition of showing street art and art that seeks the public directly. In addition to the Subway Graffitists, the artists seeking the public directly have been Paolo Buggiani, Amy Chaiklin, Peggy Cyphers, John Fekner, David Finn, Keith Haring, Jenny Holzer, Liz-N-Val, R.V., David Wells, myself, and others.

It is still surprising and unfair that the graffiti subway style has not found a more permanent home in contemporary art history or a museum of contemporary art. An important factor for the parting of ways between the larger art world and most Subway Graffitists might be the essentially different approaches of these two artistic expressions. There are notable exceptions, however. Deitch Projects in New York City exhibits graffiti writers regularly. Jeffrey Deitch visited Fashion Moda, and his more inclusive exhibition policy at Deitch Projects seems to have been informed by the experience.

Fashion Moda has not engaged much in the selling of graffiti. This financially disinterested approach allows for purity and innocence; it also results in the loss of potential revenue. As to the issue of why the Subway Graffitists have left their indigenous terrain to exhibit in galleries, the desire and need to have money and gain media attention seem legitimate reasons.

For a graffiti writer to make paintings, a certain transition process might be necessary. Many succeed splendidly. LEE and LADY PINK are good examples. Some well-known Subway Graffitists, on the other hand, have never done subways, KOOR and RAMMELLZEE among them.

The End of Modern Art

In the modern art world predating the 1970s, some creative styles were acceptable, others not. The traditions included Impressionism, Cubism, Expressionism, Futurism, Dadaism, Surrealism, Minimalism, Pop Art, and Conceptual Art. Movements like these were what modern art is all about. Artists who worked outside these traditions did not get first billing and first-rate recognition—including high prices.

This trend constituted an authoritarian, not creative, component. It left important creative contributions out. This is not to say that no important art was created and supported in these traditions; still, it was exclusive of other significant art. In addition, the financial structure of the art world and the commercial structure of the galleries leaves out art that cannot be sold as readily, or art that is made not to be sold at all. Important movements have been forgotten, de-emphasized, and their historical impact altered, because they did not produce saleable objects. There is an art historical bias and emphasis favoring paintings for this reason. The conceptual art of the 1960s and 70s has been reduced to the objects that can be sold, while, in fact, conceptual art originally emphasized ideas and the dematerialization of the object. Graffiti has a related fate.

When the Fashion Moda museum opened its space in the South Bronx in 1978, it consciously broke with the traditions of exclusivity in art. The exhibitions at Fashion Moda, among them the exhibitions featuring Subway Graffiti artists and writers, mark the end of Modernism and Modern Art—"The death of Modern Art."[4]

Since then, not one style or movement has become the dominant force that artists must adhere to in order to be considered seriously in the art world. Fashion Moda, including the graffiti exhibitions, emphasized and exemplified this point by implementing a radically open exhibition policy. Enlightened curatorial policy facilitated exhibitions and art that is more open, more vital, and often better than the more traditional modes. The South Bronx location freed Fashion Moda from certain art world traditions.

The Times Square Show (1980), the emergence of the East Village galleries in the 1980s, and Subway Graffiti in the art world are a result of the Fashion Moda concept and its implementation.[5] Other lasting changes and initiatives were implemented as Fashion Moda "consciously eschewed the modernist aesthetic and installation 'style,' supplanting it with another style"; the way exhibitions are hung has also changed.[6] And there continue to be transformations in the art world's involvement with fashion and the fashion industry and vice versa, originally initiated by Fashion Moda.[7]

The art works and the style exhibited in the East Village galleries and the Soho galleries in the 1980s in New York differed. The different scenes represented different styles, different approaches, different attitudes. When Fashion Moda had its first show of Subway Graffitists in 1980, it drove home this point of an independent art form, and an independent mode of expression.

The end of modernist dogma!

1. As an introduction, the images on pages 30, 58, 104, 106, 107, 113, 132, 133, 139, 143, and 149 might be helpful.
2. "Some Posters from Fashion Moda," *Artforum,* January 1981, p. 50.
3. Lisa Phillips, *The American Century, Art and Culture 1950–2000,* Whitney Museum of American Art, Catalogue to the Exhibition, p. 290.
4. Henry M. Sayre, *The Object of Performance,* Chicago, London: University of Chicago Press, 1989, p. 11. See also Suzi Gablik, *Has Modernism Failed?*, New York: Thames and Hudson, 1984, p. 105, and Phillips, *The American Century.*
5. See, for example, Jeffrey Deitch, "Report from Times Square," *Art in America*, September 1980, p. 60; and Walter Robinson and Carlo McCormick, "Slouching Towards Avenue D," *Art in America*, Summer 1984, pp. 138–59.
6. Lynn Gompert, *Events,* The New Museum, Catalogue to the Exhibition, 1980/81, p. 16.
7. Confirmed in conversations with Jenny Holzer (2005) and Ingrid Sischy, editor of *Interview Magazine* (2004). Jenny Holzer exhibited at Fashion Moda and co-organized with me the Fashion Moda store at Documenta 7 in Kassel, Germany. Ingrid Sischy performed at Fashion Moda.

Preface

My journey photographing murals began in CHICO's territory on the Lower East Side of Manhattan on a wintry New Year's Day over a decade ago. It happened in the morning stillness that followed the proverbial holiday revelry. An exuberant burst of color suddenly appeared on this ghostly street in an otherwise drab neighborhood. It stopped me in my tracks. Looking down at me from an East Village wall were CHICO's playful cartoon characters conveying a message against violence and injustice. As I stood back and admired the colors and composition, I could not help but lament the transient nature of murals. That very fact inspired my obsession to document an art that despite its short life span was an integral part of New York's urban landscape. On that memorable day, CHICO's mural opened my eyes to street art and launched me on an urban expedition with no apparent end in sight. Though I am on the lookout for new murals year-round, I particularly relish the process of spotting them as I am riding my bicycle, at the first sign of spring, when fresh paintings seem to bloom everywhere.

Today CHICO, the artist whose work first fascinated me fourteen years ago, still claims the same turf, over which he presides like a feudal lord. He is a well-known member of the community, popular and active in youth programs. Schoolyards feature his murals, and so do shop fronts and restaurant interiors. The police no longer hassle him as in the old days when, spray can in hand, he established his "tag," CHICO, painting subway cars and getting arrested. His journey, like my own, has been long, thrilling, and not without risks. Clinging to roofs and trespassing to get to a wall are professional hazards we both encounter as part of the adventure of being an urban explorer, Chico as a street artist and I as a documentarist.

Chico and his fellow muralists continue to surprise me with their originality and special twist on the world that surrounds them. For the most part, they are always a step ahead of my camera. Very rarely do I catch them at work. Following their trail has taken me onto rooftops, over fences, up fire escapes, and into construction sites and back alleys. This is not to mention some very tight squeezes through impossibly narrow locked gates in forsaken industrial areas of the Bronx, Queens, and Brooklyn. Getting to all these places, I always keep an open eye for graffiti art on highways, overpasses, underpasses, and off-ramps. By now I've developed a sort of sixth sense for spotting murals. The thrill of discovering a new one has rarely brought me face to face with its creator. Though I have come to know and recognize the styles and tags, in most instances I rarely have the chance to meet the artist or artists.

From my initial encounter with CHICO's mural, one could say it was love at first sight. Before I knew it, I had gone through four rolls of film. I realized at that moment that I had found a new mission, though I did not fully grasp that it would turn out to be such an enduring enterprise. Yet when I think about it, it was a natural progression: I have an affinity for Latin music and culture. I was reminded of listening to Xavier Cugat, who was the "King of Rumba" in the 1930s and 1940s, on my father's jukebox.

Looking at the murals I recognized the Latin rhythms and exhilarating energy that had captivated my imagination when I was a child growing up in New Jersey. I was immediately smitten by the lively colors and their uplifting effect. To this day, I take special pleasure in going back to the Latino neighborhoods of New York City where most of these murals are found. I feel I am in a familiar element.

"All I want to do is beautify my neighborhood." The words roll out of CHICO's mouth like a mantra when we first meet on a cool autumn day in a schoolyard on the Lower East Side. CHICO was born in Puerto Rico and has lived in the East Village in downtown Manhattan for most of his life. Soon, I find out his desire to redecorate the neighborhood did not occur by chance. He is eager to admit that "it was because of a girl. The area was scary to her. Abandoned buildings. Vandalism. I couldn't get her to hang out with me here. So I decided to do something about it." That was more than twenty years ago.

Over three thousand murals later, it is no wonder that CHICO has become a legendary figure in his fiefdom, extending from Madison Street on the Lower East Side to 34th Street, and from the East River to 4th Avenue. He remains fiercely independent, having turned down all offers to belong to a muralist cooperative.

"I am CHICO. That's it. No one else." To make ends meet he works for the New York City Housing Authority and paints murals part-time. Though the city is his canvas, his ambition is to exhibit in a gallery, a goal that has eluded all but a few graffiti artists, most notably two late icons, Jean-Michel Basquiat and Keith Haring.

Art classes in high school proved mostly boring to the very gifted CHICO. Nonetheless, he regrets that family financial hardships kept him from graduating from the Fashion Institute of Technology, which he attended for a year on a scholarship.

CHICO with spray can in hand is a sight to behold. He is using a skill clearly mastered on the street. He exudes confidence, concentration, and celerity. There is no hesitation on his part despite the technical challenges of spray-can art. Within a few minutes a blank wall in a restaurant blooms with giant daisies. Around the corner, over one afternoon, a bleak schoolyard becomes home to a slew of popular cartoon characters. His objective, whether he has been commissioned or not, is to enhance an impersonal, oftentimes dreary landscape.

While CHICO toils in the southern tip of Manhattan, another famous muralist, JAMES DE LA VEGA, echoes the same sentiments in Spanish Harlem's El Barrio. Another proud son of Puerto Rican parents who has found fame as a street artist, DE LA VEGA is a graduate of Cornell University. That in itself is a rarity among street artists. A former teacher, DE LA VEGA nowadays is a sought-after art lecturer. In private he comes across as unpredictable and contradictory. He can be monosyllabic, mince few words, or launch into a lengthy diatribe about the social issues that consume his art and time, most notably prejudice and poverty.

The ephemeral nature of murals does not concern him. "Isn't life also temporary?" he asks. His serious demeanor turns into a smile when he compares himself with the legendary folk hero Zorro. They share not only the surname DE LA VEGA but also a passionate concern for their people.

DE LA VEGA's sanctuary for many years was his gallery and studio on 104th Street and Lexington Avenue. A victim of gentrification, he lost his lease and moved downtown to St. Mark's Place in the East Village. His spin on celebrated art masterpieces such as Picasso's Guernica or Leonardo's Last Supper borrows freely from the themes and images of Spanish Harlem in a deliberate effort to connect with the Latino sensibility and heritage that surround him. DE LA VEGA's political agenda is rooted in El Barrio's economic hardship and the struggle to upgrade its standard of living. As an activist and teacher, DE LA VEGA has the goal of galvanizing the public into action to bring about sorely needed improvements to the neighborhood.

Many of DE LA VEGA's striking murals were vandalized during the summer of 2002. This does not seem to bother him. Instead he points to the fact that his is a fluid art, public in nature, which serves as a kind of popular bulletin board, providing a platform for comments and an ongoing discourse. Far from being upset, he thrives on the opportunity to provoke and be provoked.

It comes as no surprise then, that upon our first meeting, DE LA VEGA dons a huge rust-colored Afro wig and sunglasses, and pronounces this caricature to be DE LA VEGA the artist and public persona. This getup affords him a degree of privacy and mystique while keeping his interlocutors on their toes. In a sense, he is much more than an urban muralist. He is a provocateur and a philosopher. His musings have one objective: to make people stop and think. He is a successful and multitalented entrepreneur, a consummate performer, and a complex conceptual artist.

Whether it is his street chalking or the ingenious sidewalk masking-tape designs or his witty or cryptic aphorisms such as "Beauty magazines make my girlfriend feel ugly," DE LA VEGA has a muscular and deliberate approach, guaranteeing that you notice him and his work. He would rather risk being disliked than being ignored or forgotten. Though his demeanor may seem stern, it is in sharp contrast to his store, which is very colorful and jam-packed with artifacts, paintings, T-shirts, mugs, and other items that have caught his imagination.

Anything at all can serve as a canvas to this prolific artist. Incredibly, despite his notoriety and his own efforts at self-promotion, his work has never been exhibited at the neighboring Museo del Barrio, an institution with strong ties to the Latino community and culture. On the other hand, DE LA VEGA's work has been shown at the Caribbean Cultural Center, and the Cooper-Hewitt National Design Museum displayed a DE LA VEGA mural about Latino Los Angeles. The fact that the art world may not be hurrying to recognize him does not seem to faze DE LA VEGA. His murals profess in no uncertain terms where he is, who he is, and that he will not tolerate being taken for granted.

Though only a few miles separate CHICO's Lower East Side from DE LA VEGA's El Barrio, their communities face different challenges. In recent years, the East Village has become a fashionable address with skyrocketing rents. This is jeopardizing the future of CHICO's reign over its walls as well as the existence of a Latino community. In contrast, many residents of Spanish Harlem would gladly opt for the attention and development that comes with "gentrification."

Nevertheless, preserving the ethnic identity of their communities is of primary concern to both artists. In addition to changes in their neighborhoods, their work has been the target of unsympathetic mayors hostile to graffiti murals and intent on eradicating them. This is an unwelcome adversity facing urban muralists.

Being an urban mural photographer is a seasonal endeavor for me. During the cold New York winters, street artists hibernate, for the most part. As soon as the weather begins to warm up, murals start to blossom everywhere. One of my first destinations each spring is the celebrated Graffiti Hall of Fame wall on 106th Street and Park Avenue, not far from DE LA VEGA's territory. Located in a schoolyard, this is New York's graffiti mecca, where self-taught muralists such as the Bronx's famous TATS CRU often showcase their talents.

The original members of TATS CRU, named NICER, BIO, and BG 183, have been spray-painting the town for over two decades. However, much has changed since they began their exploits. They are no longer considered notorious graffiti vandals persecuted by the police. Today, they run a successful business from their studio in the Hunts Point section of the Bronx. Such major sponsors as Coca-Cola, Avirex, and MTV are among many clients, some with long-term contracts. It is a far cry from the days when painting memorials was their full-time activity, that began with a commission in 1984 to honor the late hip-hop artist M.C. Cowboy. To this day, TATS CRU's homage to beloved rapper Big Pun, who, at seven hundred pounds, died in 2000, remains a venerated site.

When you cross the Willis Avenue Bridge, which connects Spanish Harlem to the South Bronx, you find yourself in TATS CRU country. Though I am on the lookout for new murals year-round, during the summer months I enjoy crisscrossing the boroughs on my unusual recumbent titanium bicycle. The bike attracts attention and makes it easy to strike up conversations with strangers. I often get tips about new murals from residents and graffiti writers on these excursions. Even the police are helpful. On one occasion an officer gave me a long list of works in progress! That kept me busy for an entire summer. In recent years I have found that the police have become more sympathetic to muralists. It is the new, more affluent arrivals in the neighborhood, the so-called "yuppies," who consider street art offensive.

The Bronx, with its myriad large walls, showcases numerous monumental murals. FX CRU, a leading group of aerosol artists, is an important presence with their large-scale murals. Some of the best writers around belong to the noteworthy FX CRU. However, few would dispute that TATS CRU are truly the reigning kings here. Over twenty years have passed since the original three members began their artistic careers spraying subway graffiti. Thus began a journey that eventually transformed this art form.

Other talented aerosol artists come from all over the world vying to intern with them. TATS CRU are also involved in a mentoring program at the Hunts Point Community Center, as are many veteran muralists. They share a sense of commitment and pride in the community, promoting issues such as education, social justice, public health, and the glory of their culture. This is precisely the bone of contention between those who see street art as a social statement and expression of community values and those who perceive it only as a nuisance and a destruction of property.

When I cross over from the Bronx to Queens I could not ask for a better guide and graffiti historian than Gregory Sessoms (also known as PCKIDONE). Originally from Manhattan, Greg and his large family are longtime residents of Queens. The youngest of seven siblings, Greg has been part of the aerosol art movement for close to thirty years. His mentor in the 1970s was the late graffiti pioneer CAINE ONE (Edward Glowacki), a Polish artist whose original approach and style changed graffiti writing. During the 1970s and 1980s the Number 7 train of the New York City subway system was PCKIDONE's favorite canvas.

Tagging a subway car was more than a question of spraying a design on a large surface; it entailed stealth and some danger entering the yards and avoiding the police, which was not always successfully done. Taking these risks was a badge of honor in the community of taggers. Even though they tried to avoid getting caught, getting arrested was nonetheless considered a badge of honor. To hear it from PCKIDONE or CHICO, tagging subway cars was an exhilarating rite of passage, as competition among them was rife. Each artist tried to outdo the other.

Today, PCKIDONE is an accomplished painter and illustrator whose murals are commissioned by private clients as well as community organizations. His recollections, spanning over three decades, are almost encyclopedic in nature. Names, dates, places—he recounts all in such vivid detail you visualize the evolution of graffiti art as he speaks. To hear it from PCKIDONE, it all began with the famous message left by GIs, "Kilroy was here," which appeared as graffiti throughout Europe and the Pacific during World War II. Many years later, in the 1960s, EARL and CORNBREAD, two Philadelphia writers, were instrumental in taking graffiti to its next level: notoriety for the tagger. Their exploits of leaving their tags all over the place were written up in the publication *Black Culture,* and began a trend among gangs intent on marking their turf.

Next, we found homeboys in different boroughs inventing nicknames they displayed as public signatures to establish their identities. The most notorious, TAKI 183, from Manhattan, rode as many subways as possible and wrote his name everywhere. The effort ultimately earned him an interview with the *New York Times.* His notoriety began a whole new wave: "getting up," as the writing was labeled, became a mission. Those who tagged most often and in the most out-of-the-way places became, in the graffiti world, urban heroes.

Eventually, in the late 1970s, graffiti moved aboveground, and a whole new story began to unfold. Influences could be seen in advertising and fashion. PCKIDONE continues to be an integral part of this history, and his evolution mirrors the progress of the movement as a whole.

Looking back, I can see that my first glance at CHICO's mural in 1991 was indeed a life-changing experience. That encounter has spawned close to two thousand photographs and has transformed a hobby into an obsession: to preserve this extraordinary art by creating the largest archive of New York City murals. It has also inspired travel to other cities—in the United States, to San Francisco, Baltimore, and Los Angeles, and, abroad, to Cuba, the Czech Republic, Austria, Germany, and Poland.

I am painfully aware of the dangers that threaten the continued existence of street art, and thus I realize that my work in documenting New York City murals can no longer be seen as an option; it has become a duty.

It was a daunting task to select a mere one hundred or so photographs for this book. It's not easy to pick favorites when you have thousands of images and you love all of them.

Peter Rosenstein
New York City
April 2005

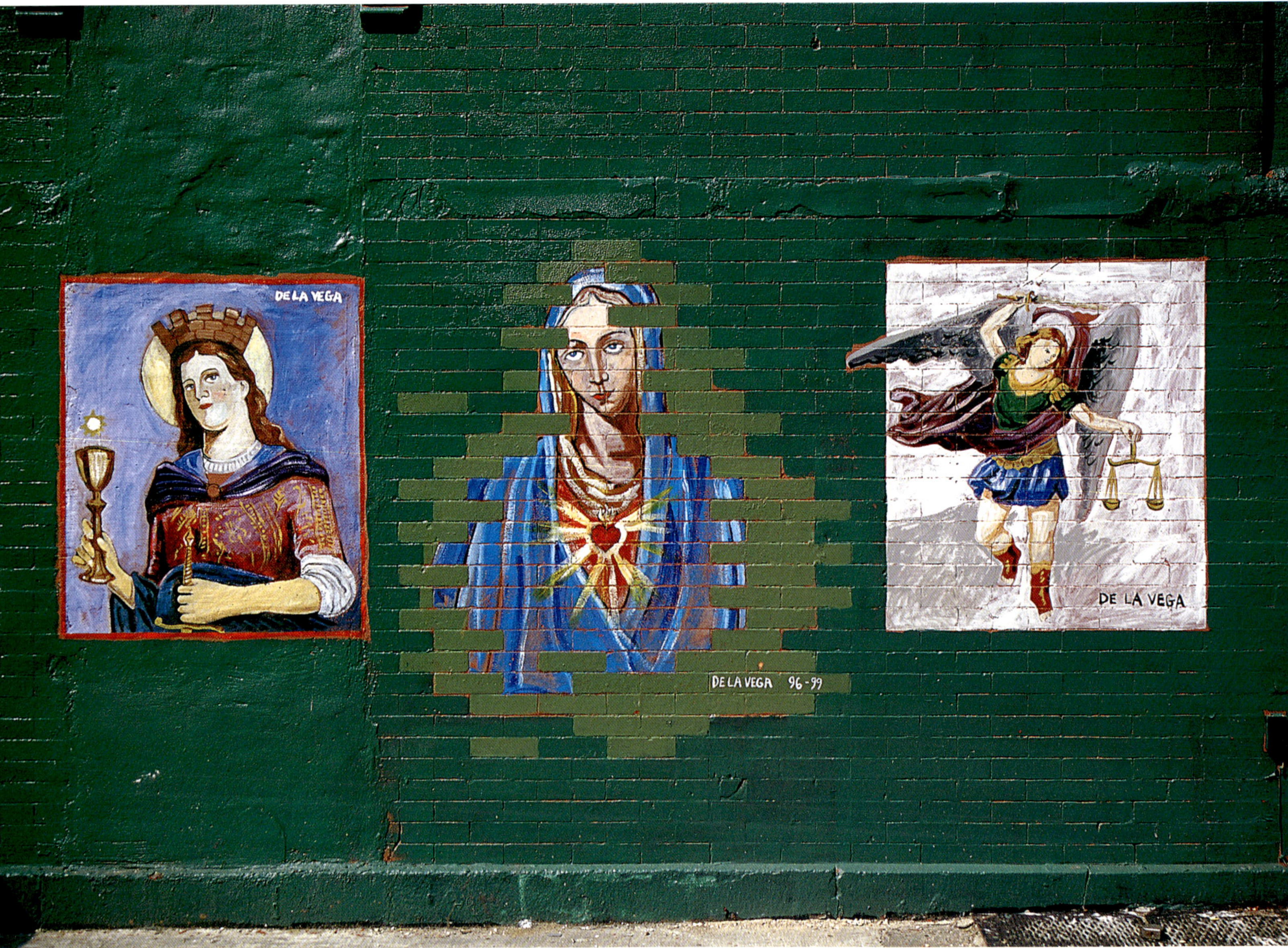
DE LA VEGA
DE LA VEGA 96-99
DE LA VEGA

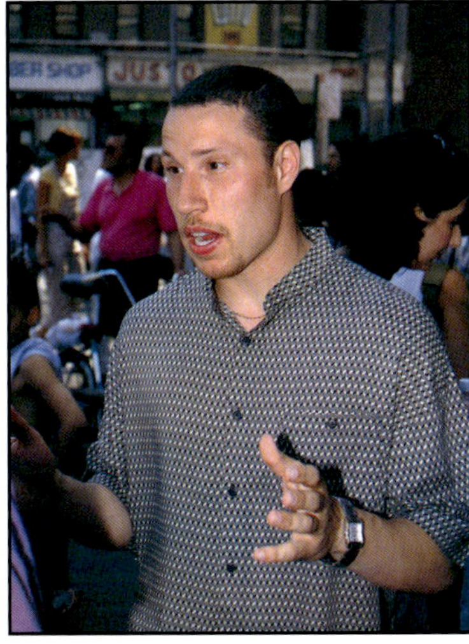

De la Vega's work extends beyond what he did to get an art degree from Cornell University and his many indoor exhibits. In addition to his East Harlem murals, he can be found writing adages on sidewalks, either with chalk or masking tape. He vows to keep doing it.

Interview with Artist James De La Vega

About the history of murals, graffiti, and tagging:

I can't give an accurate account for the making of murals in New York City, but I do remember seeing them throughout Spanish Harlem, on trains, in buildings. It was definitely an important part of the street experience. Most young guys I knew kept fat markers in their pockets and were always eager about leaving their mark everywhere.

I remember people always trying to come up with cool names for tags (CRIME, EZ BOB, SWEET, NOR, LEPSKI, SPON, etc.). These names worked their way onto the world in simple bubble letters or disguised in cubist-like works of art.

Why do people choose to do murals and tag?

Painting on walls was a way to communicate with the people in the neighborhood, get fame, or honor someone's death. It was a way to fight, to bring beauty, make others think, leave your mark, get respect, compete, build, destroy.

How do painters, aerosol artists, and writers get started?

I was influenced at first by cartoons, copying the characters. Tom and Jerry, Batman, Superman, the Smurfs. I enjoyed the ability to accurately reproduce some of these characters. When others receive your work with approval, at a young age, it is encouraging. I copied photographs, magazine ads, anything where I could develop my drawing skills. My mom sent me to after-school art programs.

How do painters choose their subject?

A subject matter can come from anywhere. It can be recognizable or metaphorical. I choose subject matter that interests me but that can also send a huge political or inspirational message to the world. I've explored portraits of well-known cultural or political leaders, ordinary people usually ugly or of strong character, my mom, to more abstract things like fish jumping in and out of bowls. I've always been interested in art as a tool for education and improving not only the environment but also people's lives.

What separates murals from graffiti?

The law. Both murals and graffiti are works of art created on public or private wall space. Graffiti is considered illegal. But the highly developed graffiti art is beautiful and very inspirational to young children. Most young children in Spanish Harlem, Harlem, and the other poor neighborhoods I've worked with are always interested in the graffiti art. They are never told entirely about the consequences of creating such art without permission. Permission also separates mural work from graffiti work.

About the importance of murals in the community:

Paintings, murals have been a way to bring beauty to the abandoned neighborhoods, teach through pictures, remember someone, and express a neighborhood's issues or concerns. It is also a great way to unite a neighborhood. Murals encourage dialogue, and dialogue builds the communal experience.

What is the role of this form of expression in these particular communities?

It is rare that a young artist from these poor communities even gets the opportunity to show work in the commercial downtown galleries. So street artists create their own venues. The work needs no validation. It grows from our experience. It is how we share and teach on our streets. It is the most authentic and important art being done in most cities because it is directly involved with improving lives. It is God's work because it is a way to strengthen and liberate but also to build bridges to a world beyond our own borders.

About graffiti artist vs. muralist:

They grow from the same idea. I am as inspired by TATS CRU as I am by Michelangelo or Diego Rivera.

About murals in the other parts of the world:

It all interests me, especially the artists who make their own way and build success on their own. I am also interested in how artists combine imagery and text.

Which themes are becoming popular?

Portraiture, political commentary.

Do you see murals eventually attaining the same recognition and respect as traditional art?

Mural paintings and public art is God's work. The rest is good to look at.

About muralists becoming commercial:

Good. Artists should learn how to communicate with as wide an audience as possible. Though I like the art of not compromising.

Recommendations for young artists:

Keep a sketchbook, draw, think, write down your thoughts. Become your dream, learn from everybody, do something powerful with your life.

Muralists I admire:

Diego Rivera. He painted with the goal of affecting people's lives.

Government's attitude in New York towards murals:

They love it but are afraid to admit it so they lock up people because it's better for business. You can't own or sell a mural so there's no profit to be made. But they love it.

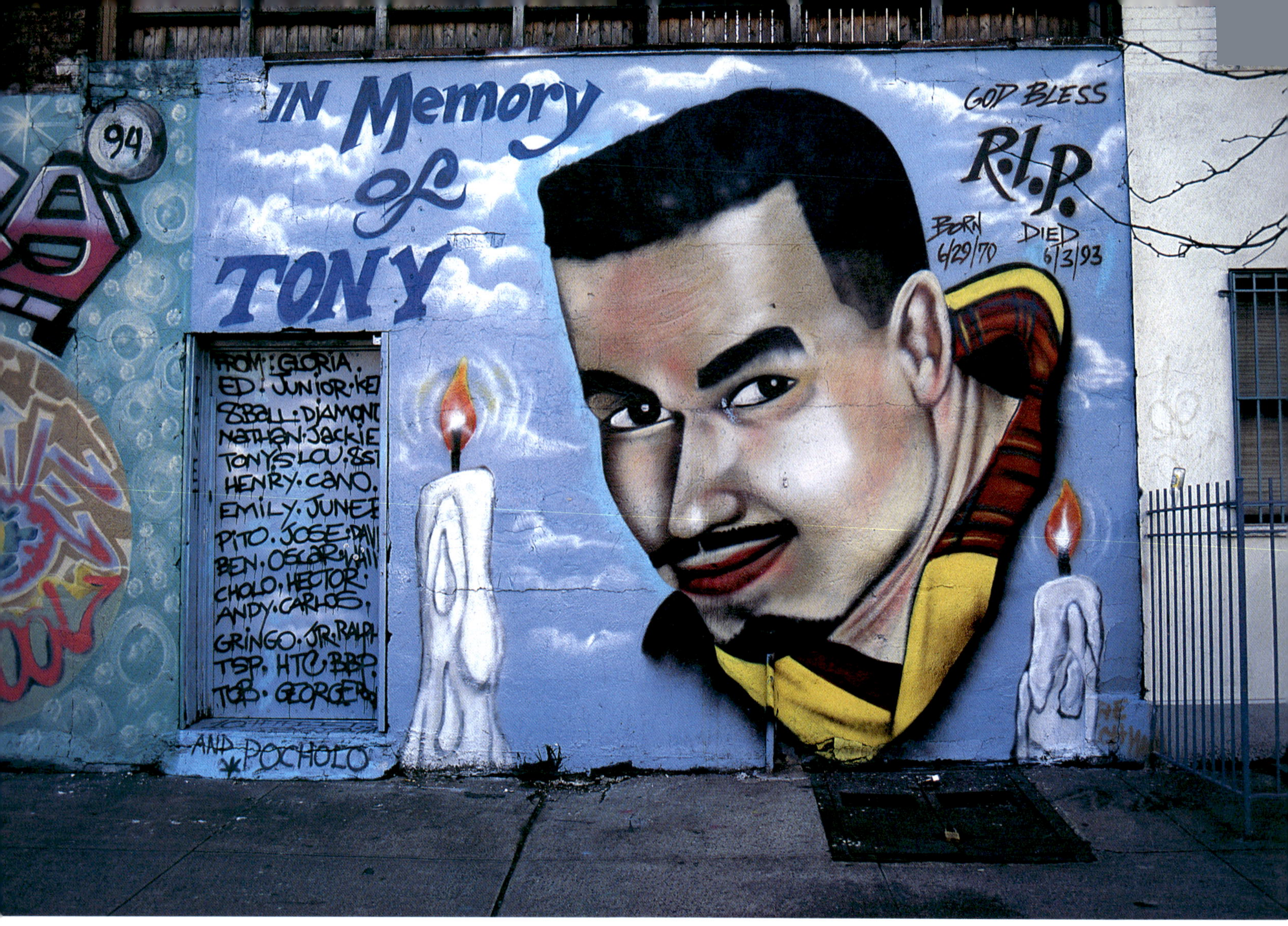

Day and night views of a strong example of a classic memorial mural. Tony lives on in the memory of his friends through this CHICO creation. The night view brings out the mural's light and shadow relief on a wall in the East Village of New York City, CHICO's territory.

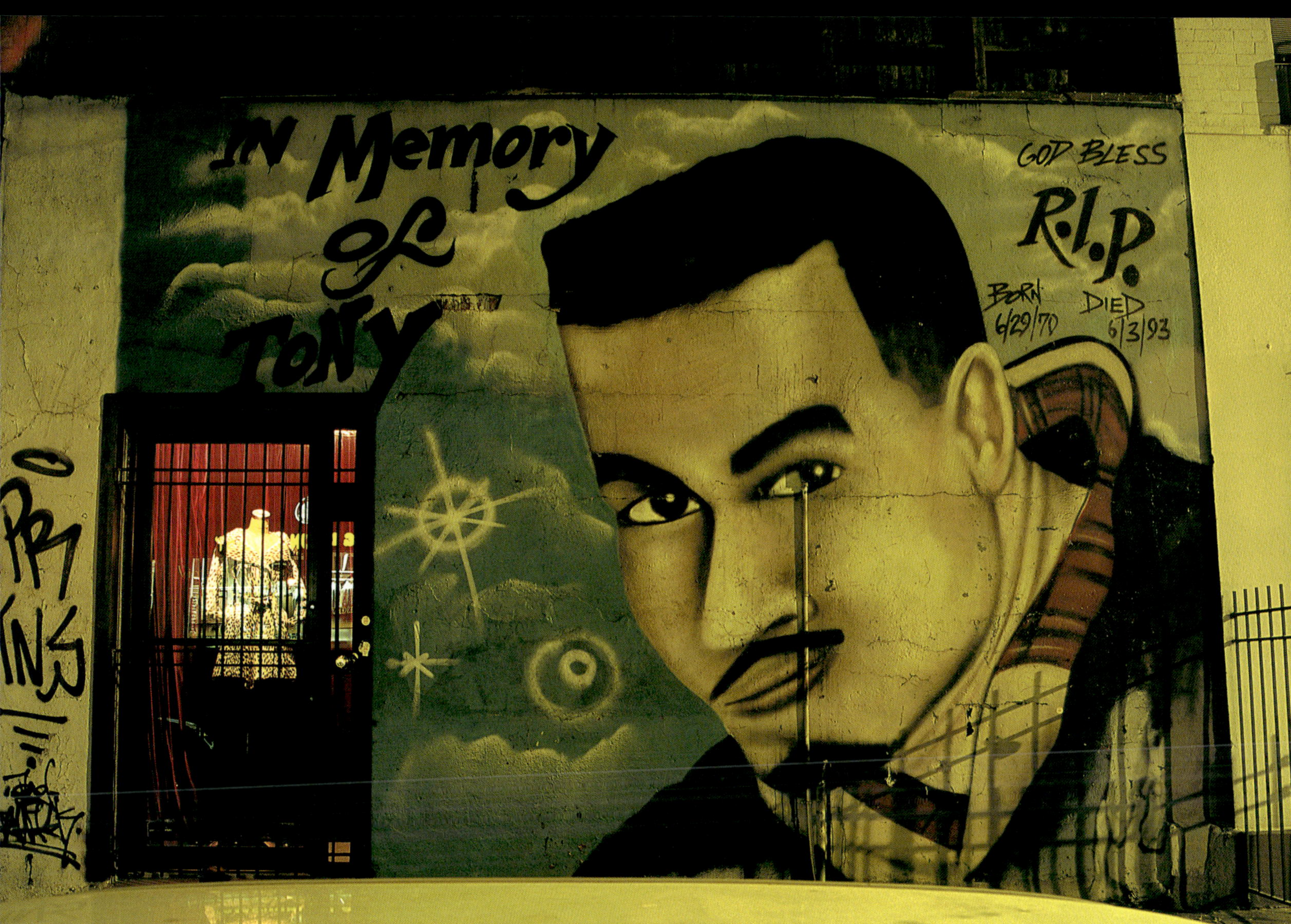
IN Memory
of
ToNY
GOD BLESS
R.I.P.
BORN
6/29/70
DIED
6/3/93

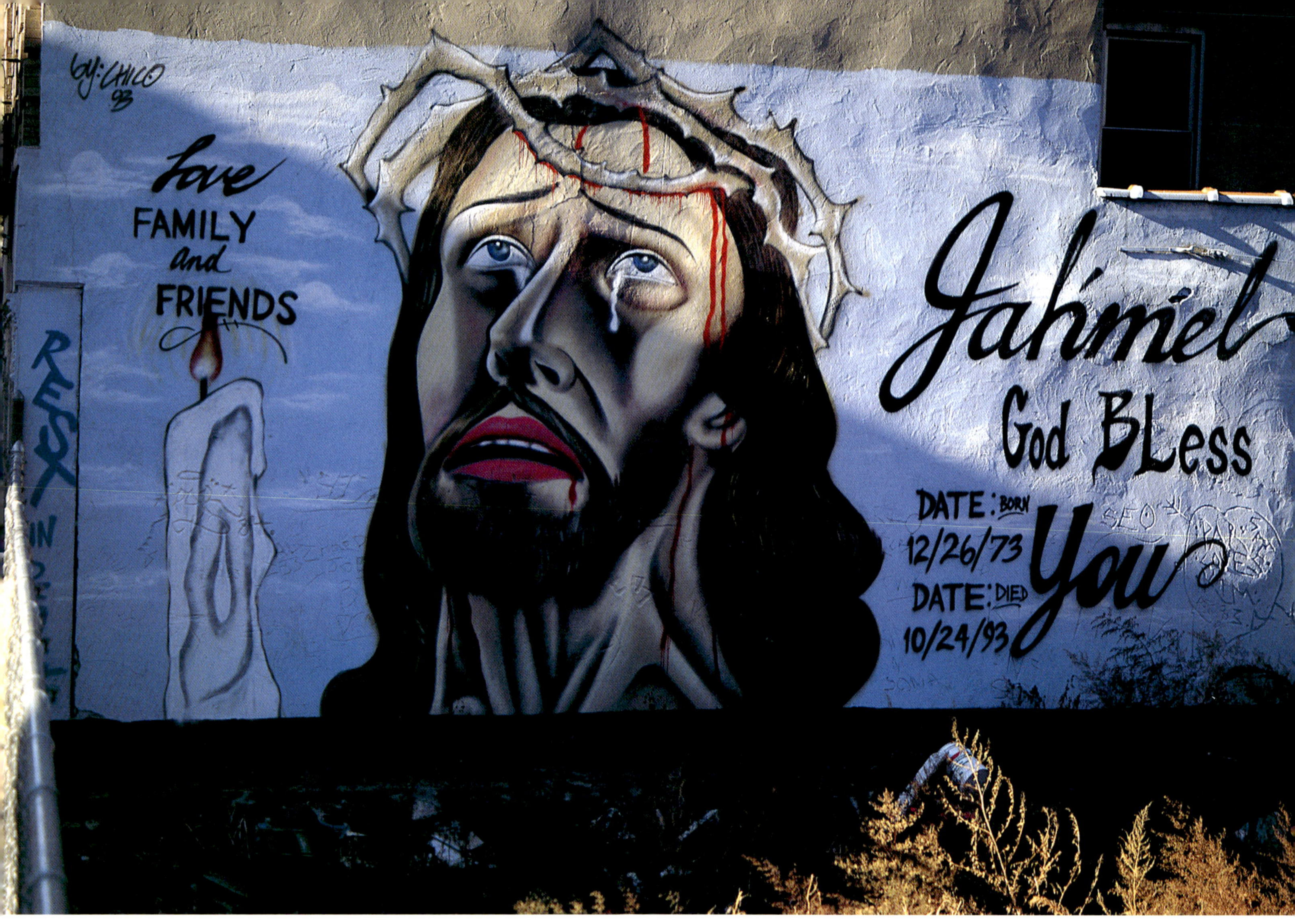

CHICO's barrio religious imagery defines his heavyhearted memorial to Jahmel, a victim of a crime of passion.

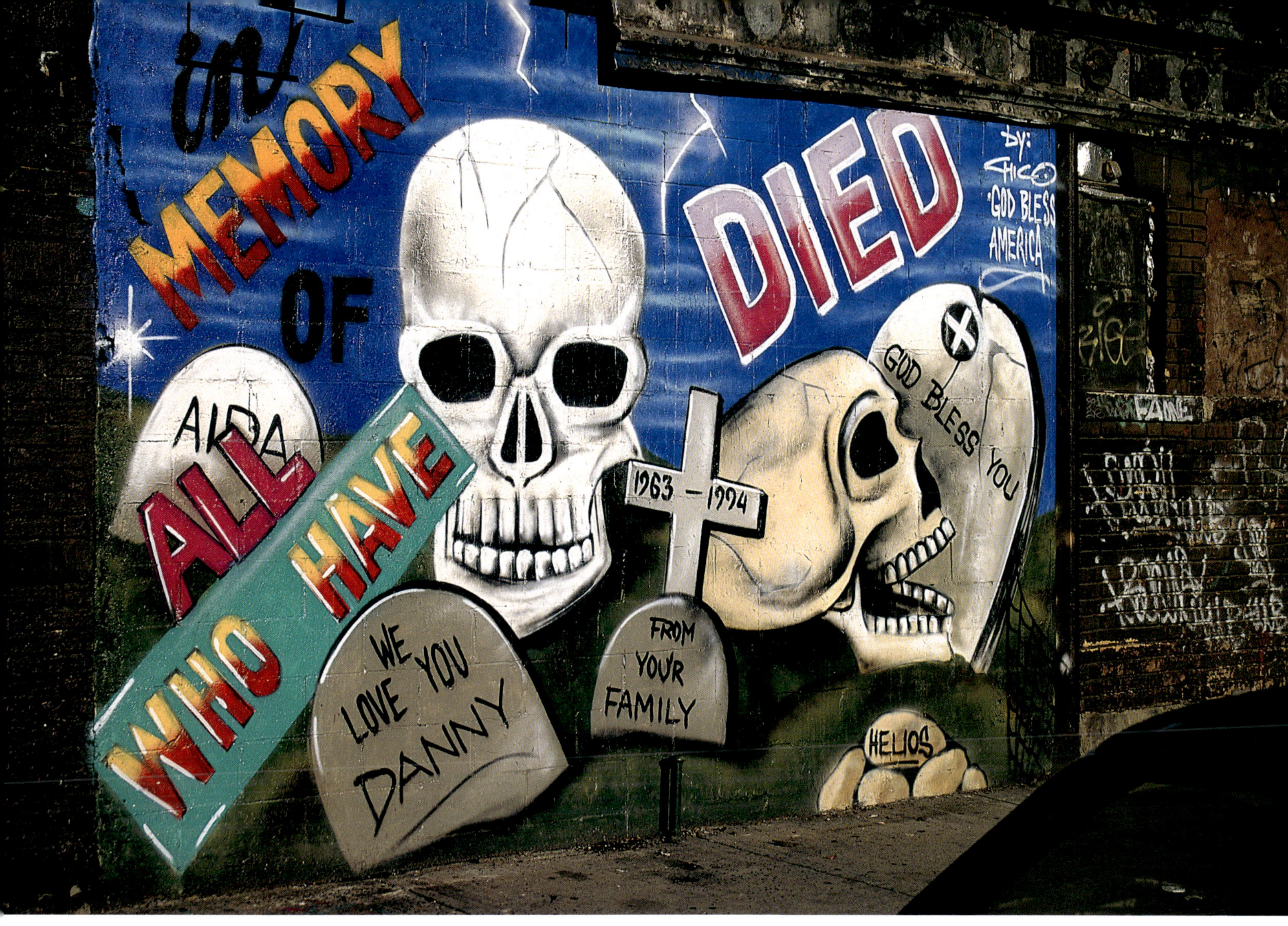

With folkloric skulls and tombstones, CHICO's memorial implies homage to his subject's homeland, where the dead and living interweave the tapestry of life.

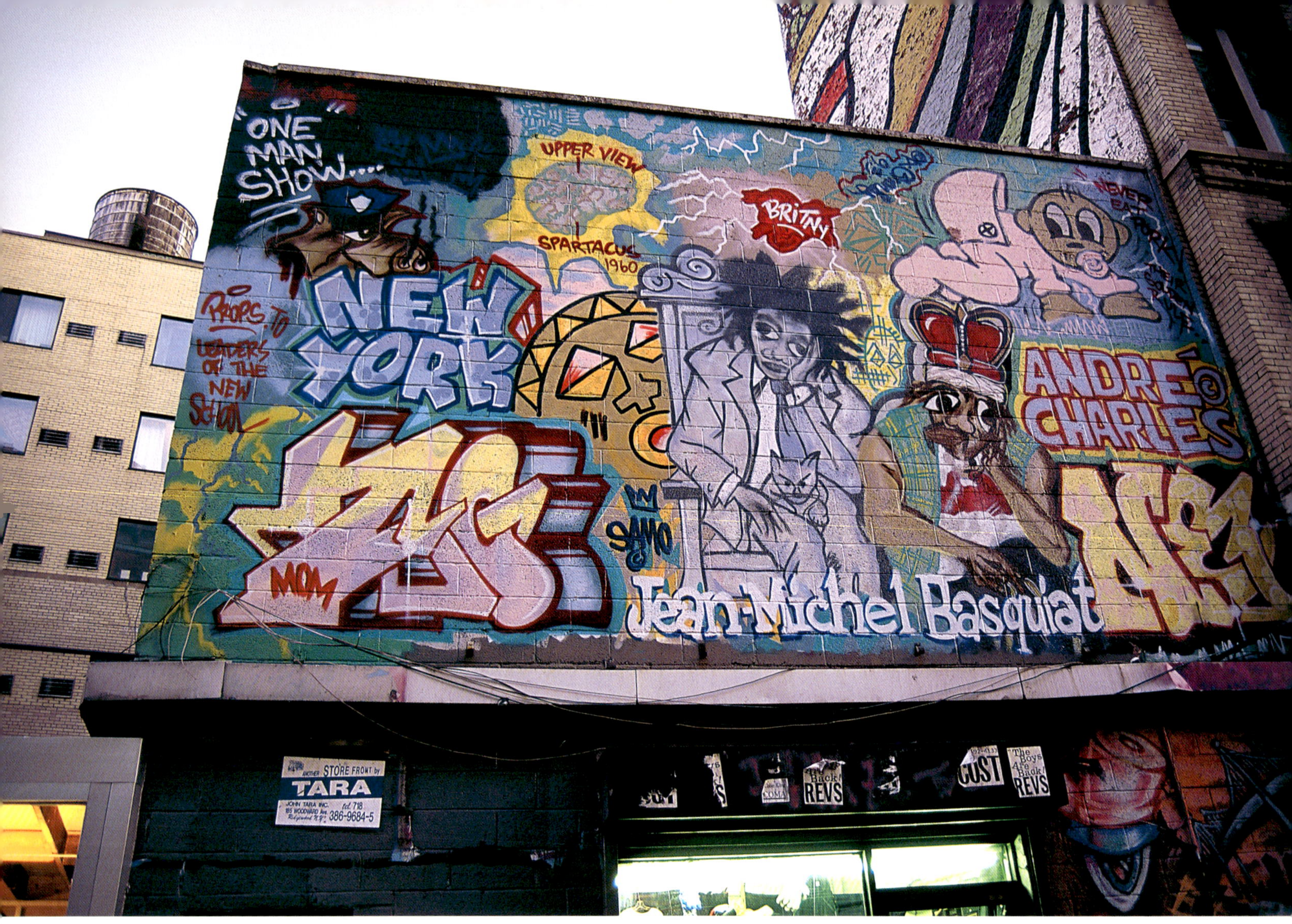

Andre Charles's memorial to famed painter Jean-Michel Basquiat shows muscular respect from one artist to another. Charles collaborated with another artist on the image of Basquiat, who died of a heroin overdose in 1988, at age twenty-seven.

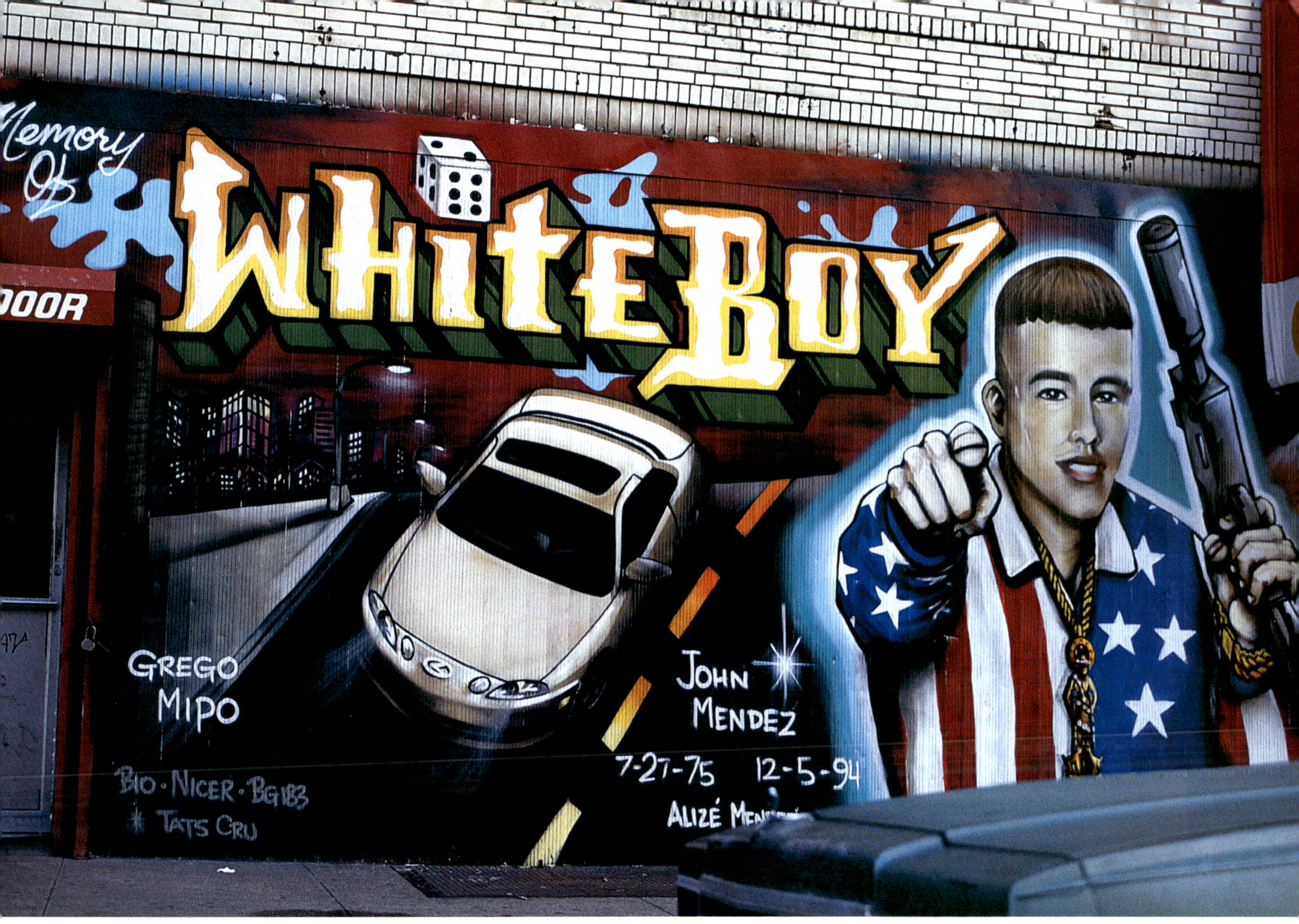

The gun is a symbol of toughness, the dice of chance, and the car of success in TATS CRU's well-known South Bronx memorial, visible around Hunts Point.

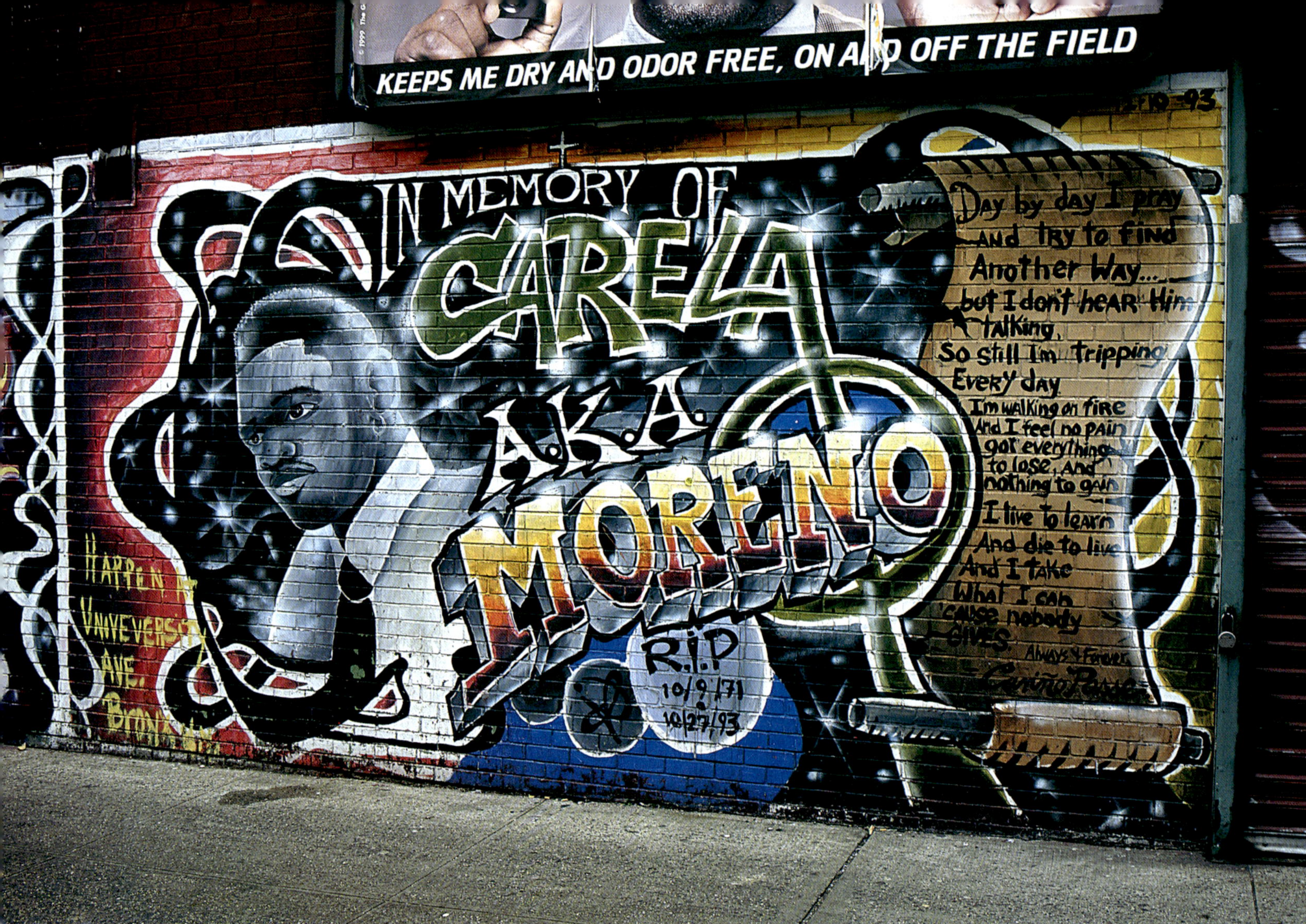

Locals say this gloomy Bronx mural memorializes the despair of a man who probably died of a drug overdose.

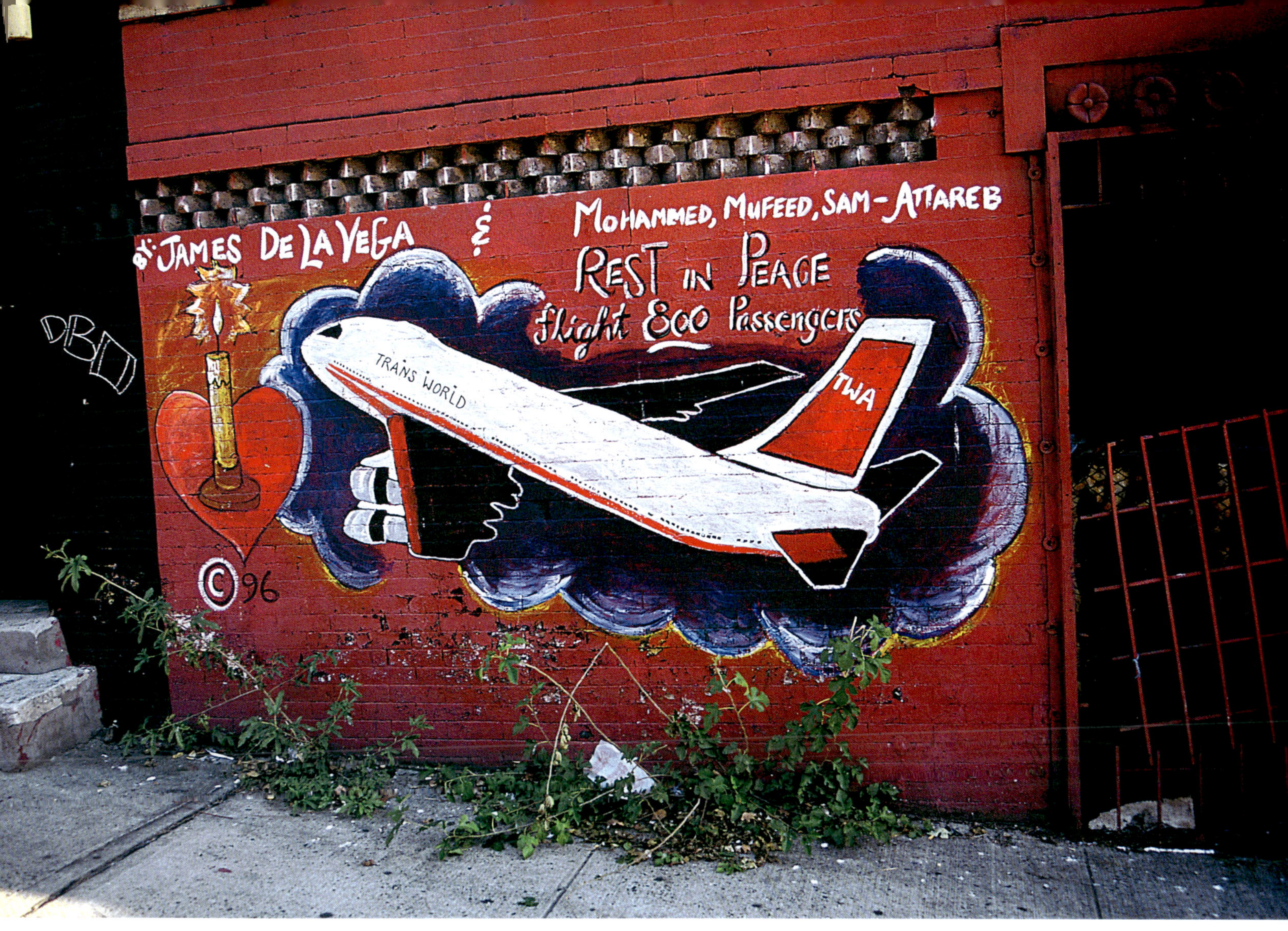

Mourning the incomprehensible is expressed through deep murky blues in DE LA VEGA's Lexington Avenue memorial to TWA Flight 800, which went down off Long Island in 1996.

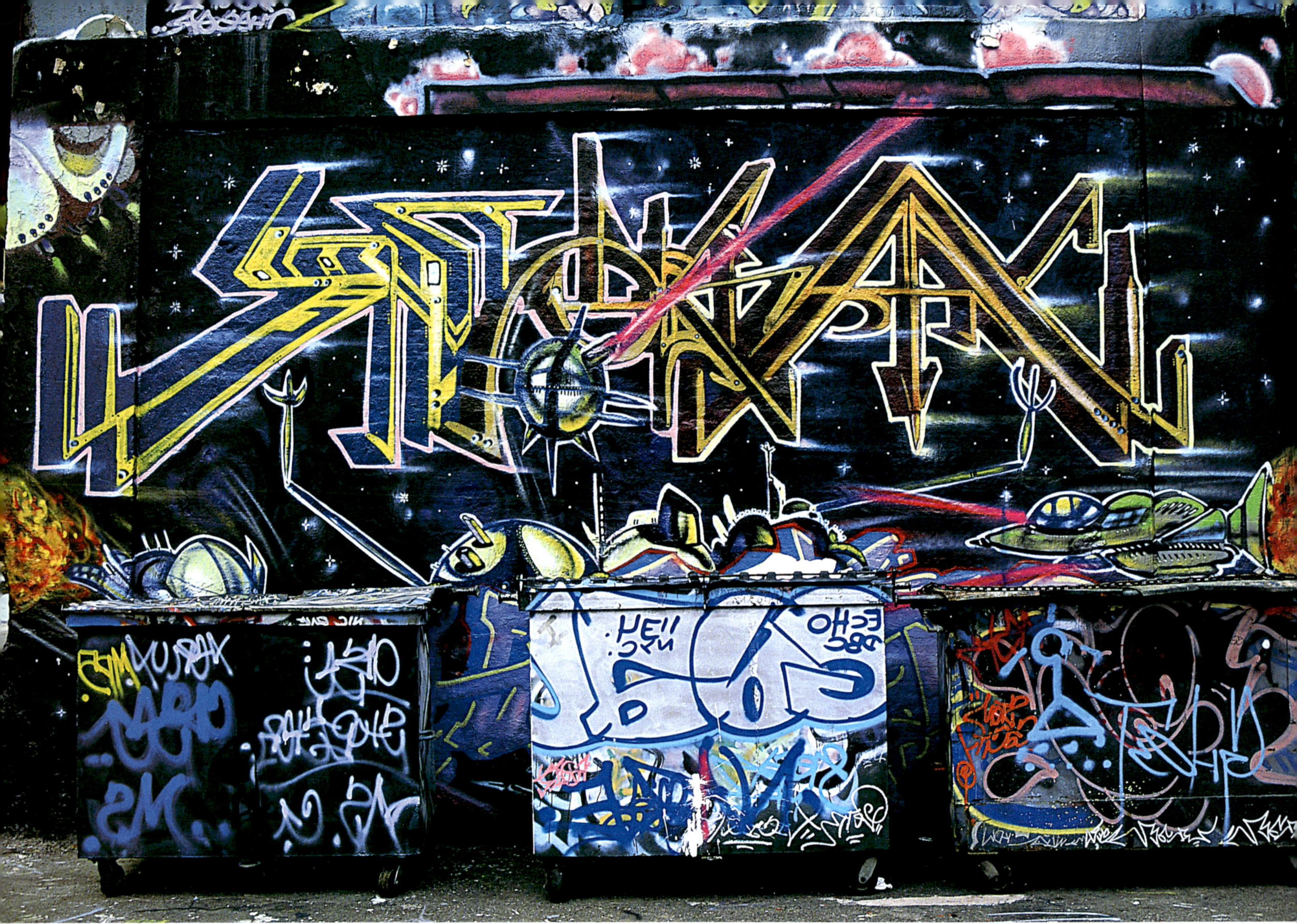

"Five Pointz," the building formerly known as "Phun Factory," sports a massive wall stretching one full block in Long Island City, Queens. Graffiti artists from all five boroughs are welcome to feature their throw-ups here, hence its moniker. The building and whatever else surrounds it are fair game to the aerosol artists. Here garbage dumpsters and a fire hydrant have become an integral part of this urban canvas.

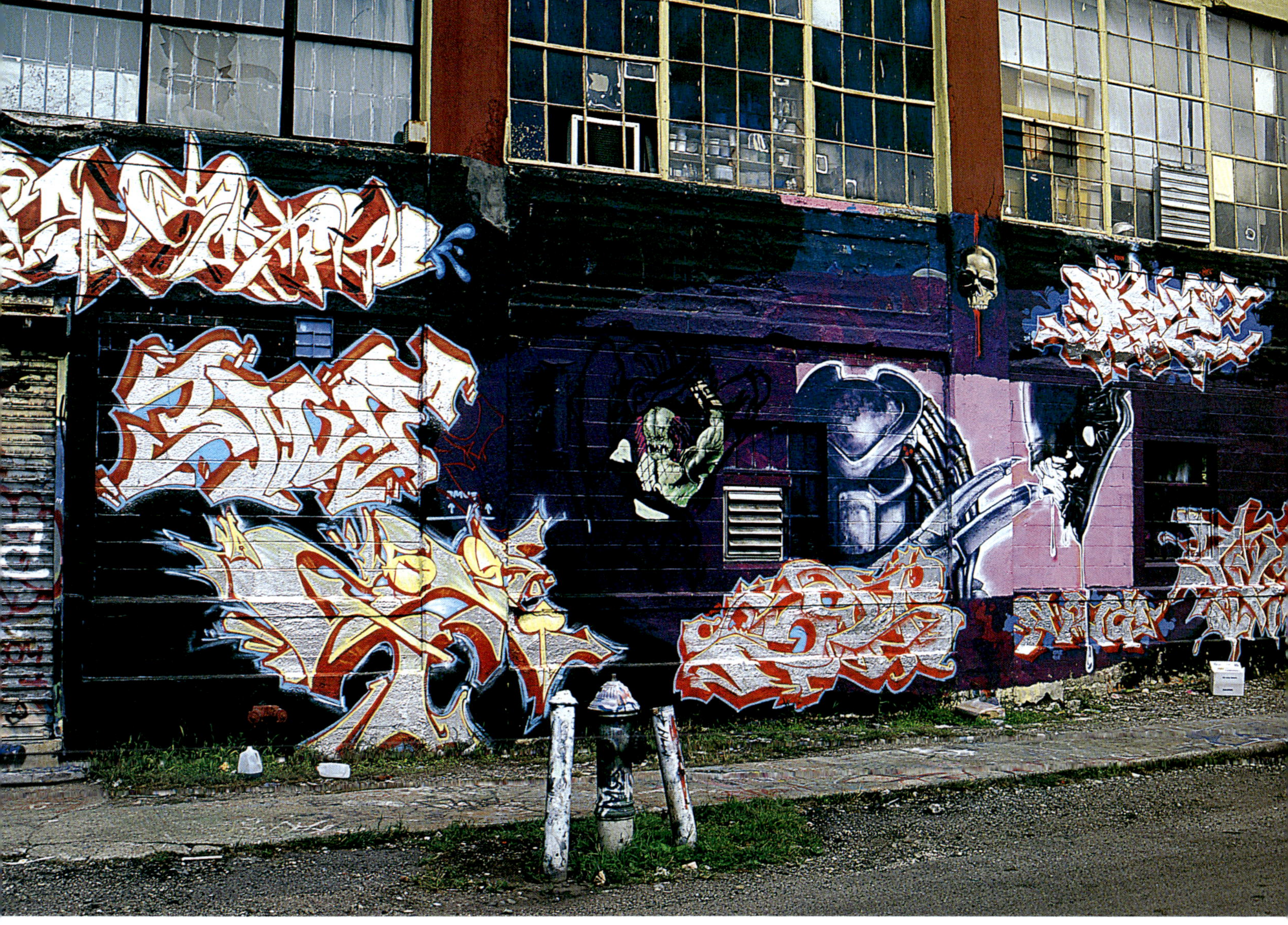

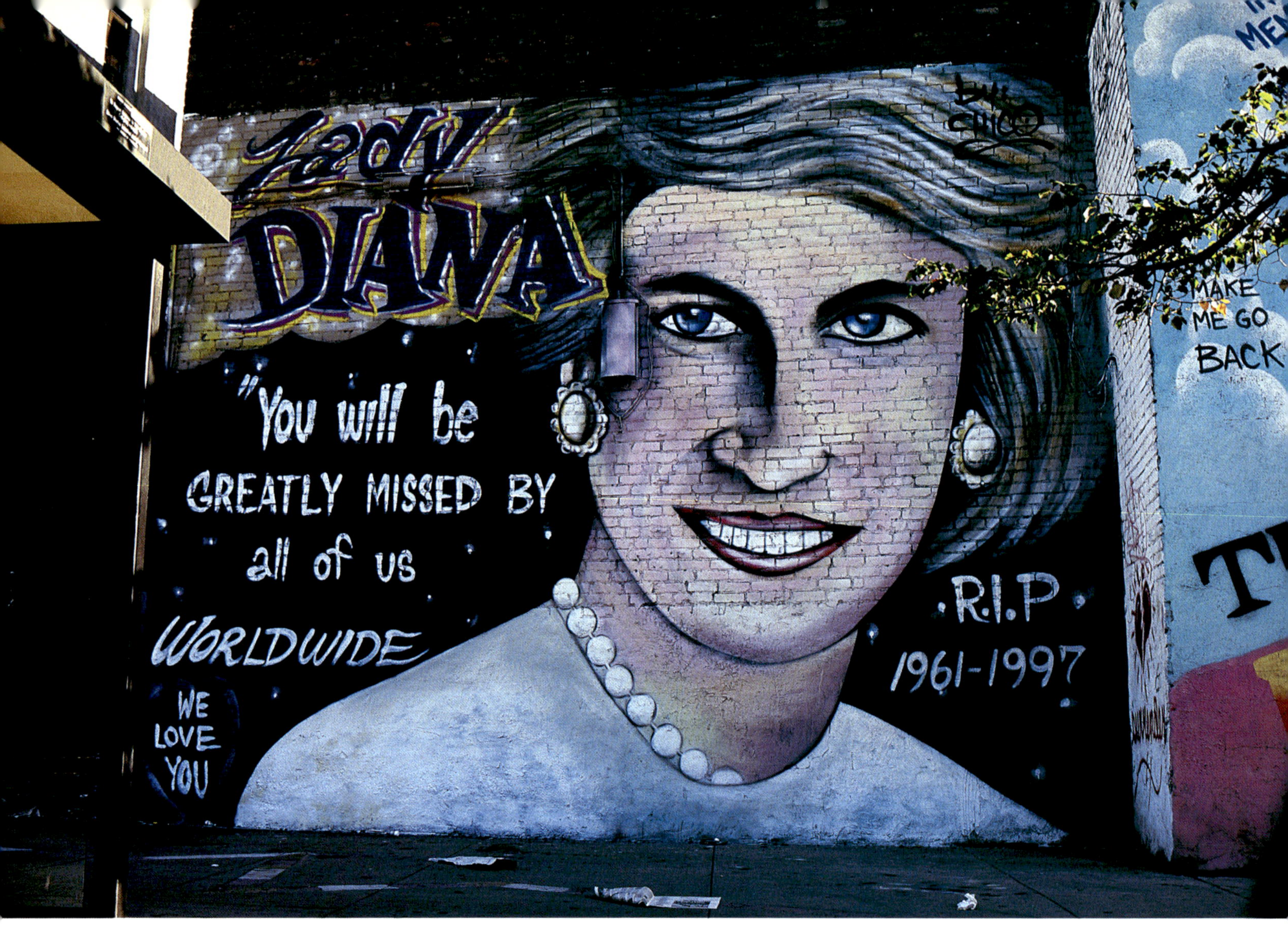

CHICO's simple memorial to Princess Diana makes an easily readable statement.

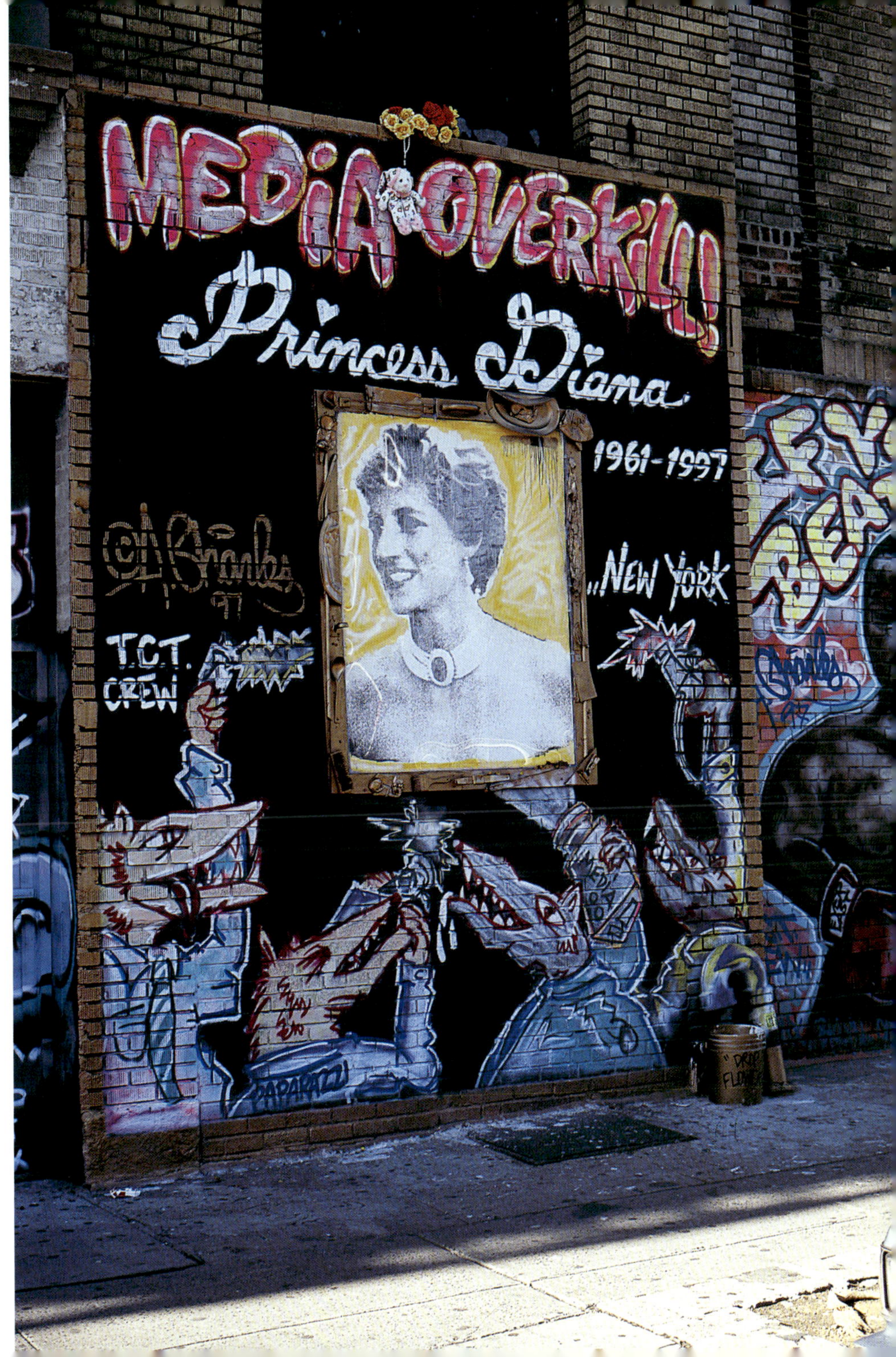

Andre Charles's edgy Houston Street mural on media overkill after the death of Princess Diana stands as an interesting counterpoint to other memorials in her honor. The collage design makes use of a paper drawing of the deceased princess.

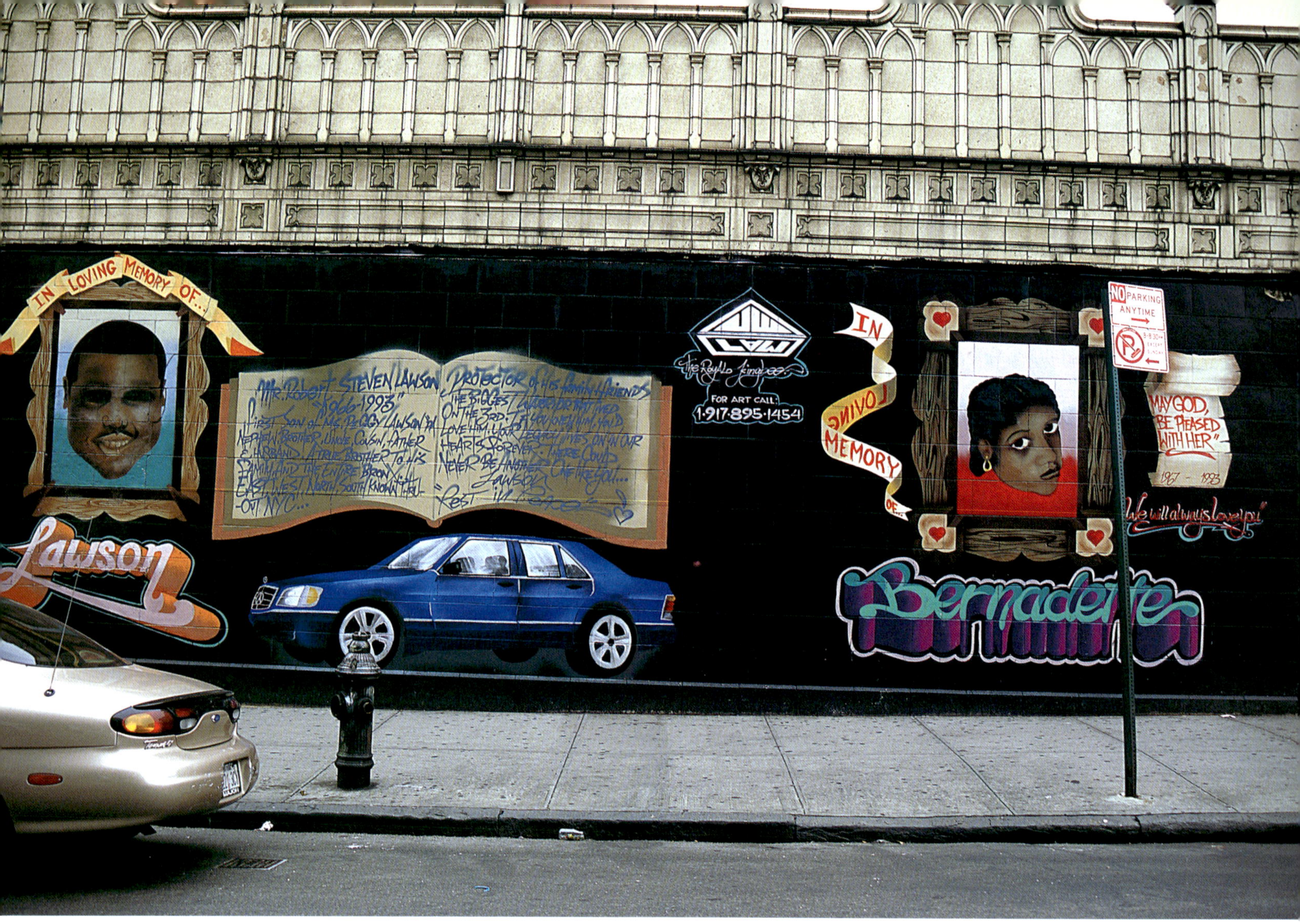

Memorial murals as a portrait gallery by different local artists. The unusual style of the Bernadette tribute has the theatrical look of a 1940s silver screen poster.

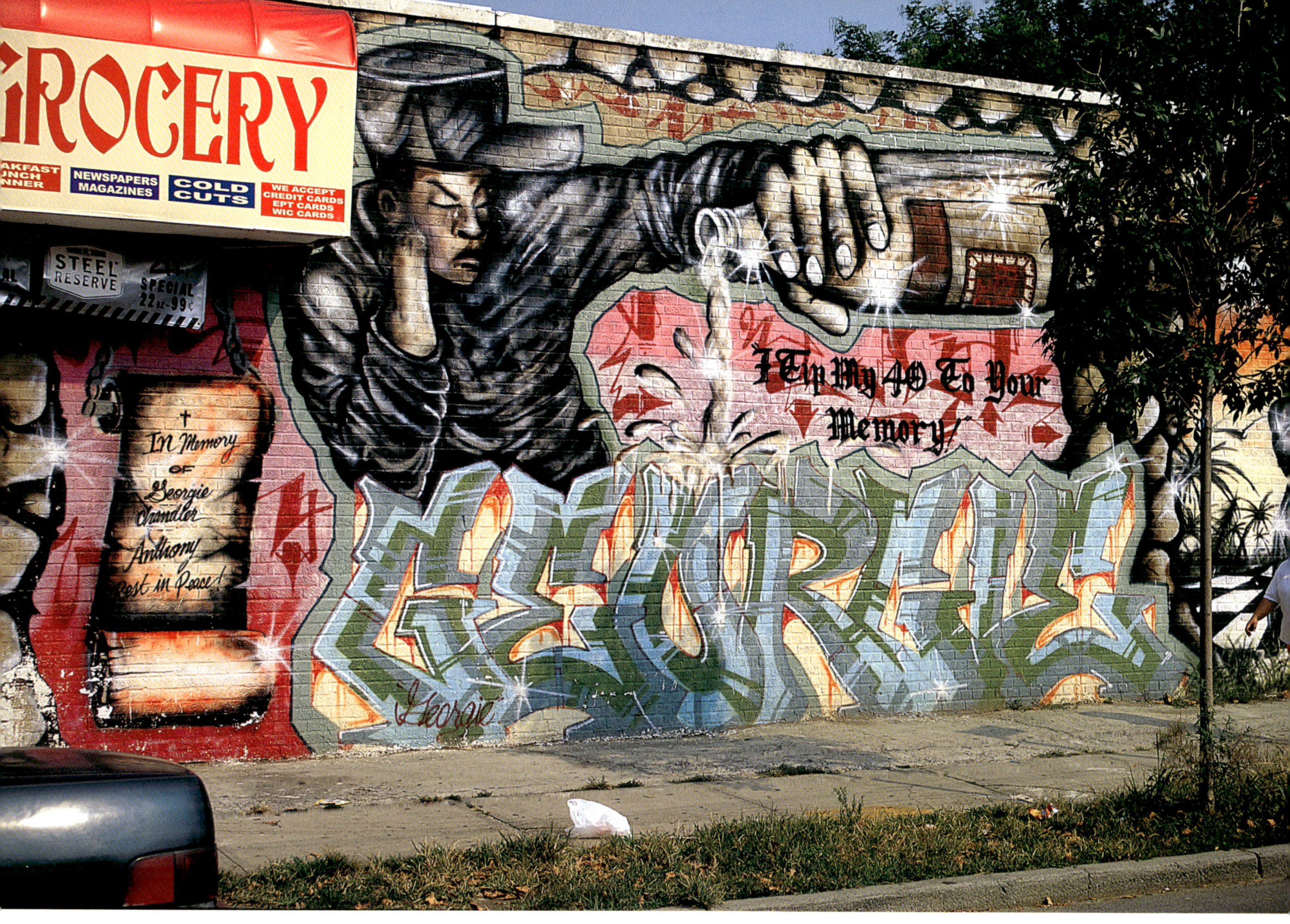

Following an old custom, a homeboy pours beer over the grave of a friend. This Brooklyn memorial mural is probably at a corner where Georgie was well known.

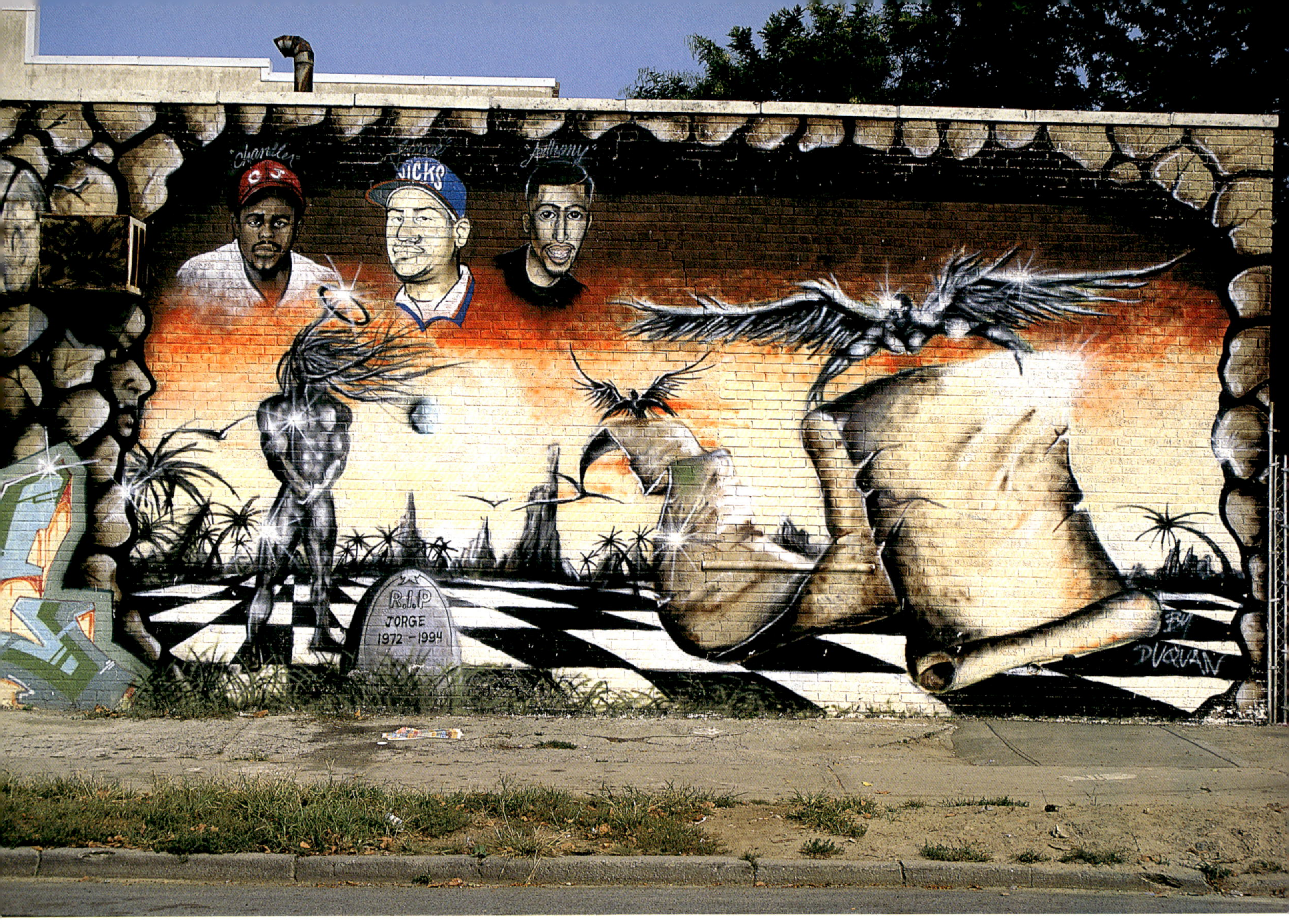

The dominant crow in this Brooklyn memorial carries the spirit to another life.

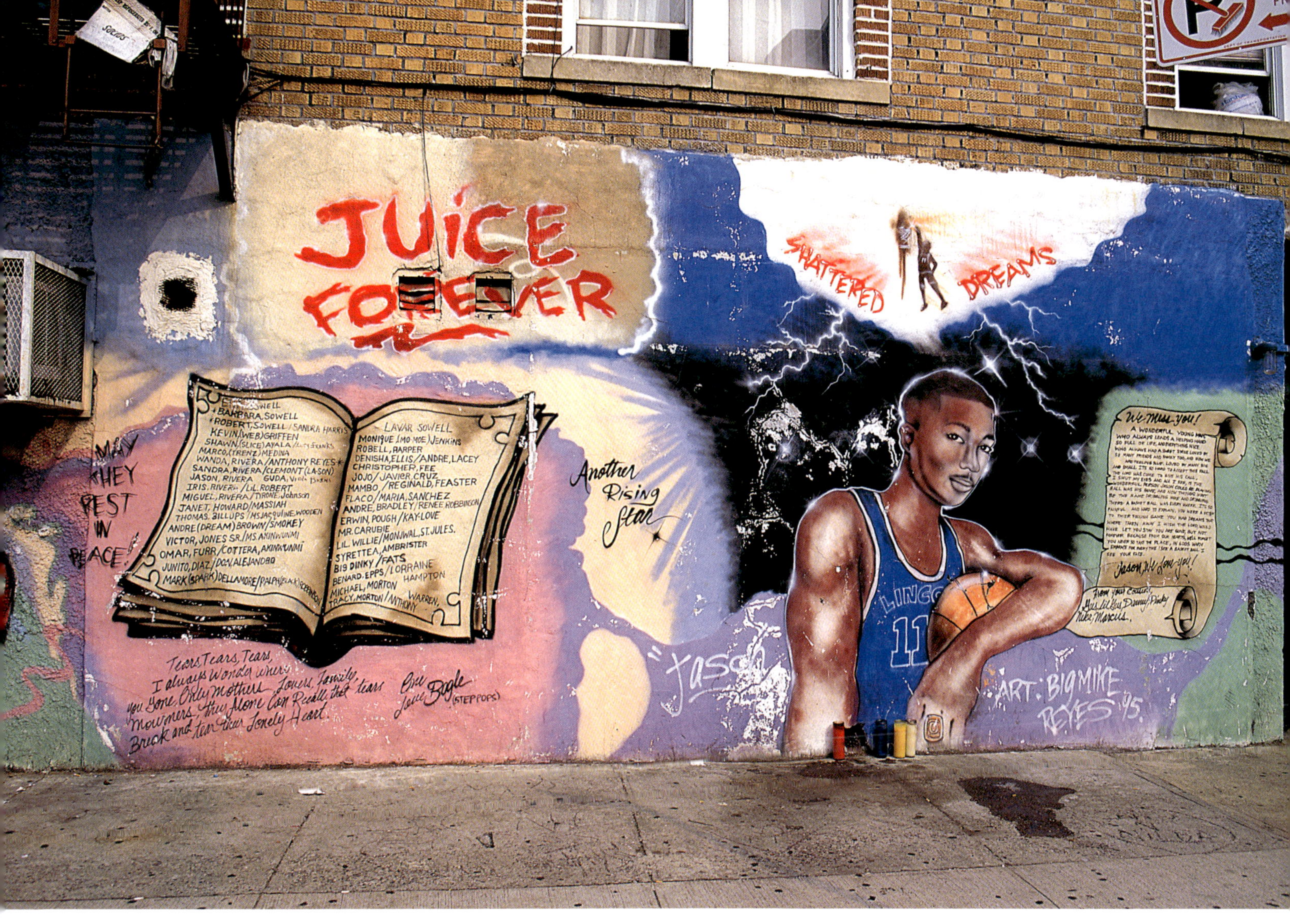

Basketball talent and a life cut short illustrate broken dreams in this Brooklyn memorial mural.

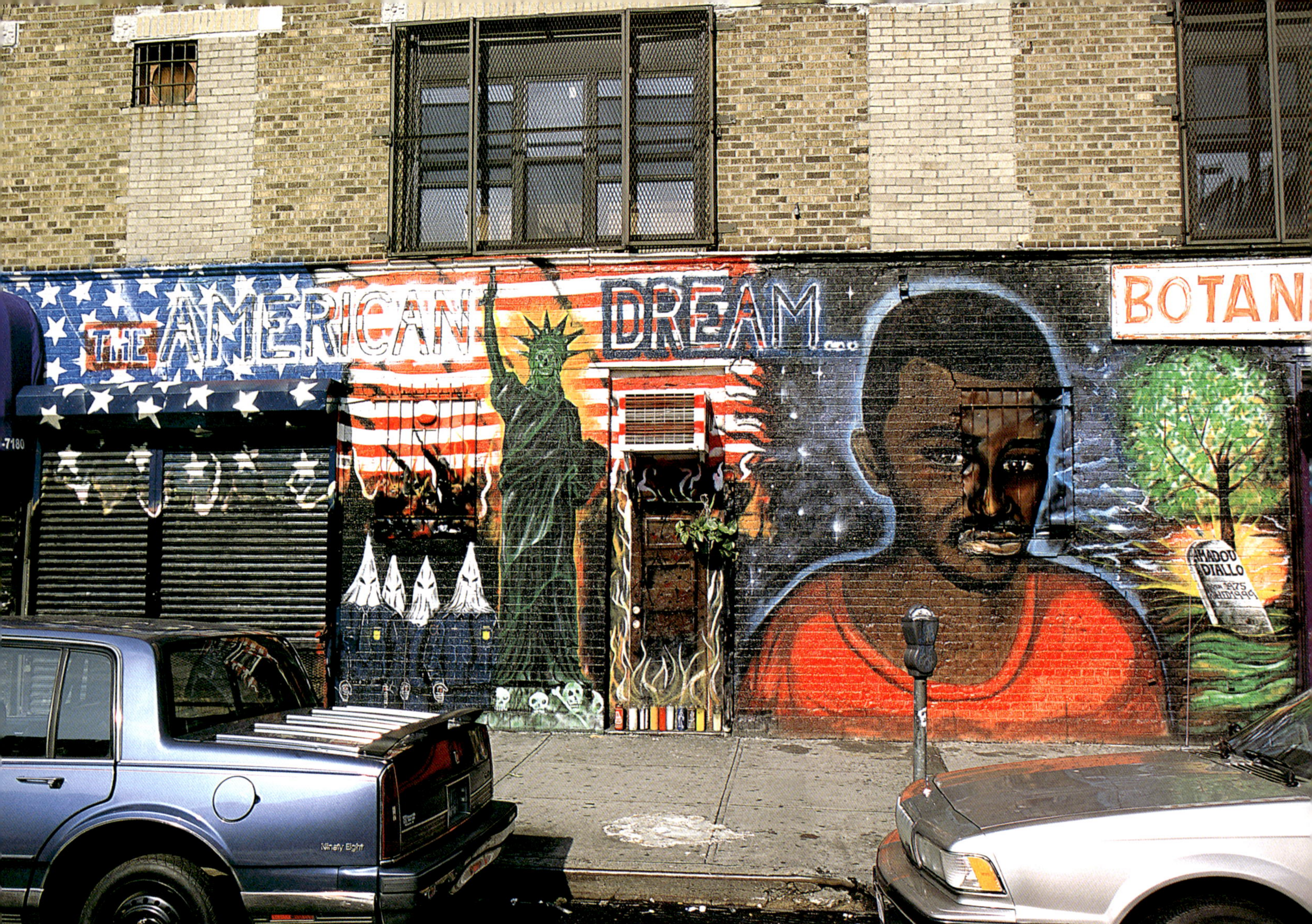

A paintbrush mural by Chicago artist Hulbert Waldroup. The controversial Bronx memorial is to Amadou Diallo, the African immigrant whose American dream ended in a pool of blood when he was killed by police in 1999 near Wheeler and Westchester avenues. The unarmed street vendor was shot forty-one times because police said they thought he had a gun. The mural bears little resemblance to the distinctive style of the barrio's other murals by FX CRU. Its visual clichés show outside influences (the incident had drawn international attention).

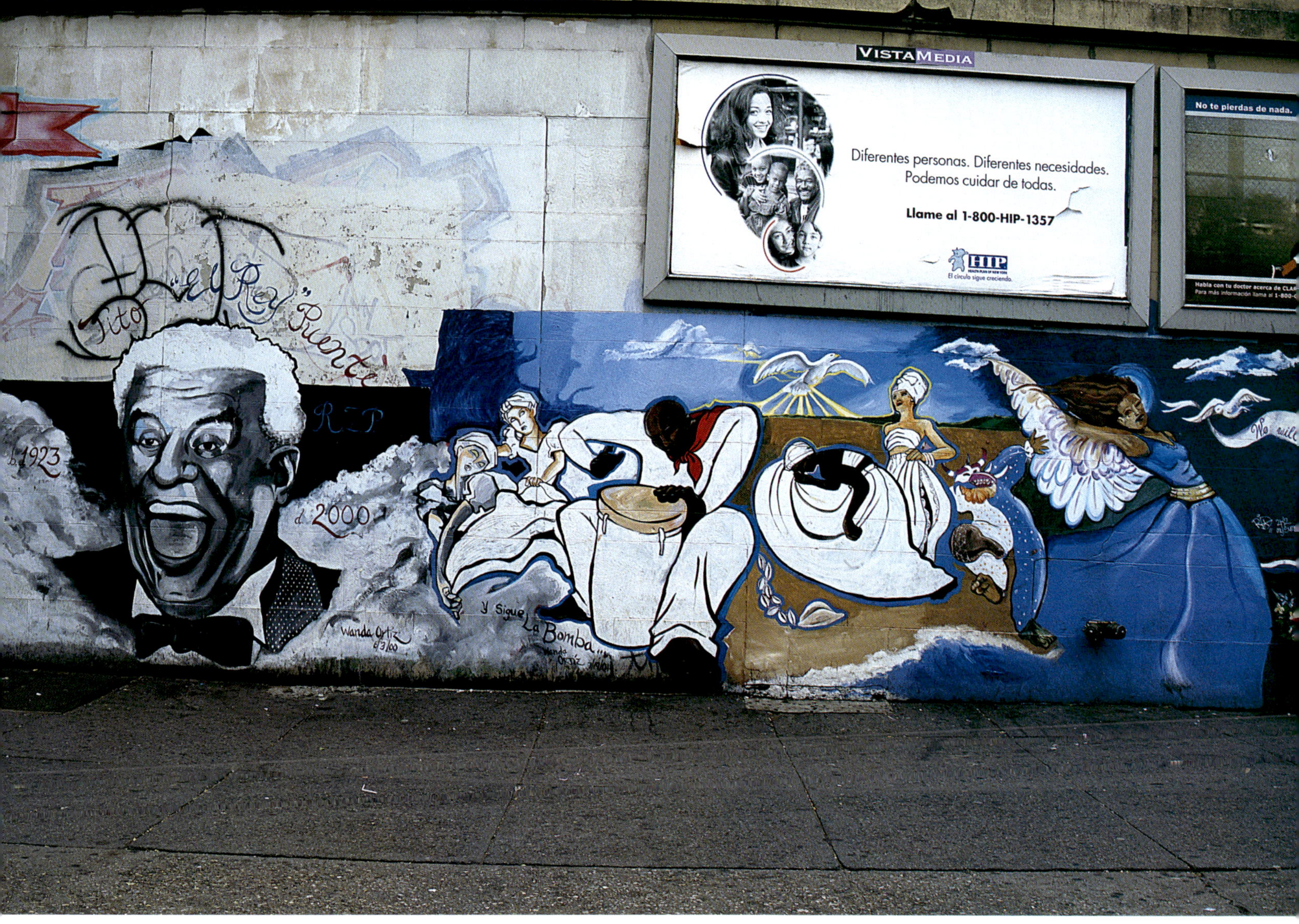

Wanda Ortiz's strong image of Tito Puente and her elegantly rendered vision of paradise suggest that his music is still playing.

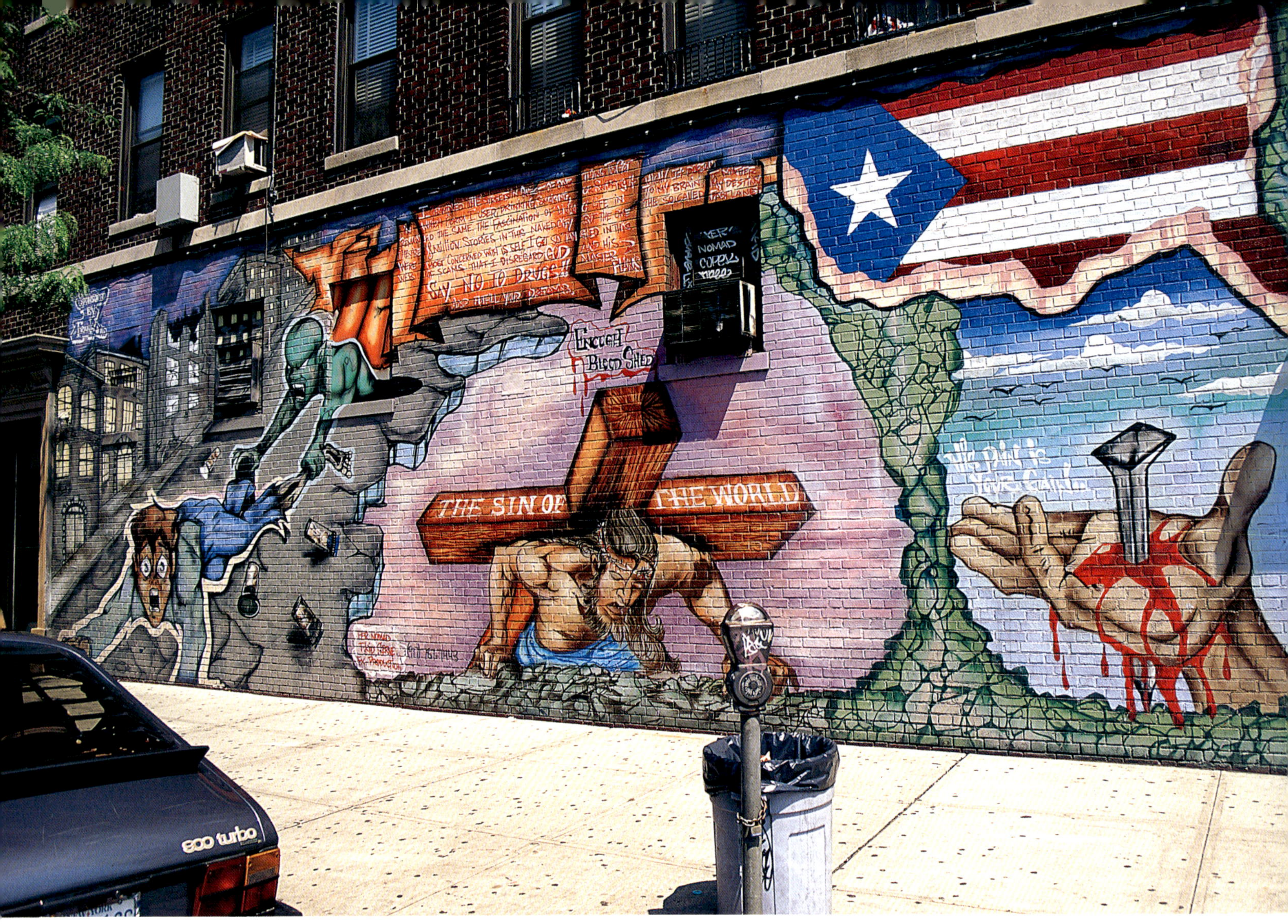

A Bronx political mural, near Yankee Stadium, where the hand of fate personified by a grasping sewer creature suggests a unified message of no escape.

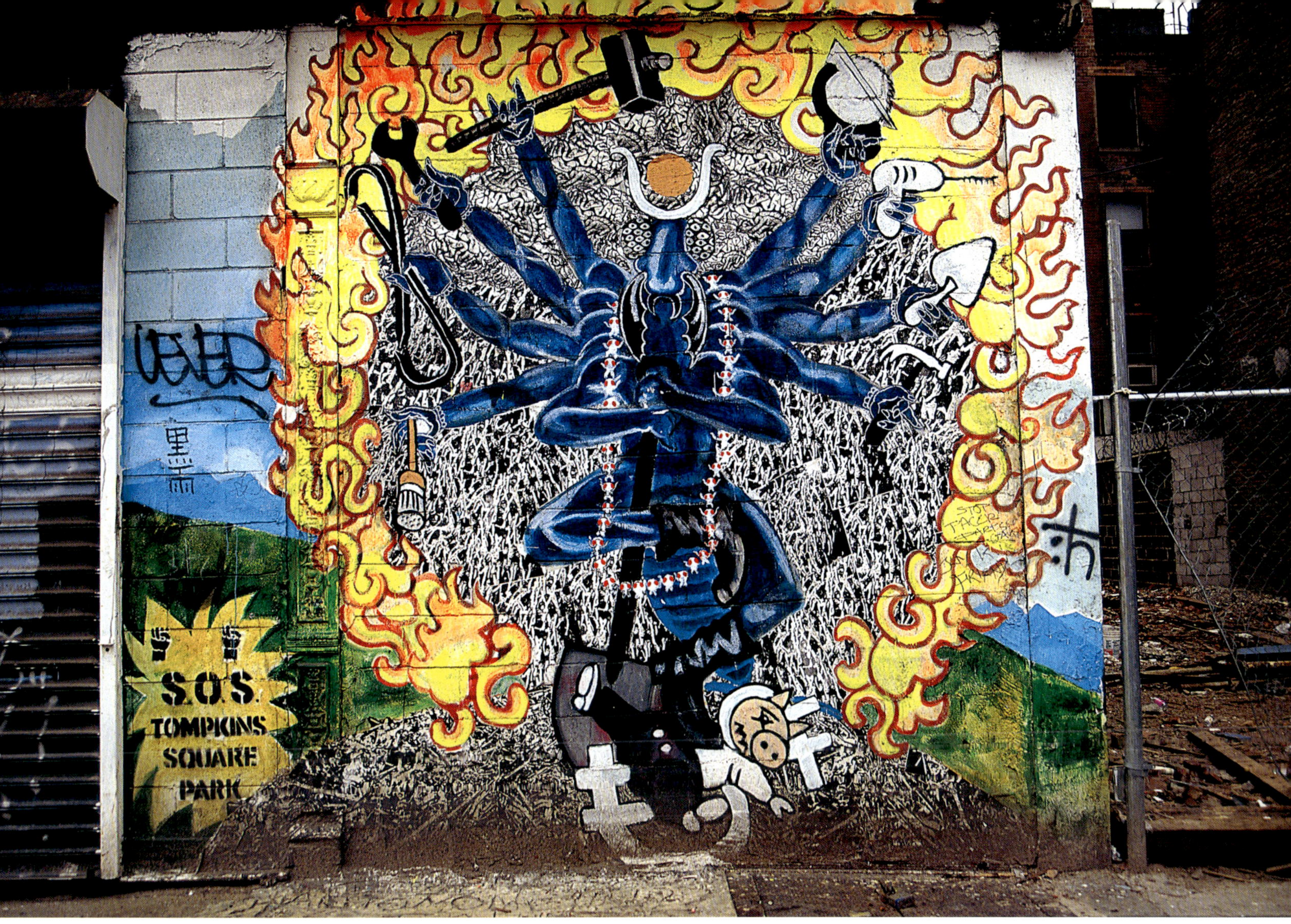

A political message to save Tompkins Square Park in the East Village is vividly presented in a local artist's mural combining hippie Hinduism and urban gardening themes.

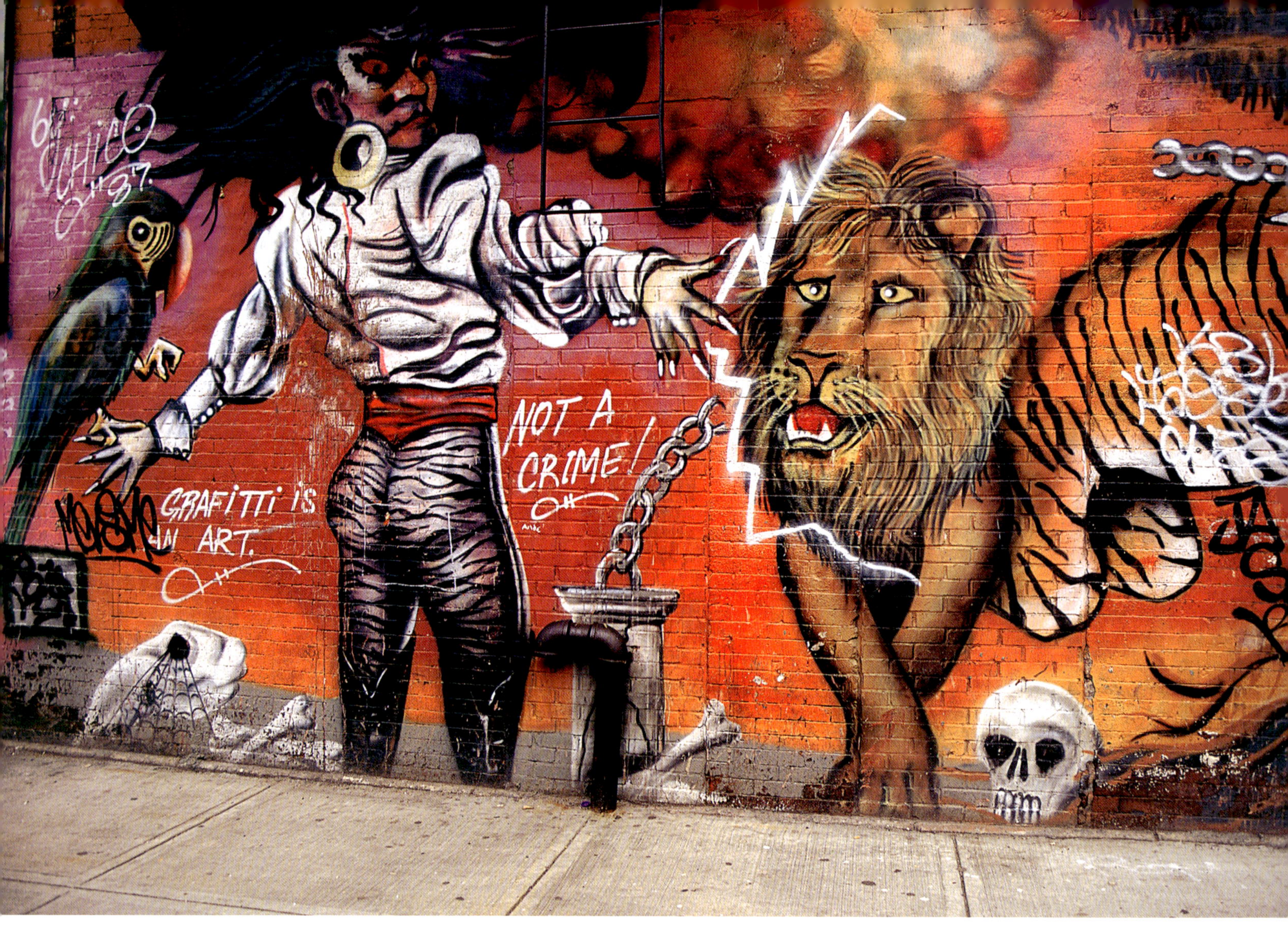

CHICO's vivid political statement defending graffiti as art, not crime, borrows fellow artist LEE's motto and takes its fiery motif from an Ozzie Osborne album, *Shout in the Dark*.

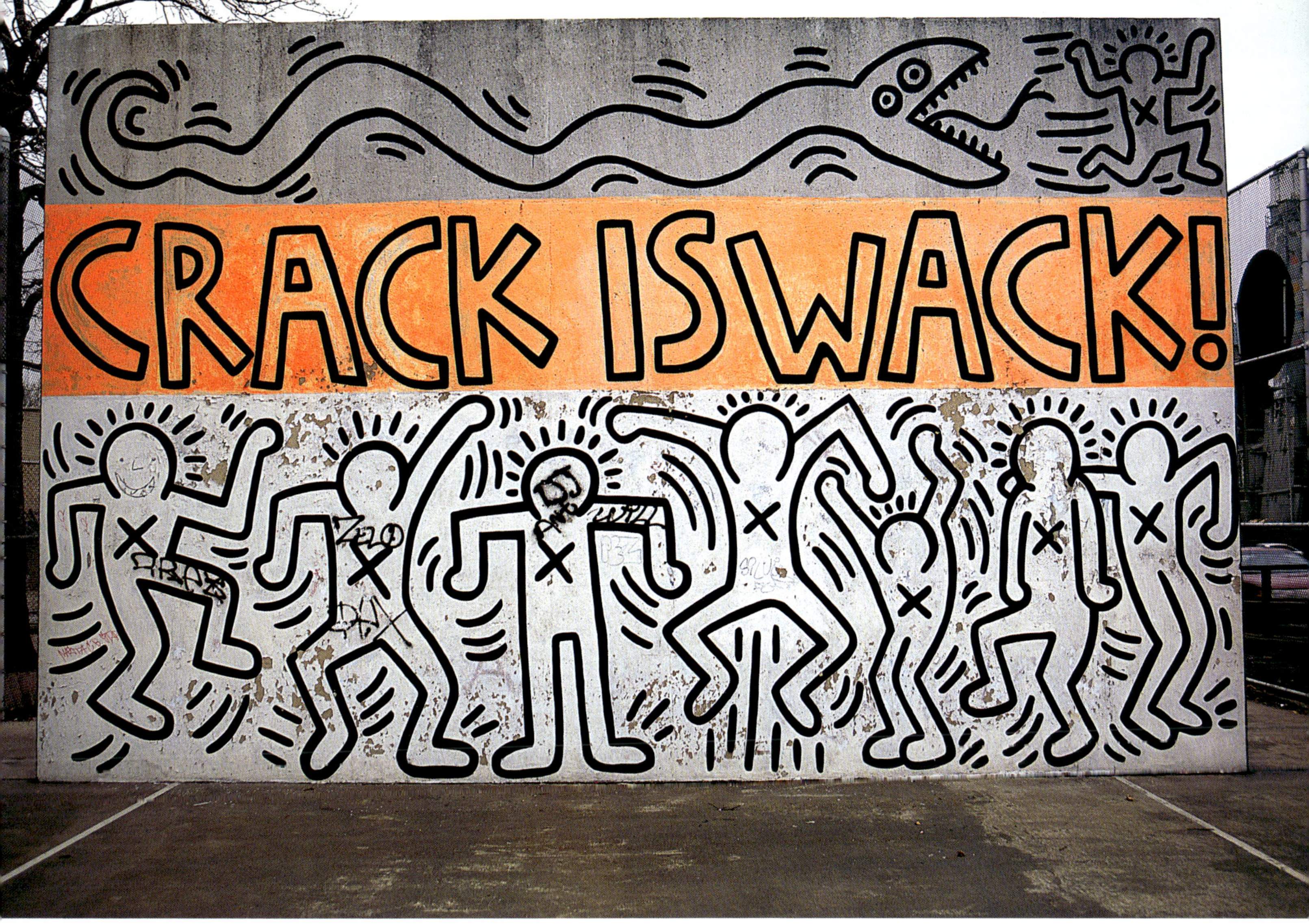

The strong, distinctive style of Keith Haring's two murals on opposite sides of a wall on a handball court on Second Avenue and Harlem River Drive present a cohesive antidrug message.

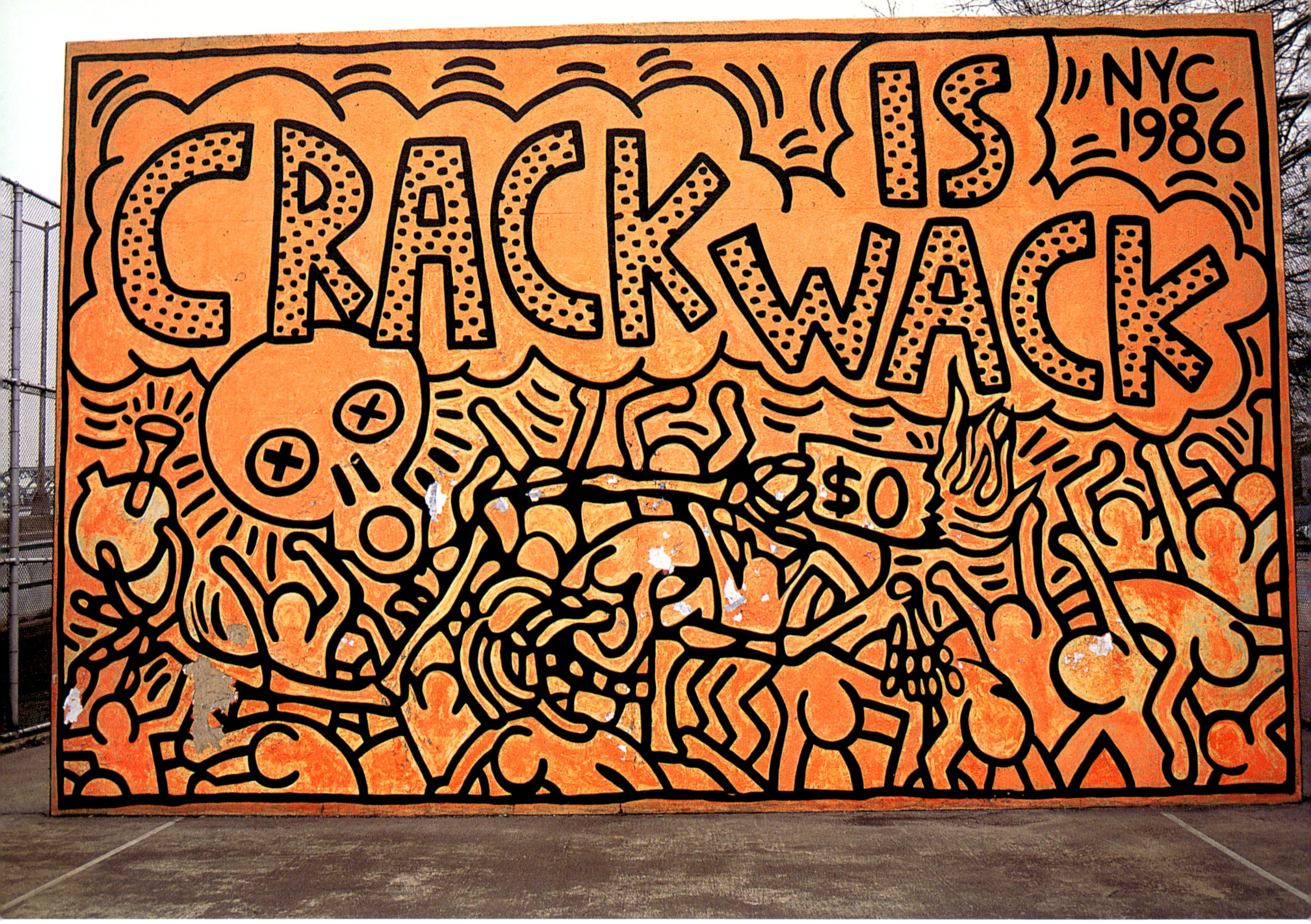

A perfect illustration of Keith Haring's activism, originality, and legacy preserved in an eye-catching set of murals on Manhattan's upper East Side.

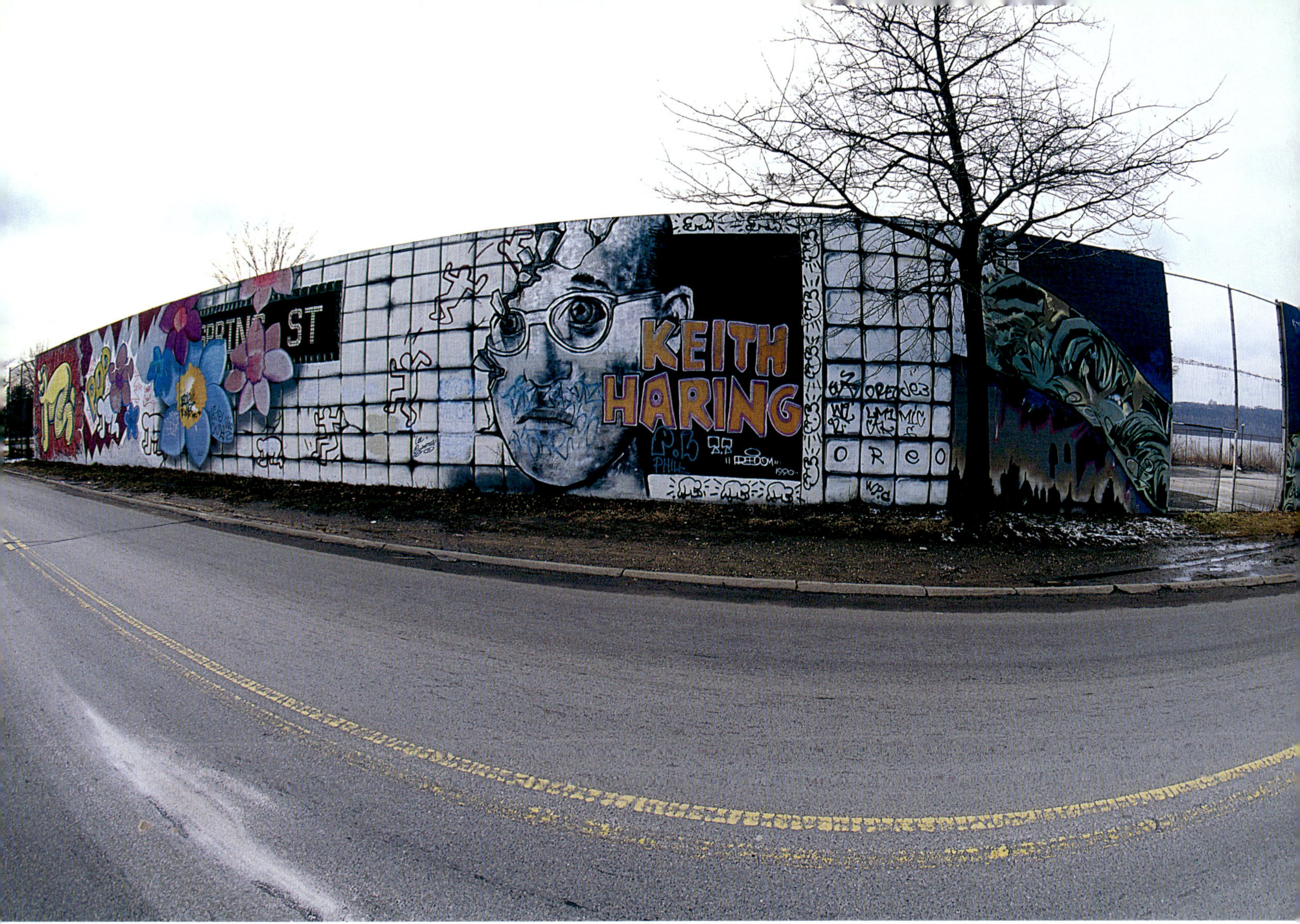

The West Side Highway's long memorial to beloved artist Keith Haring, who died of AIDS at thirty-two, in 1990, drew much anger in the community when it was painted over by city authorities. This group homage to Haring was signed by Kenny Scharf, LEE, Chris Pape (FREEDOM), and Johnny Matos (CRASH).

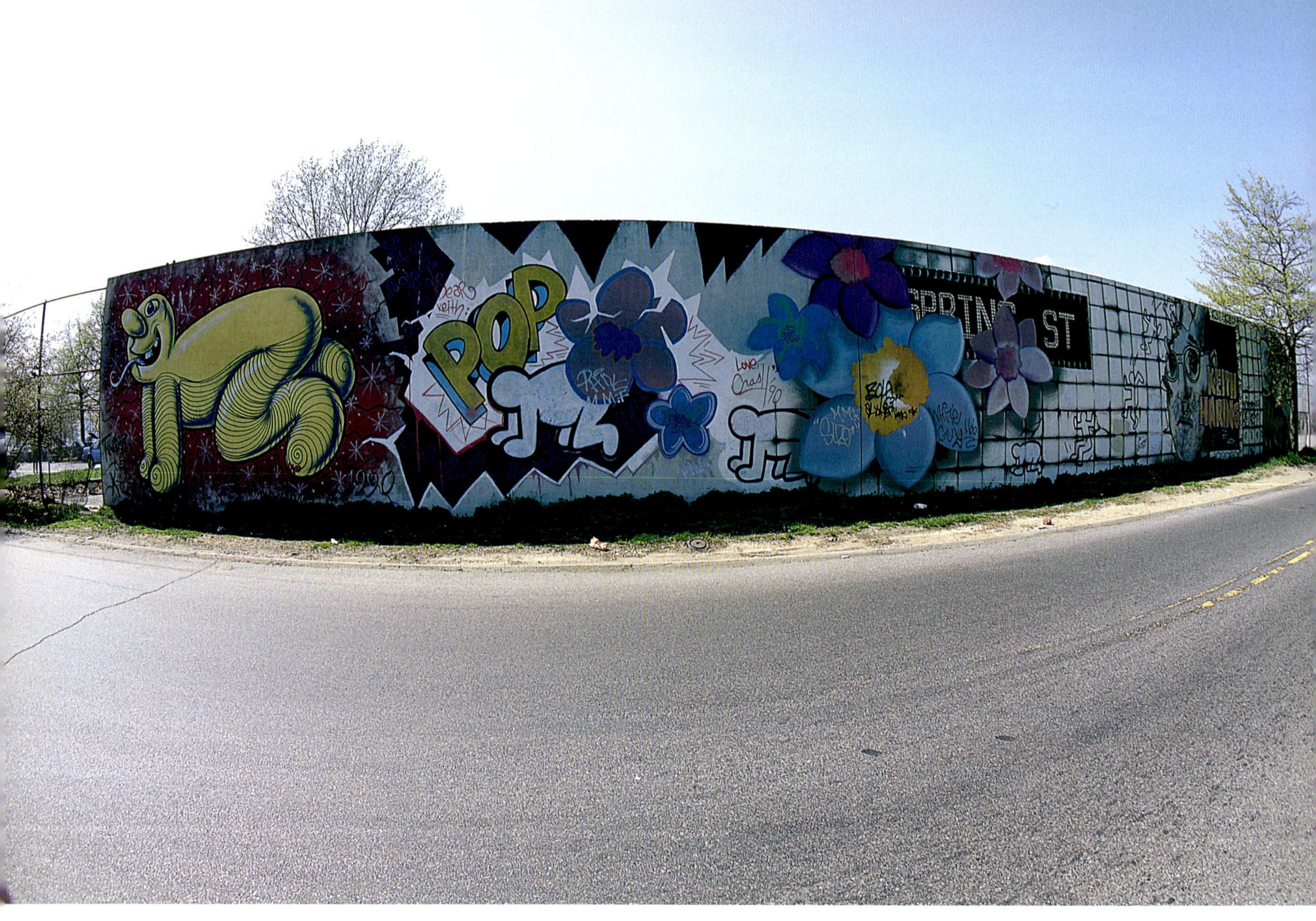

Another side of the West Side Highway memorial mural to artist Keith Haring, who died of AIDS in 1990.

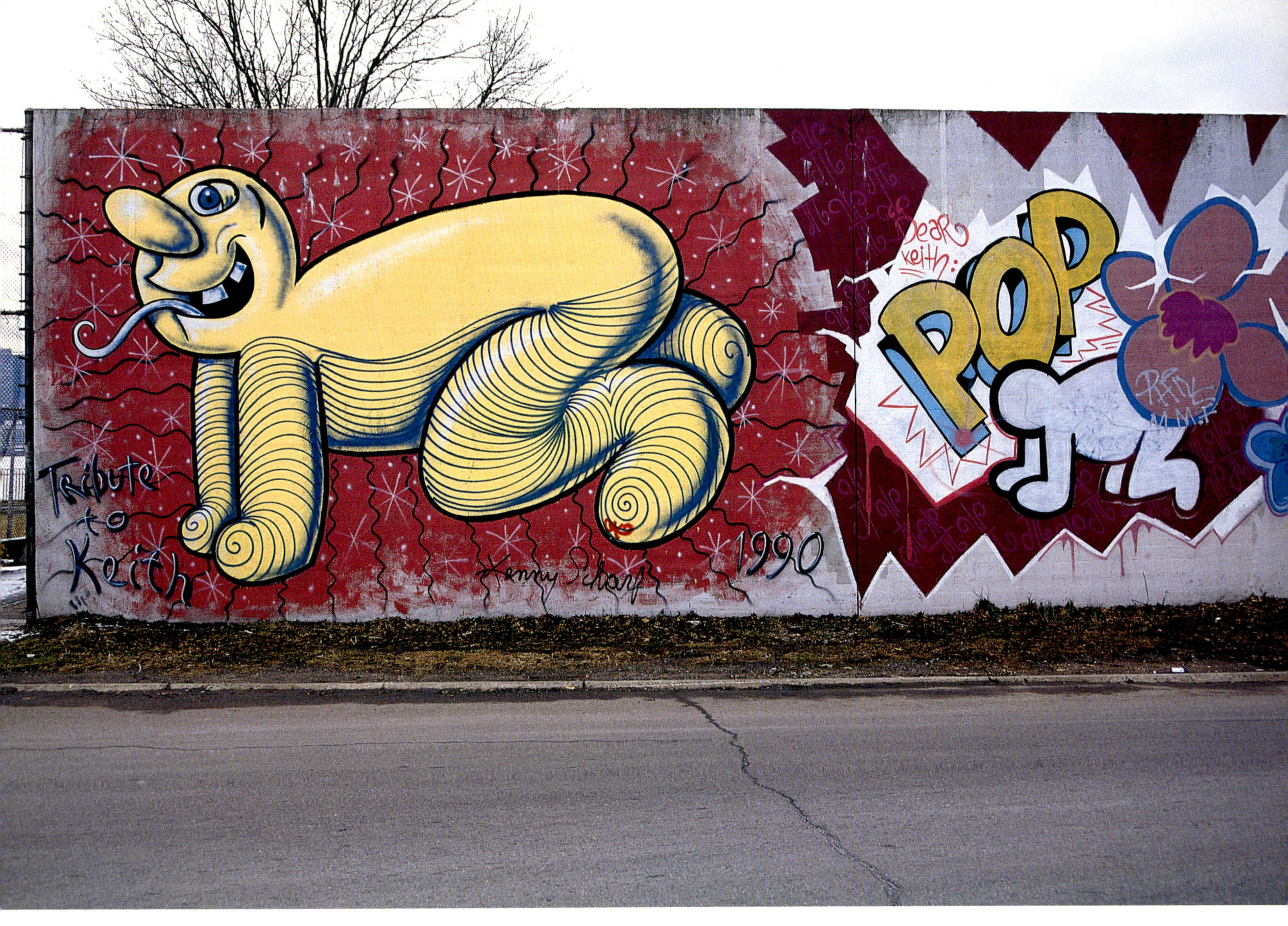

Haring's admirers pay tribute to his distinctive style with their own playful images. The toy-like figure is from artist Kenny Scharf.

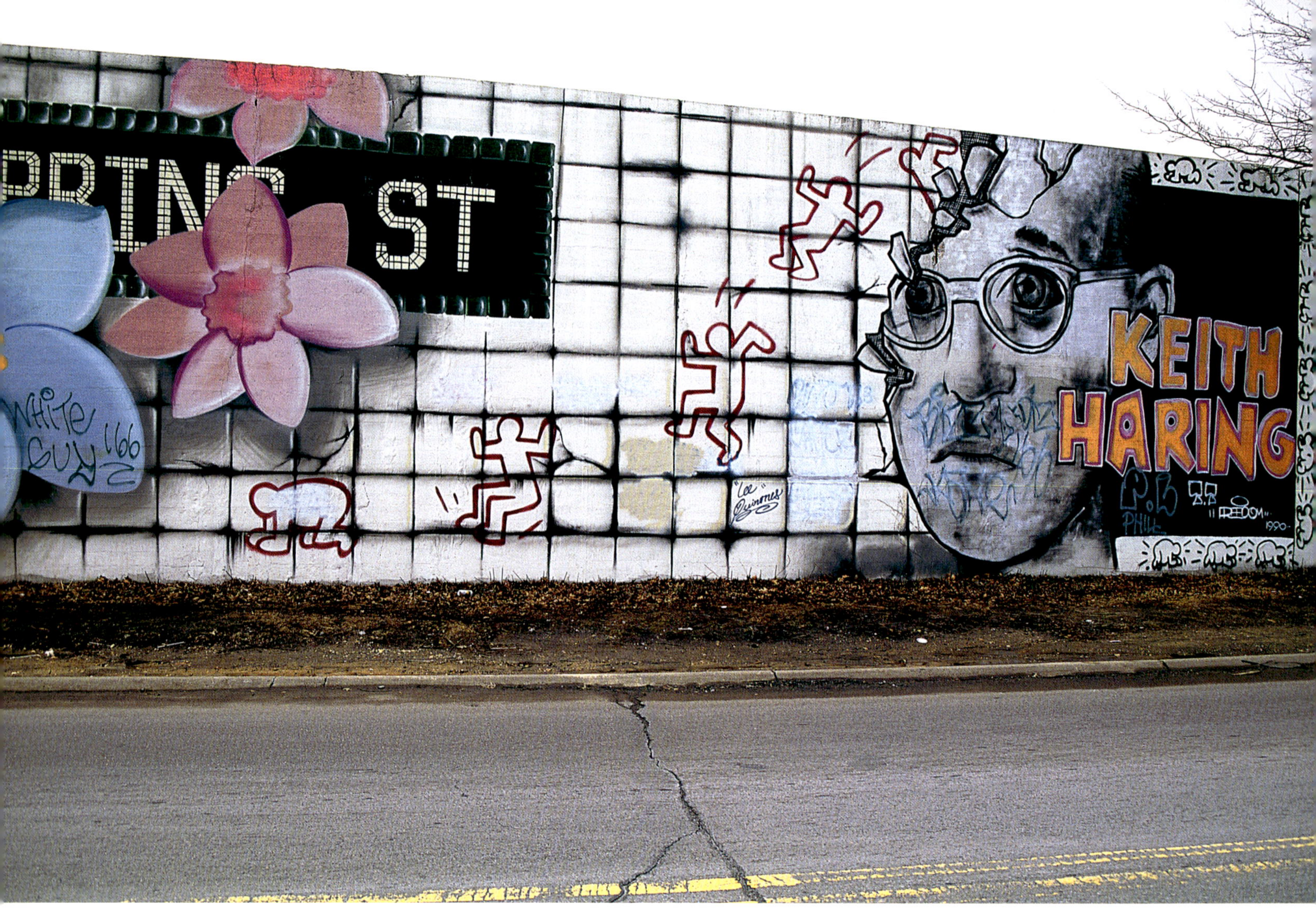

The Haring memorial drew tributes from many noted aerosol artists. Haring's portrait is the work of Chris Pape (FREEDOM).

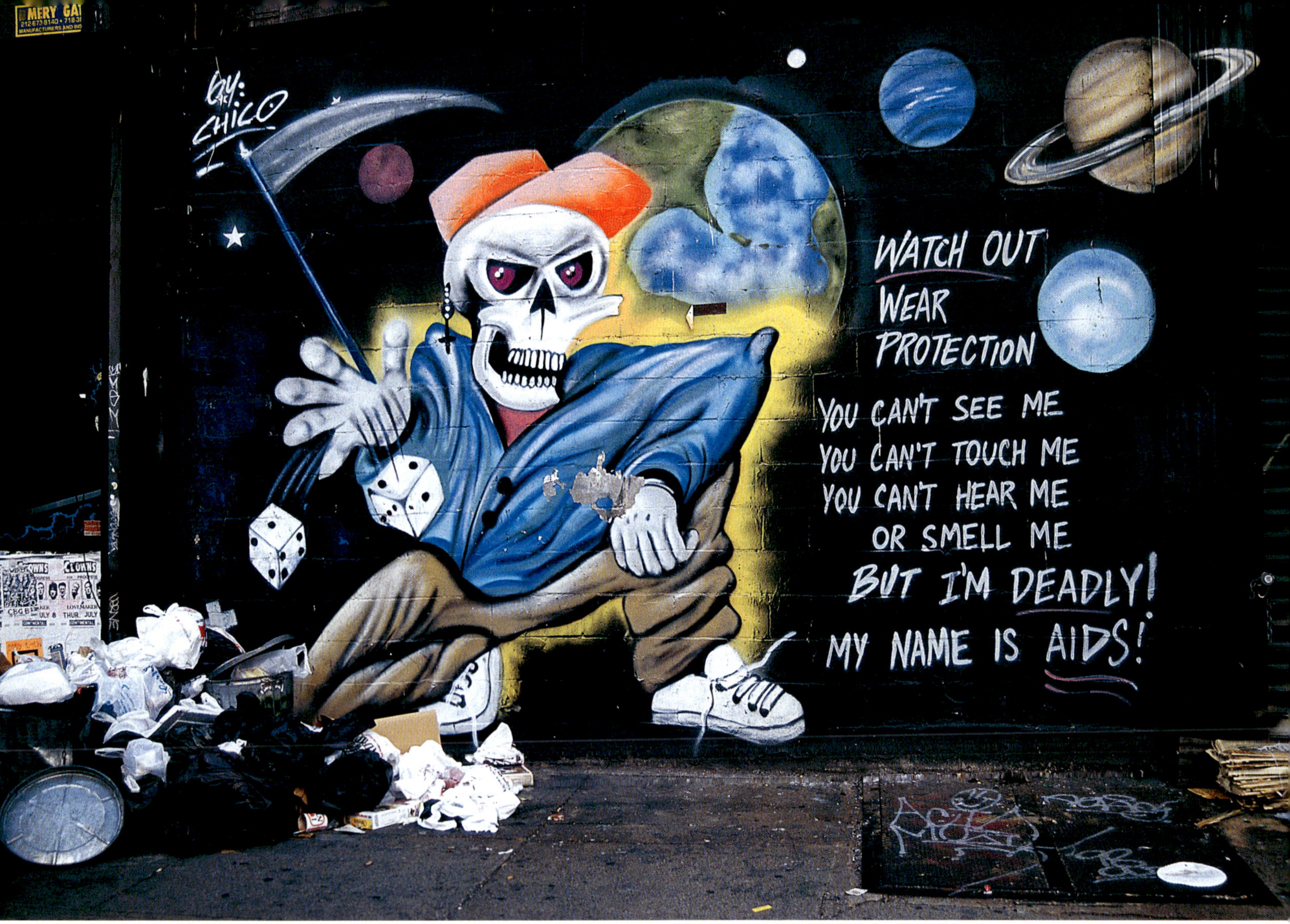

CHICO's compelling political message personifies AIDS in a menacing yellow aura. The mural incorporates the urban environment's existing elements, like trashcans, which add a decadent dimension to the composition.

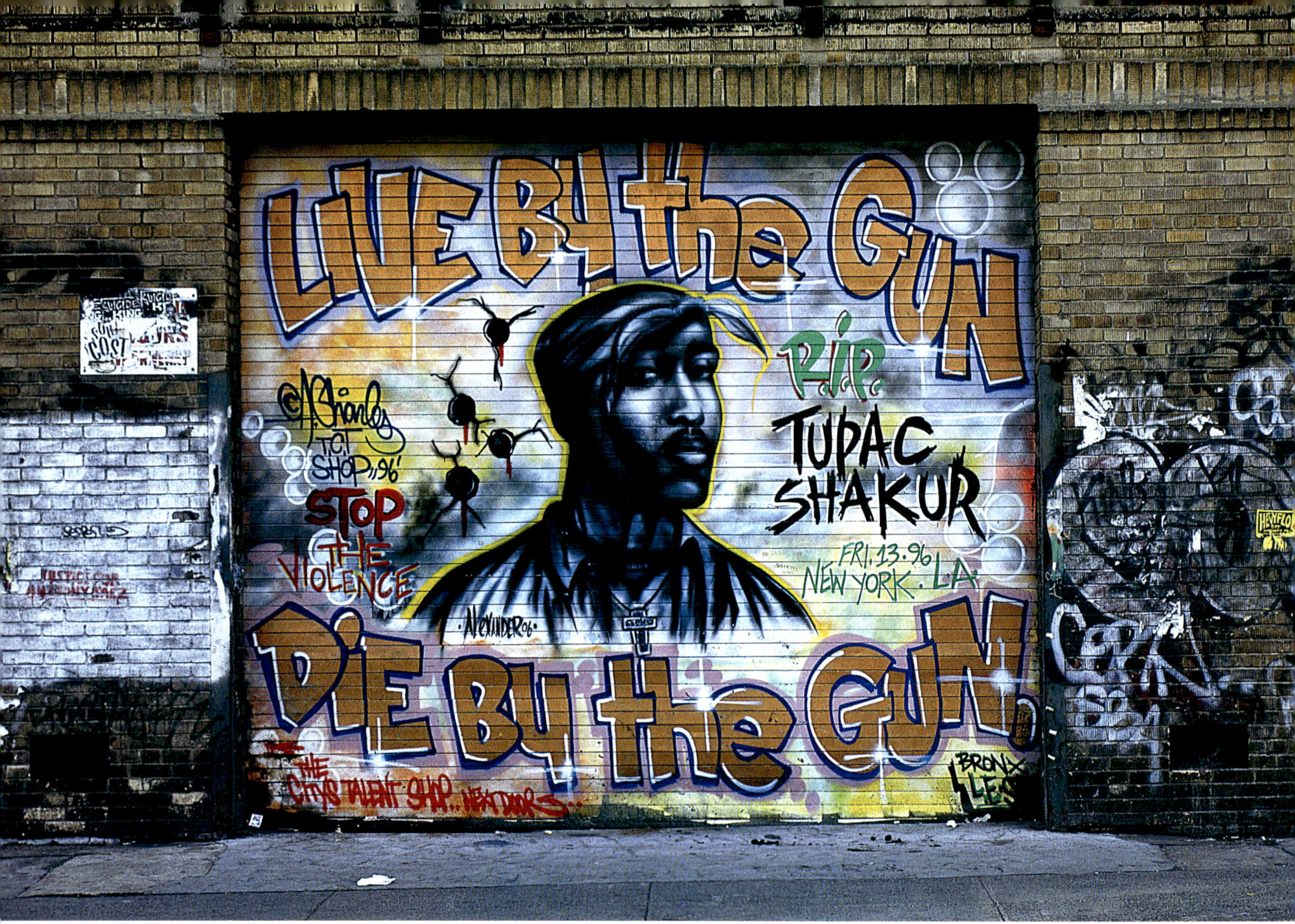

Andre Charles's Houston Street memorial to Tupac Shakur, a young rapper killed by gunfire in 1996. As with many Charles murals, the portrait was executed by another artist. Andre has been a muralist since the age of eleven.

Andre Charles's Houston Street portrait of Mike Tyson after he bit off part of the ear of a rival in a match. The mural is a good example of Charles's interest in controversial and provocative themes.

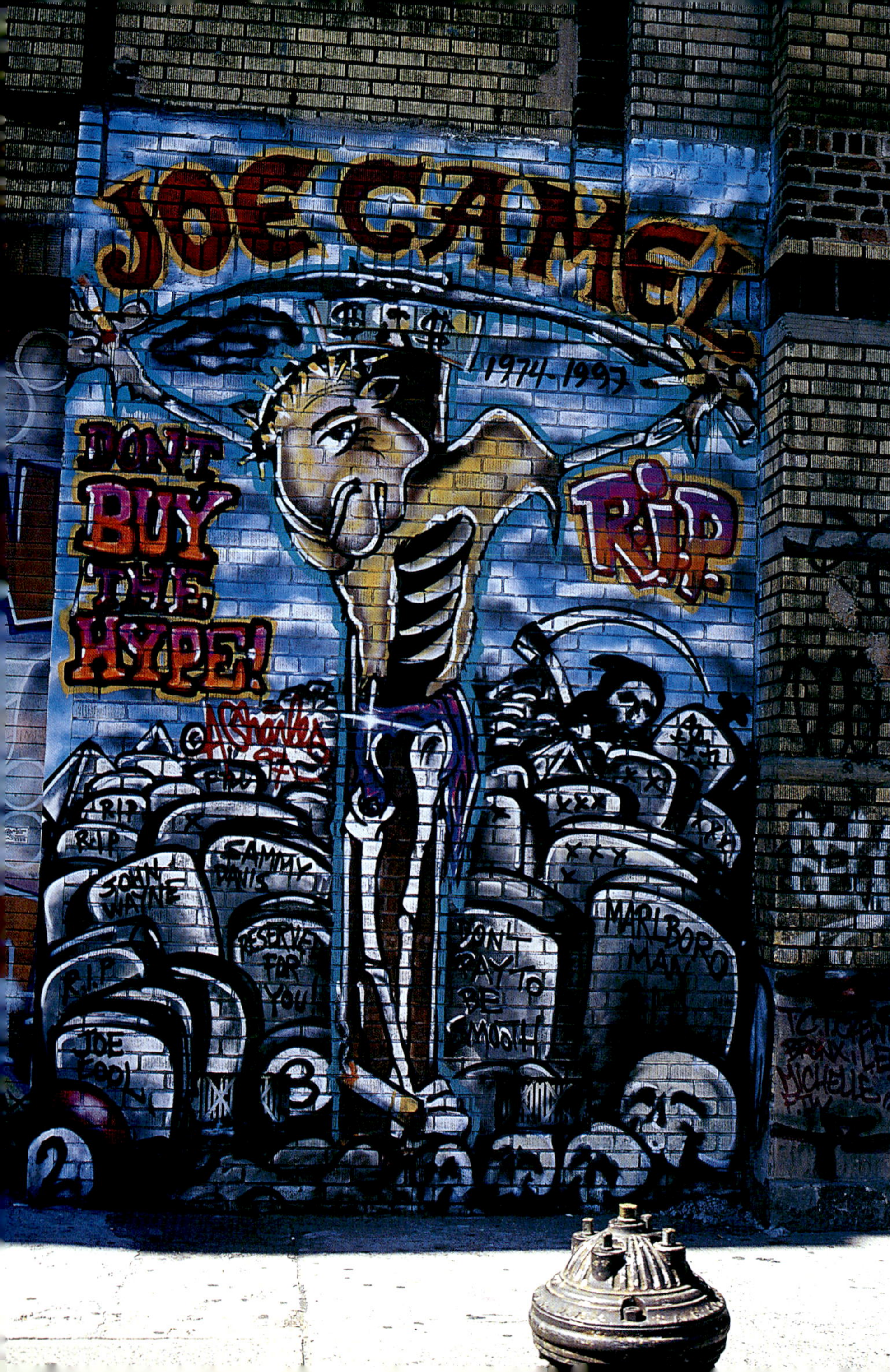

Andre Charles's strength is in logos and symbols. His Joe Camel images showcase his original mind in an antismoking message on Houston Street, his territory.

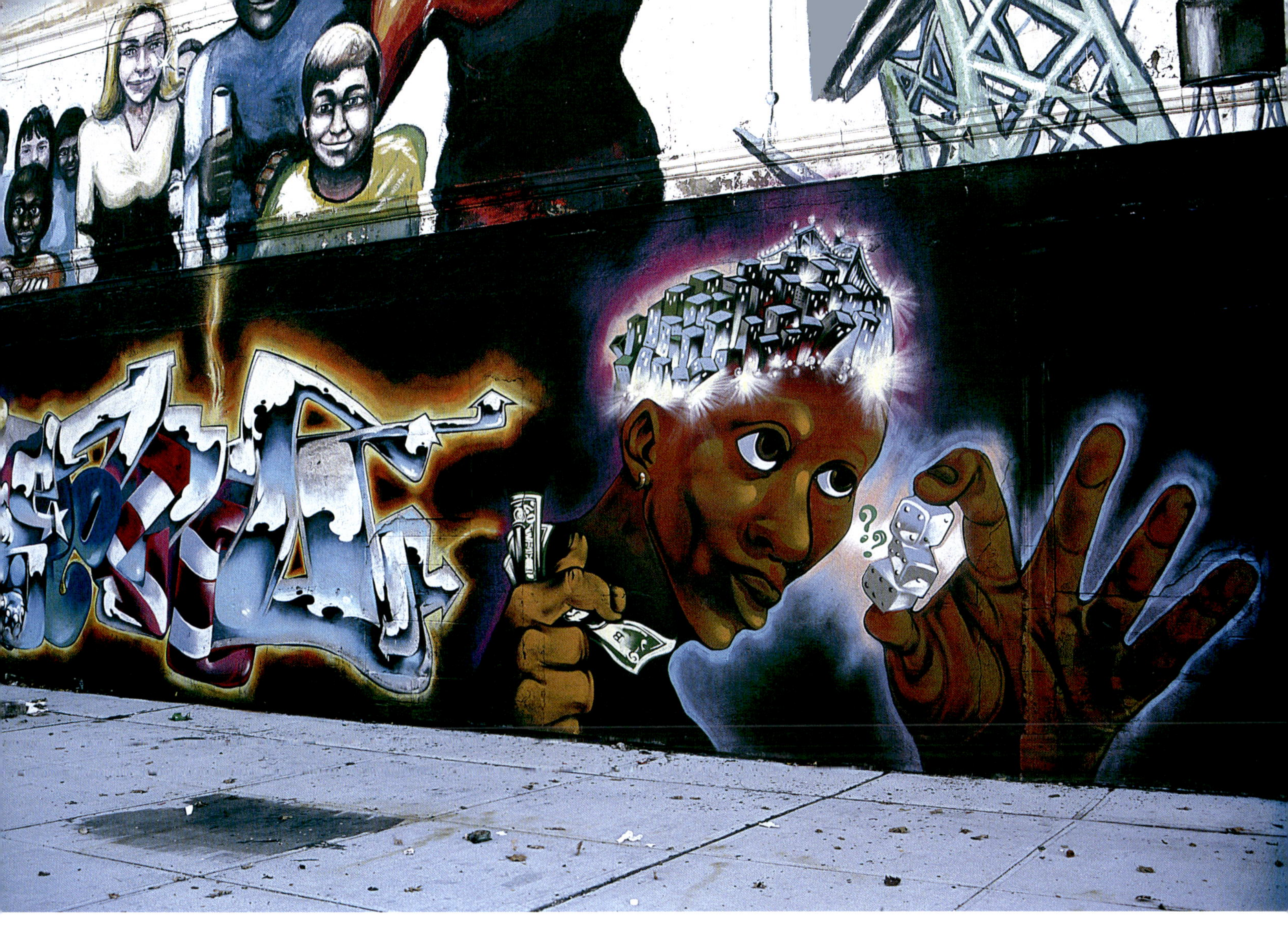

Decorative mural by EZO, whose dice theme shows that the comforts of gambling, unlike life, are in its immediate if uncertain results.

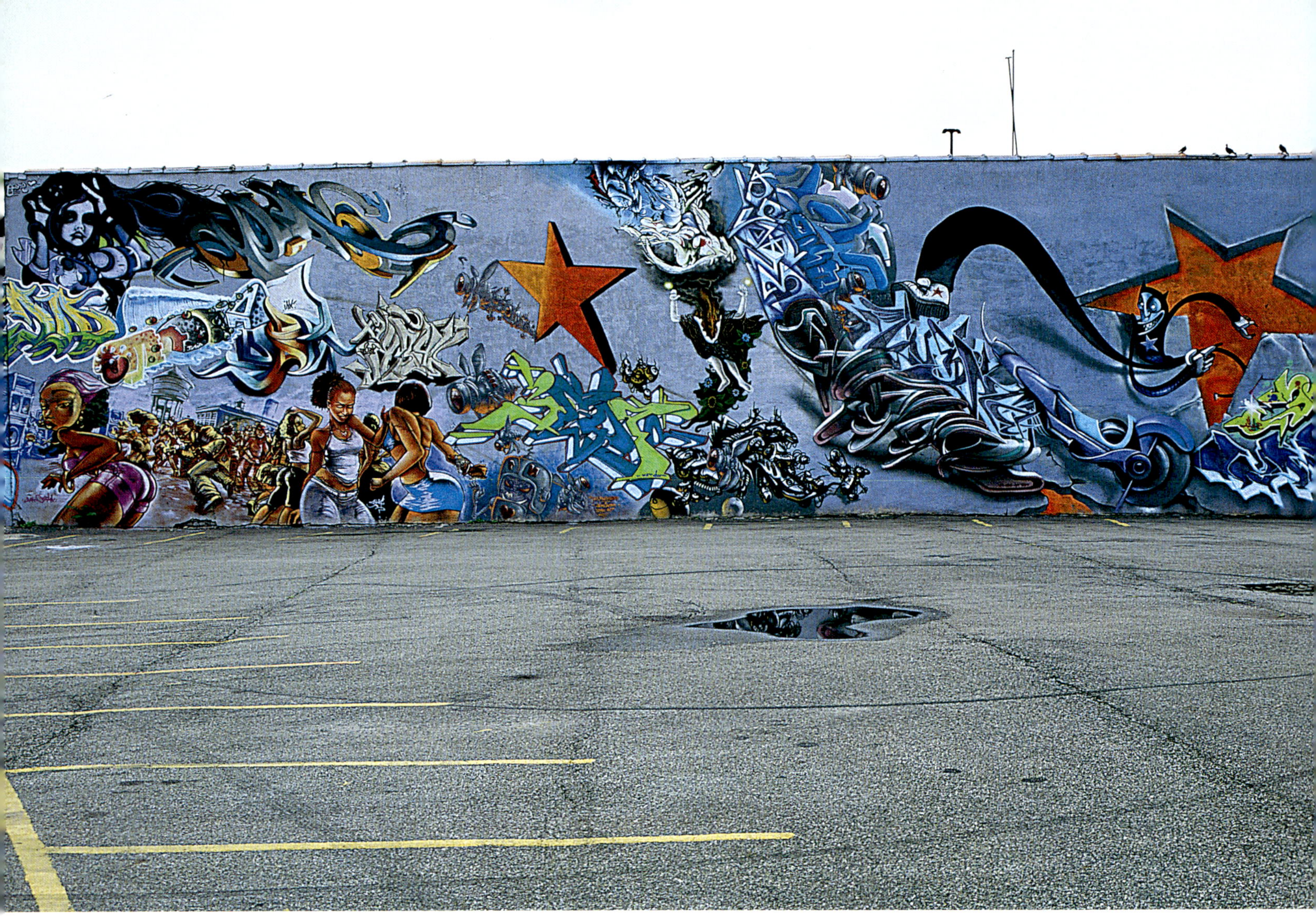

A large parking lot wall, bordering Brooklyn and Queens, is home to a mural that exhibits all the energy, urgency, and illegality of tagging and is a noteworthy example of public art in the tradition of New York subway graffiti writing, a precursor to all its street art.

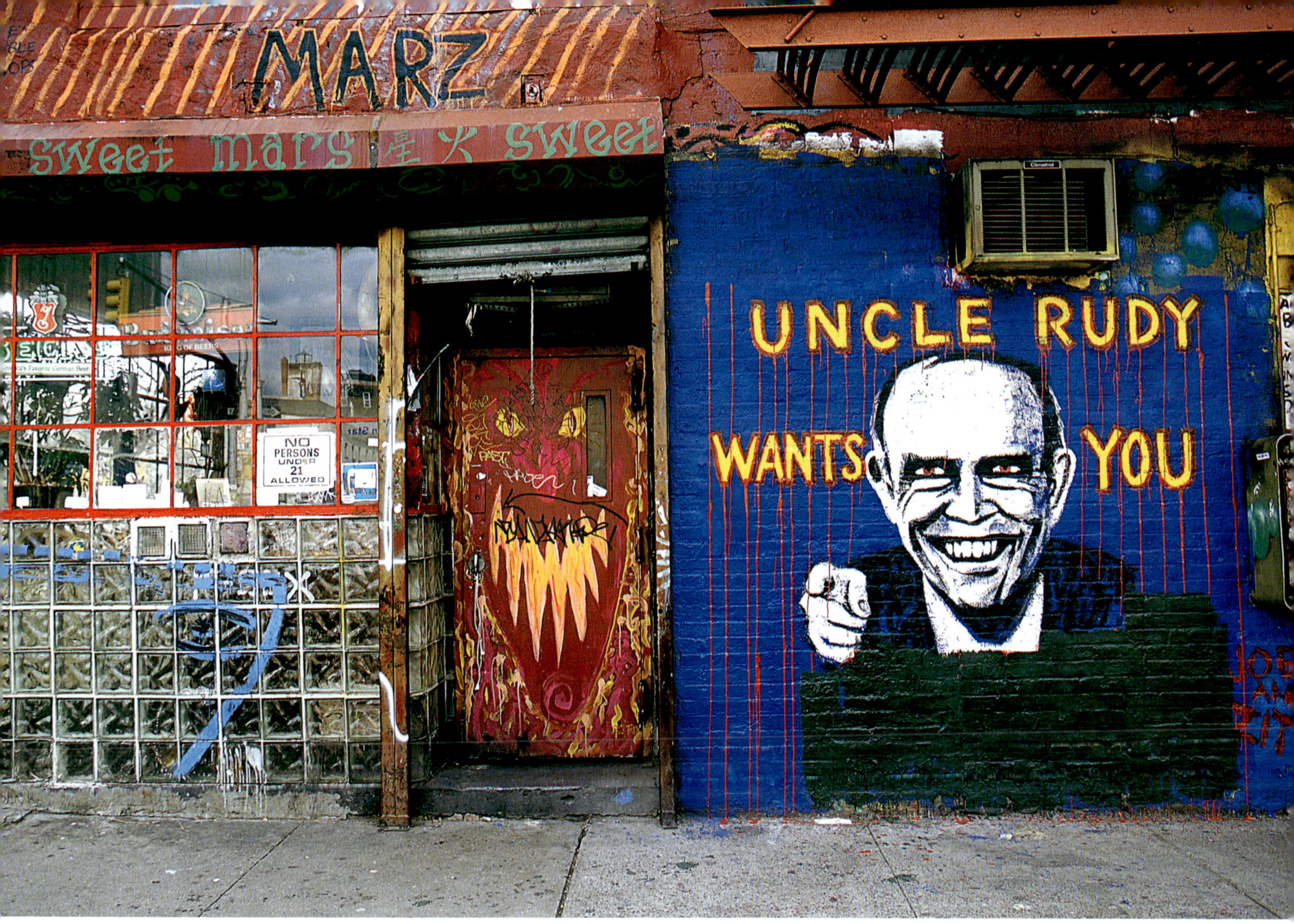

The mural, shot in 2001, depicts an often-shared sentiment among New Yorkers about former New York mayor Rudy Giuliani before 9/11. The icy, sallow visage, straight-arrow lettering, and red-line background, alluding to either blood or prison bars, have since been erased. But the Mars Bar, a magnet for graffiti, thrives on this East Village corner.

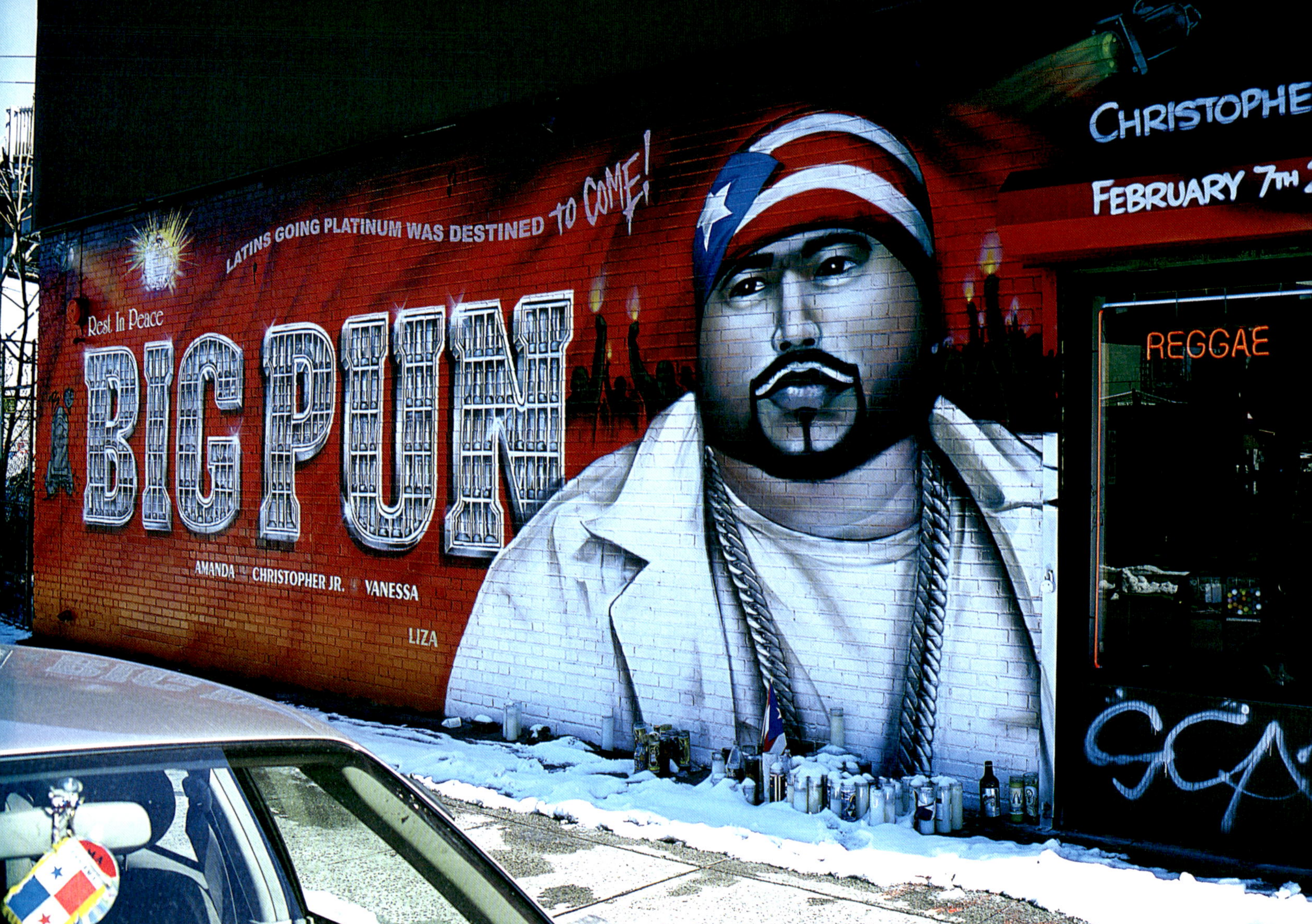

When the rapper known as Big Punisher, or Big Pun, died from causes related to his weighing seven hundred pounds, a mural went up on Rogers Place in the Bronx. His real name was Christopher Rios, and even though he sold more than a million albums, he never left the neighborhood where he was born and raised. He was twenty-eight years old. The memorial was a collaborative effort between two German artists, who created the lettering, and TATS CRU, who designed the image. Europeans often "intern" with Bronx artists.

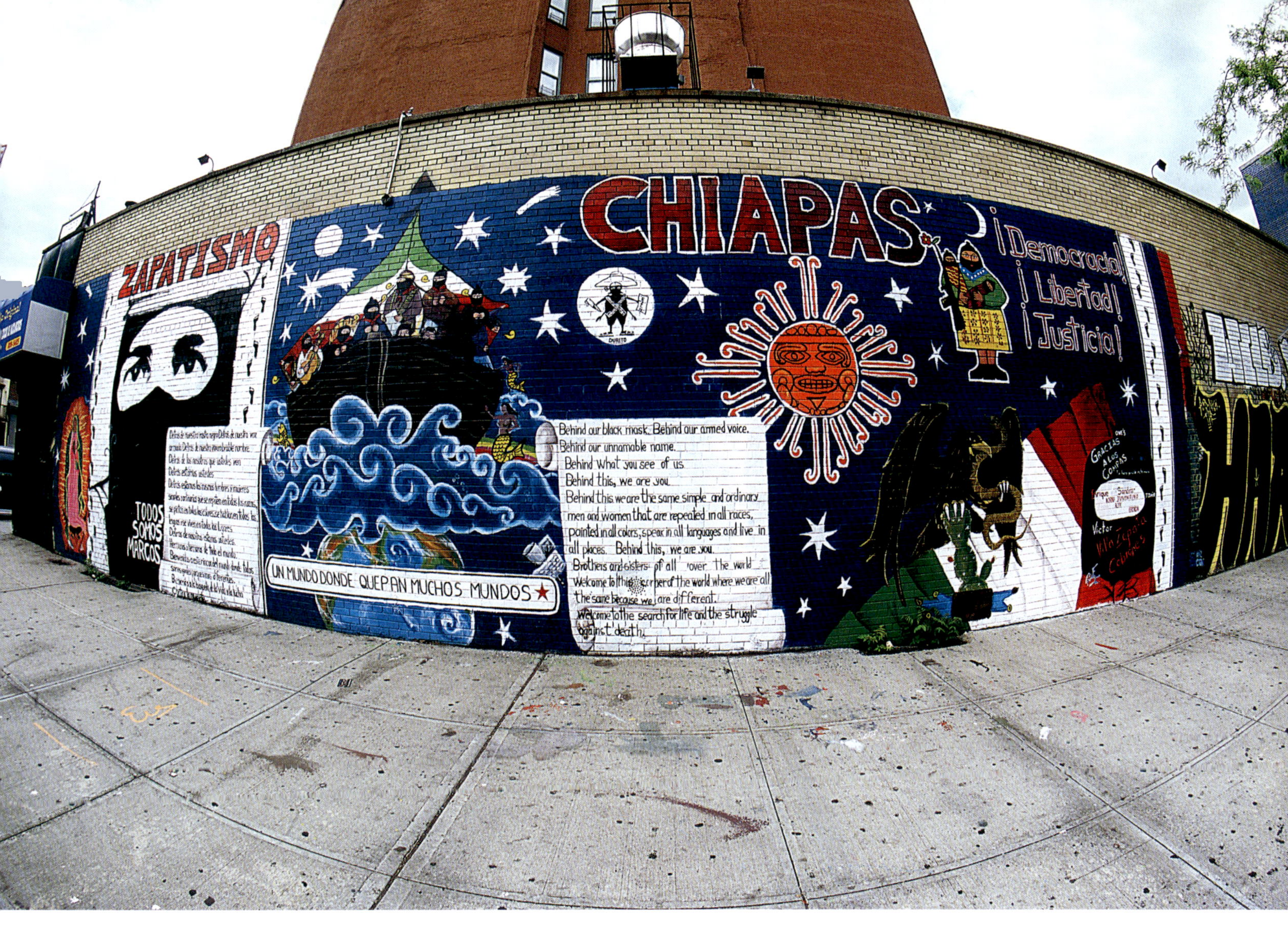

A political mural on the people's struggle in Chiapas, Mexico, incorporates many indigenous motifs in a decorative style. The creator is a local artist in the Bronx.

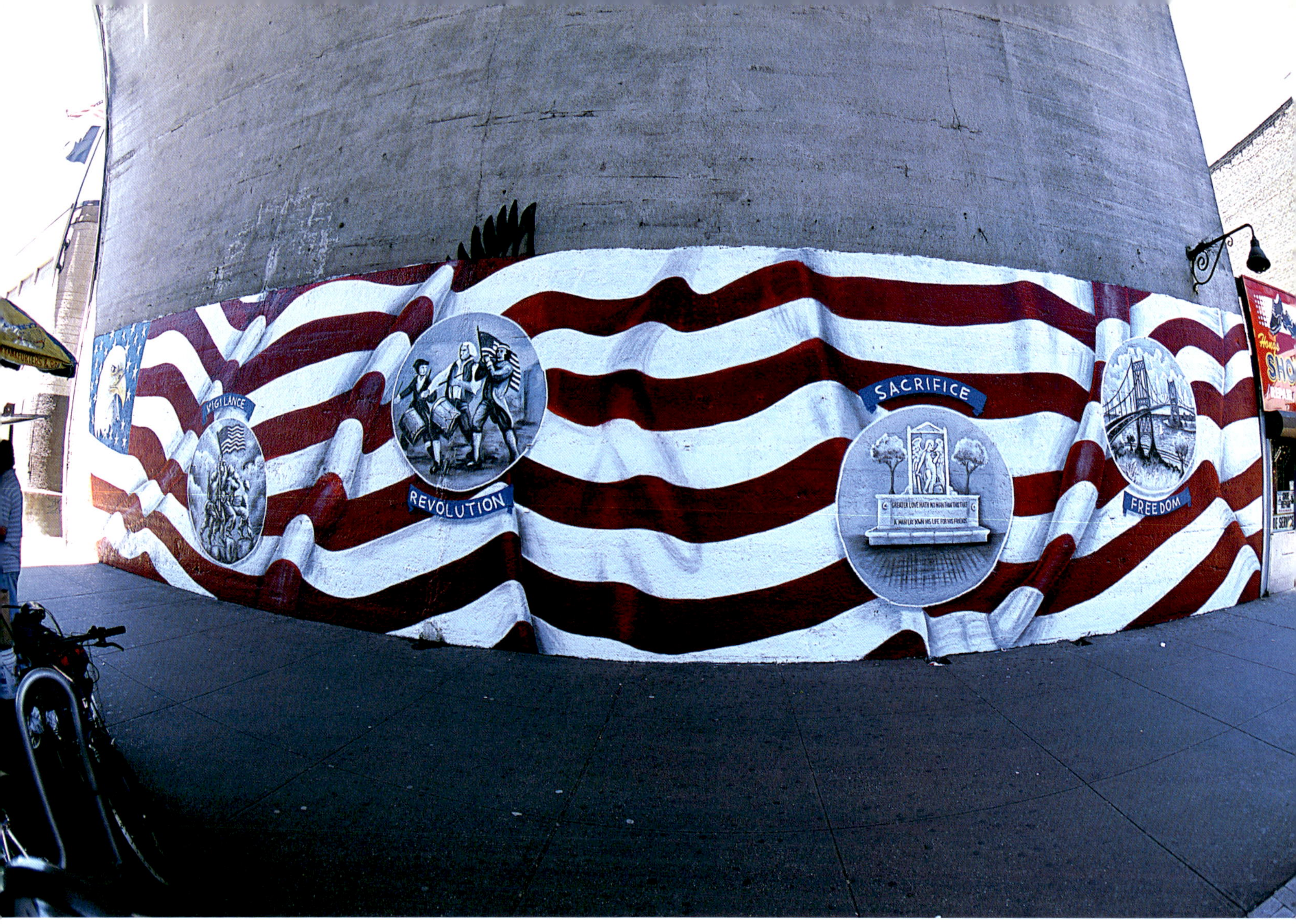

A highly stylized Queens political mural with decorative aspects by PINK SMITH.

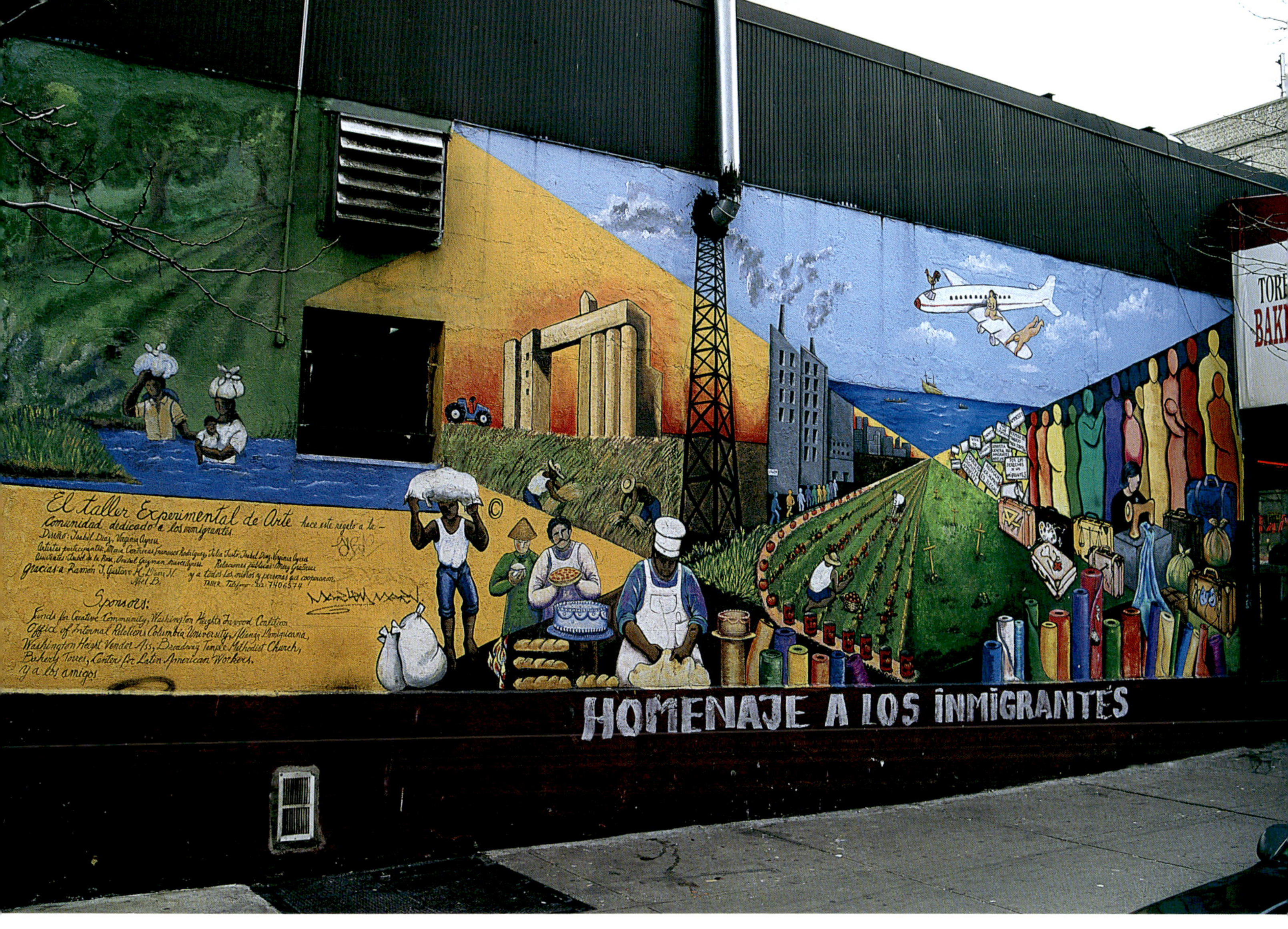

The "Homenaje a los emigrantes" in the Bronx, painted by a local artist, incorporates the traditional style of Mexican master muralists like Diego Rivera.

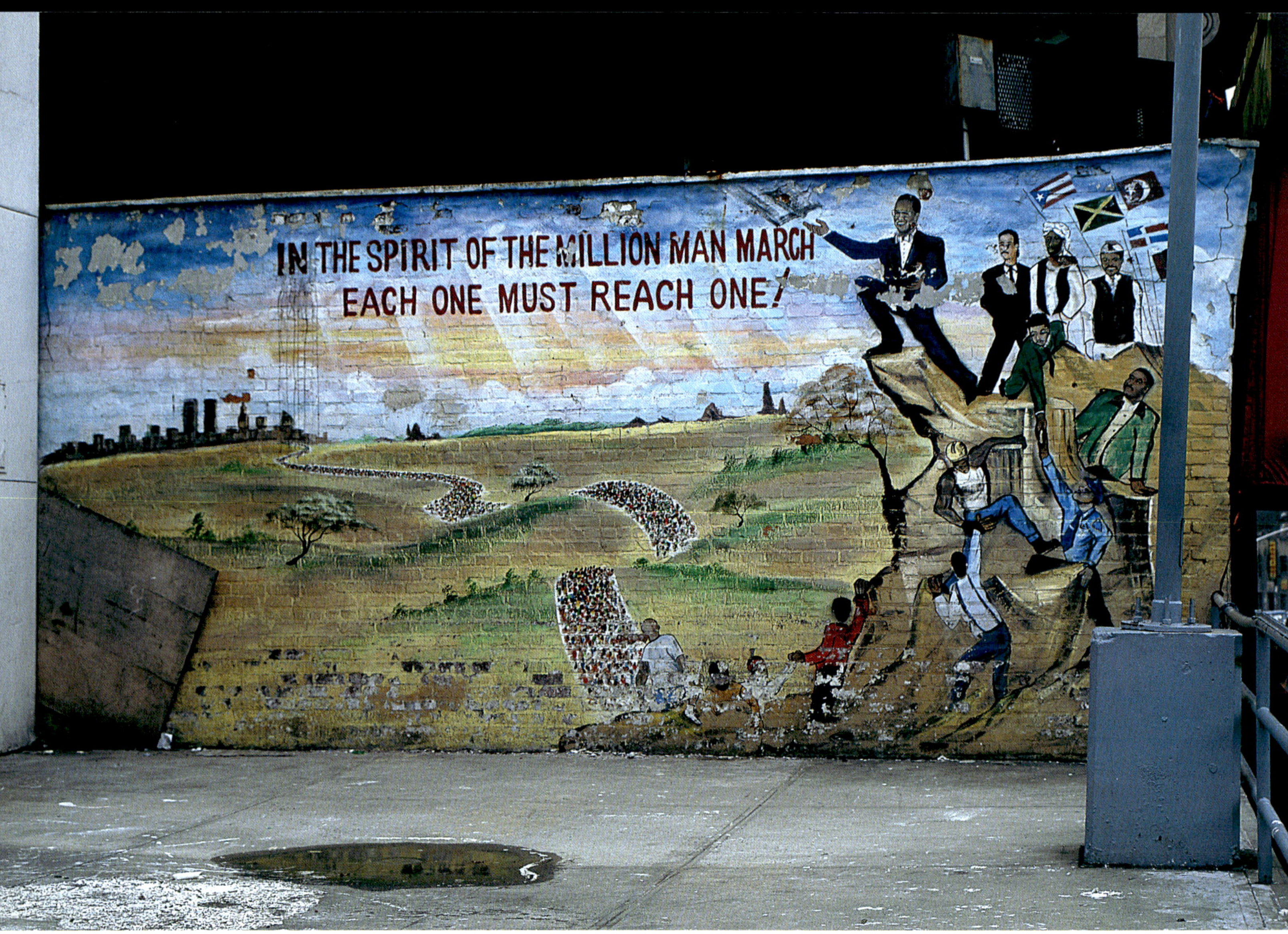

A political mural by a local Harlem artist memorializes the Million Man March held in Washington on October 15, 1995.

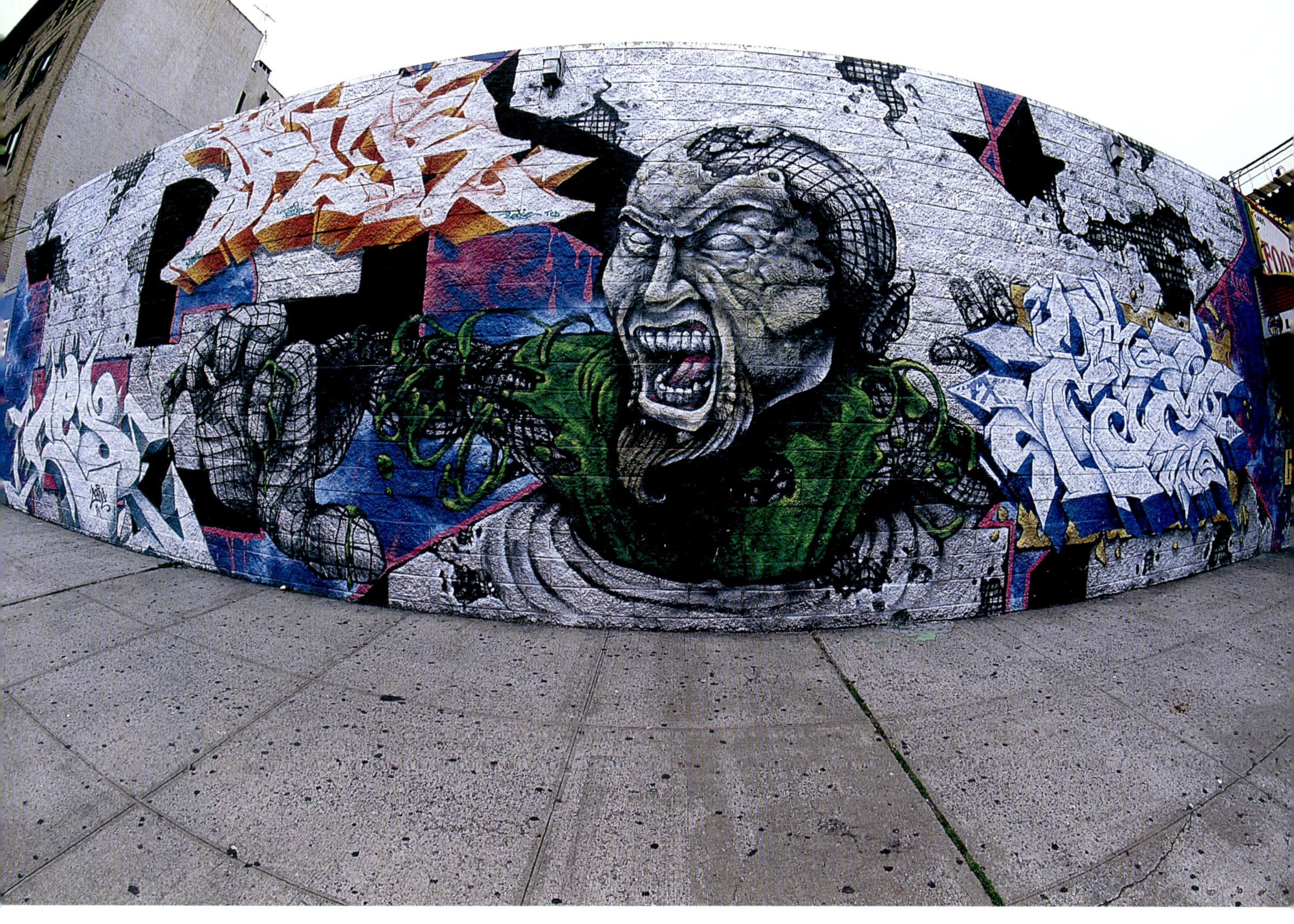

A decorative mural by FX CRU artists PER and SES on Westchester Avenue in the Bronx. Up close, this mural has sophisticated shading details, with the surrealist elements and fascination with symmetry that characterize their work.

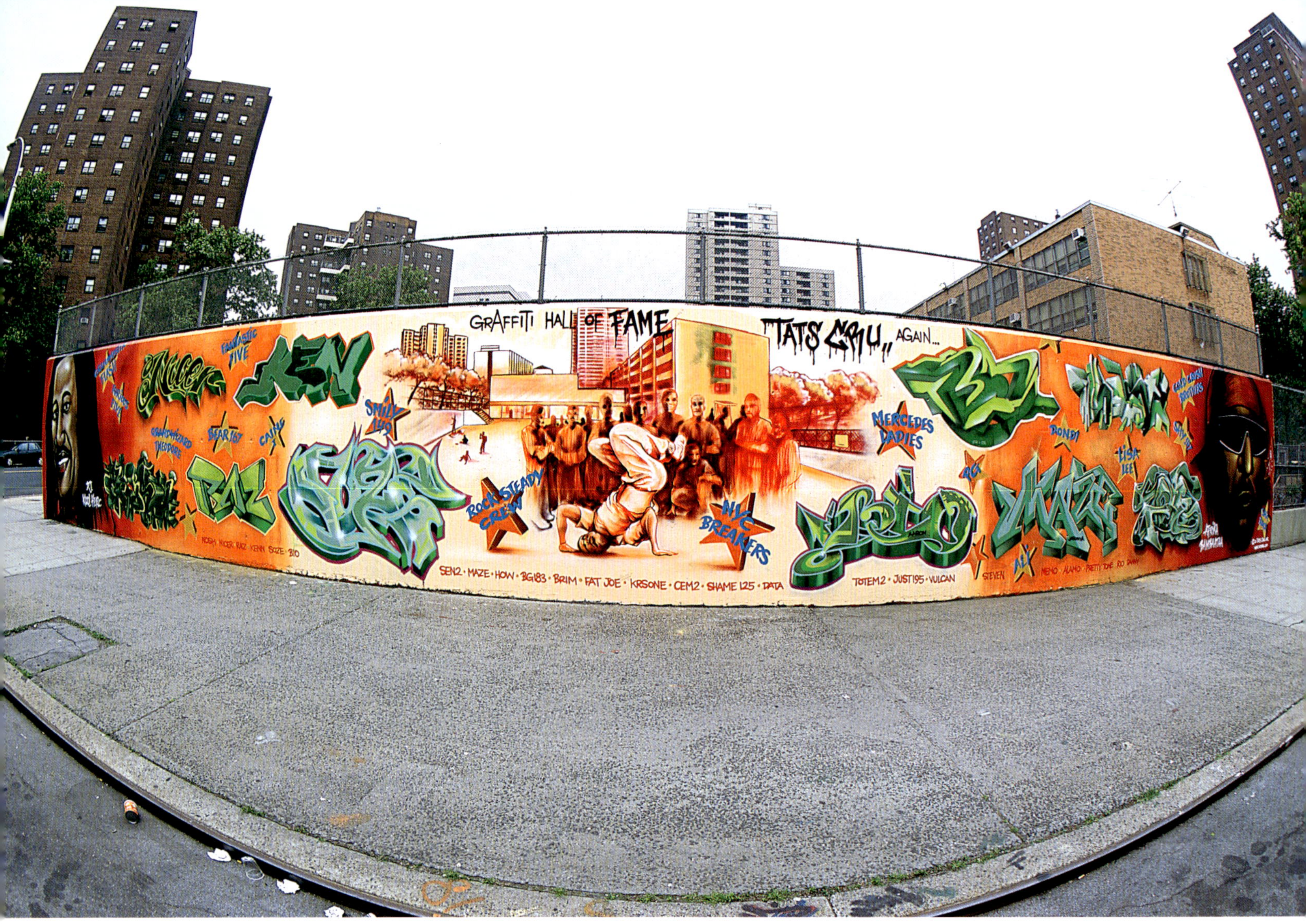

TATS CRU's decorative flashback to the great old days of hip-hop at the corner of 107th Street and Park Avenue, known as the Graffiti Hall of Fame, the mecca for aerosol artists. This notable wall, near a schoolyard, is painted and repainted every few months.

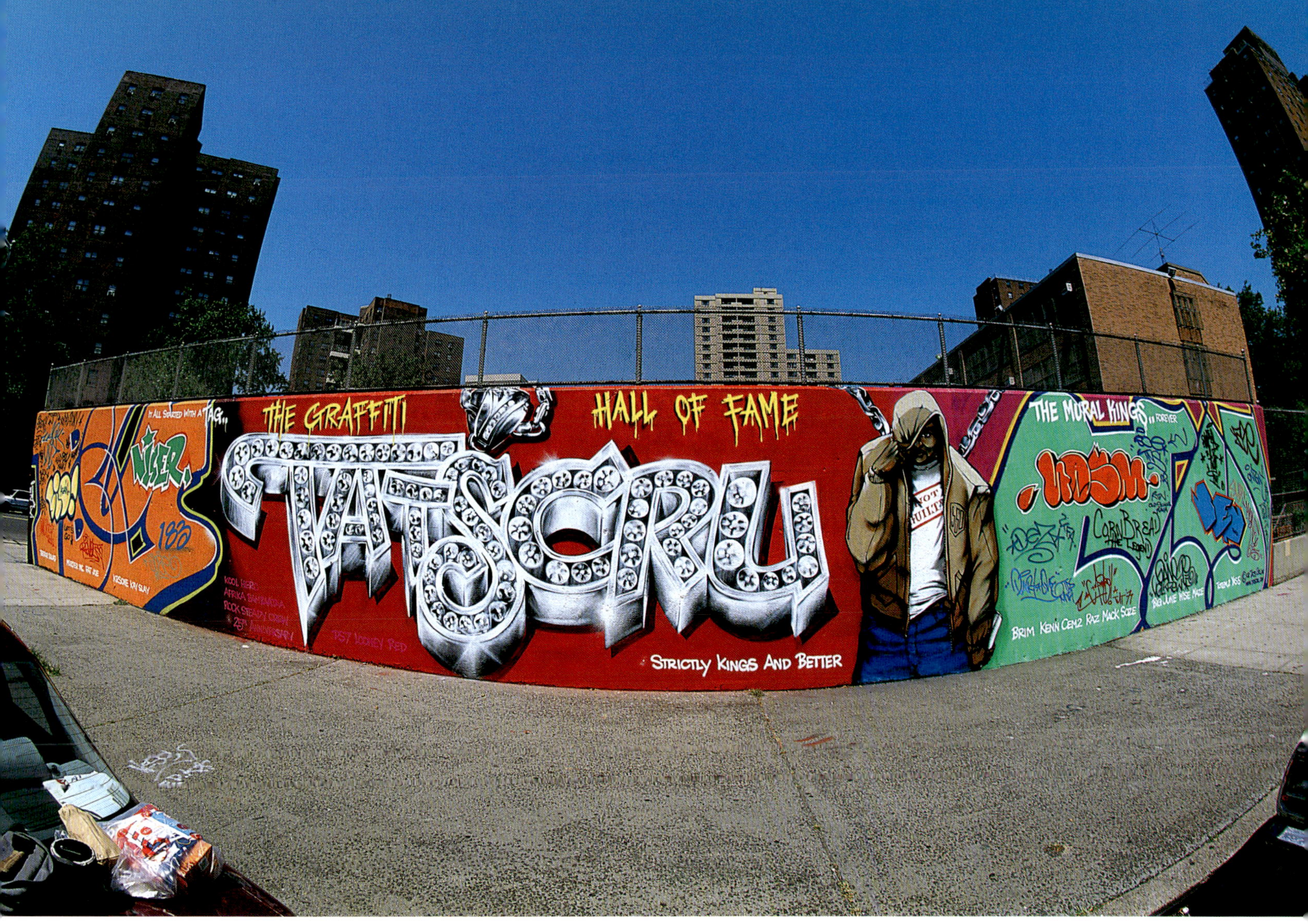

TATS CRU's stylish tag makes a strong statement on Graffiti Hall of Fame wall.

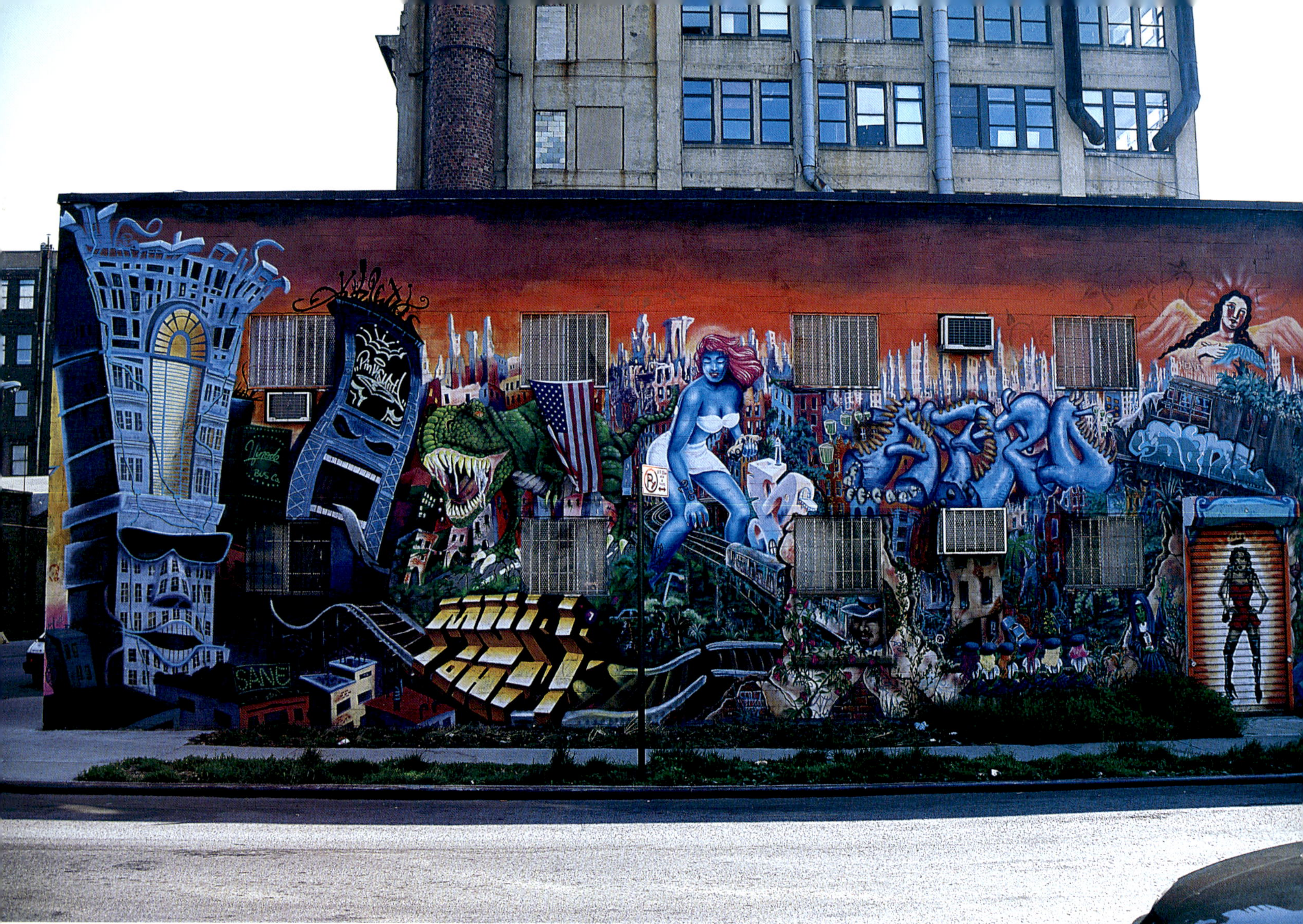

A decorative mural in Brooklyn's Williamsburg makes an effort to humanize city buildings and encapsulate urban life. The mural's roster of artists includes PEAK, CYCLE, MUSE, PINK SMITH, and OH.

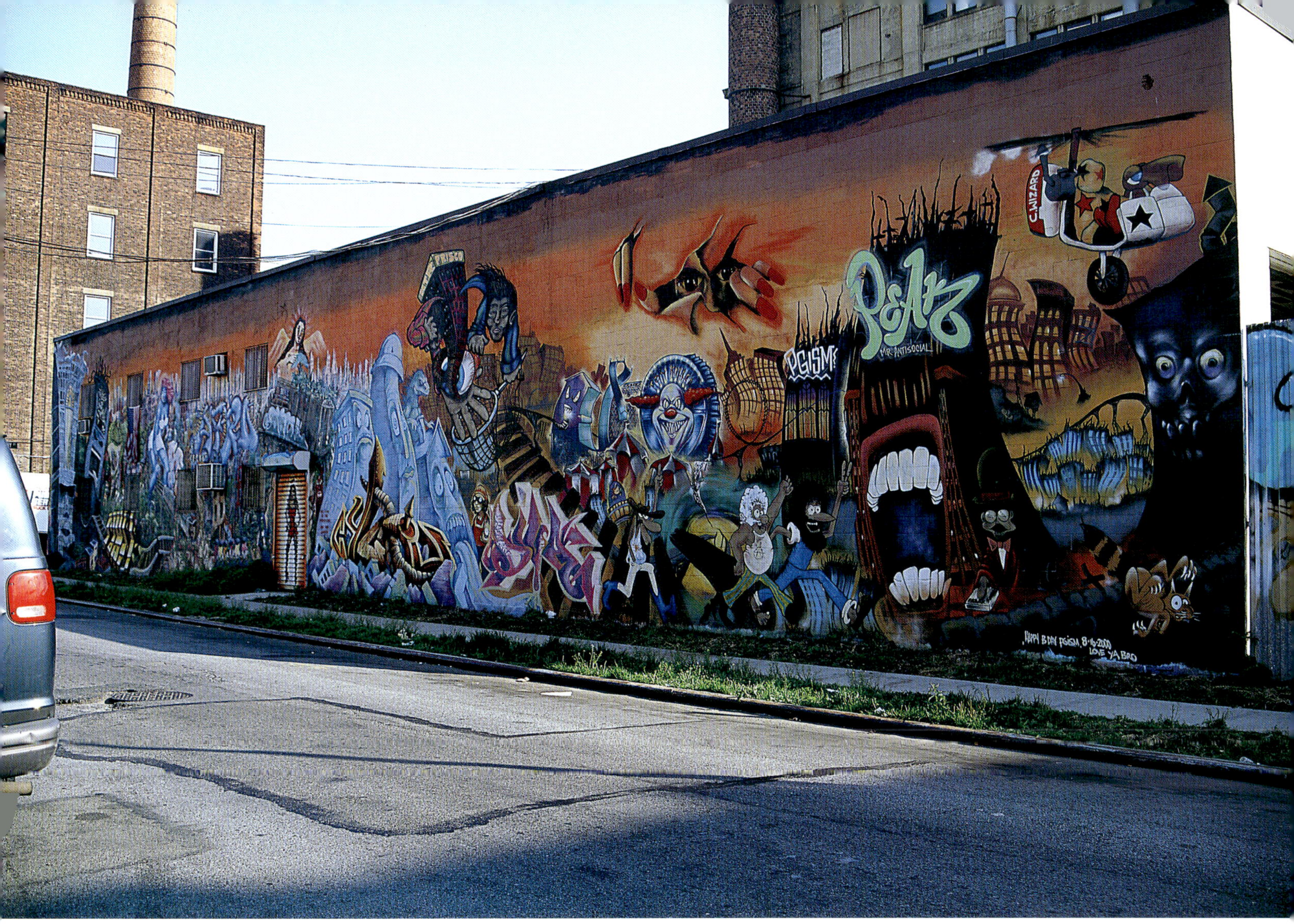
C. WIZARD
MR. ANTISOCIAL
PGISM
HAPPY B DAY PGISM, 8-16-2000
LOVE YA BRO

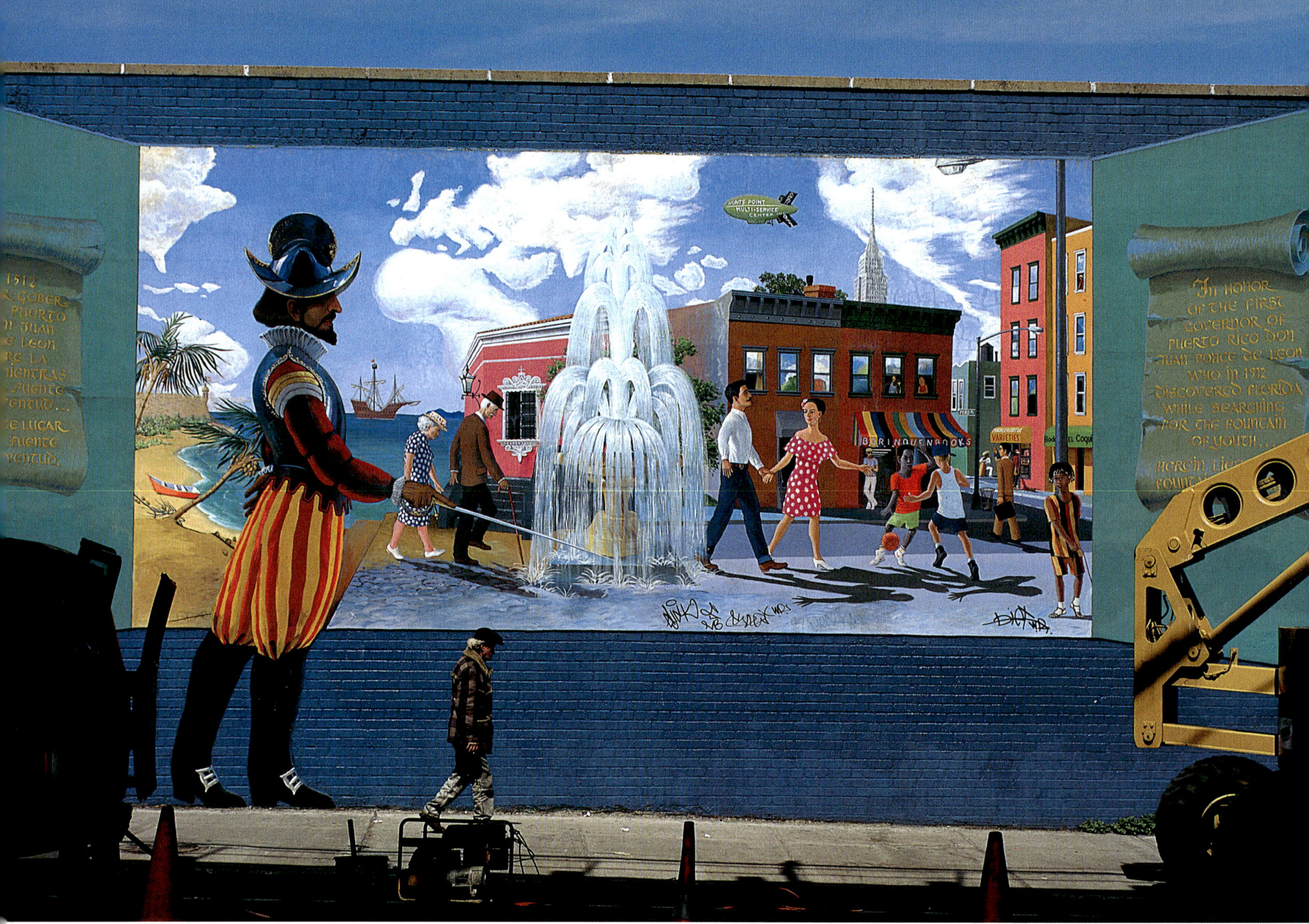

A decorative tribute to Ponce de Léon, who sought the Fountain of Youth and was Puerto Rico's first governor, is really a tribute to its emigrants who seek the same in New York City. The Bronx mural's cloud formation shows a map of the world.

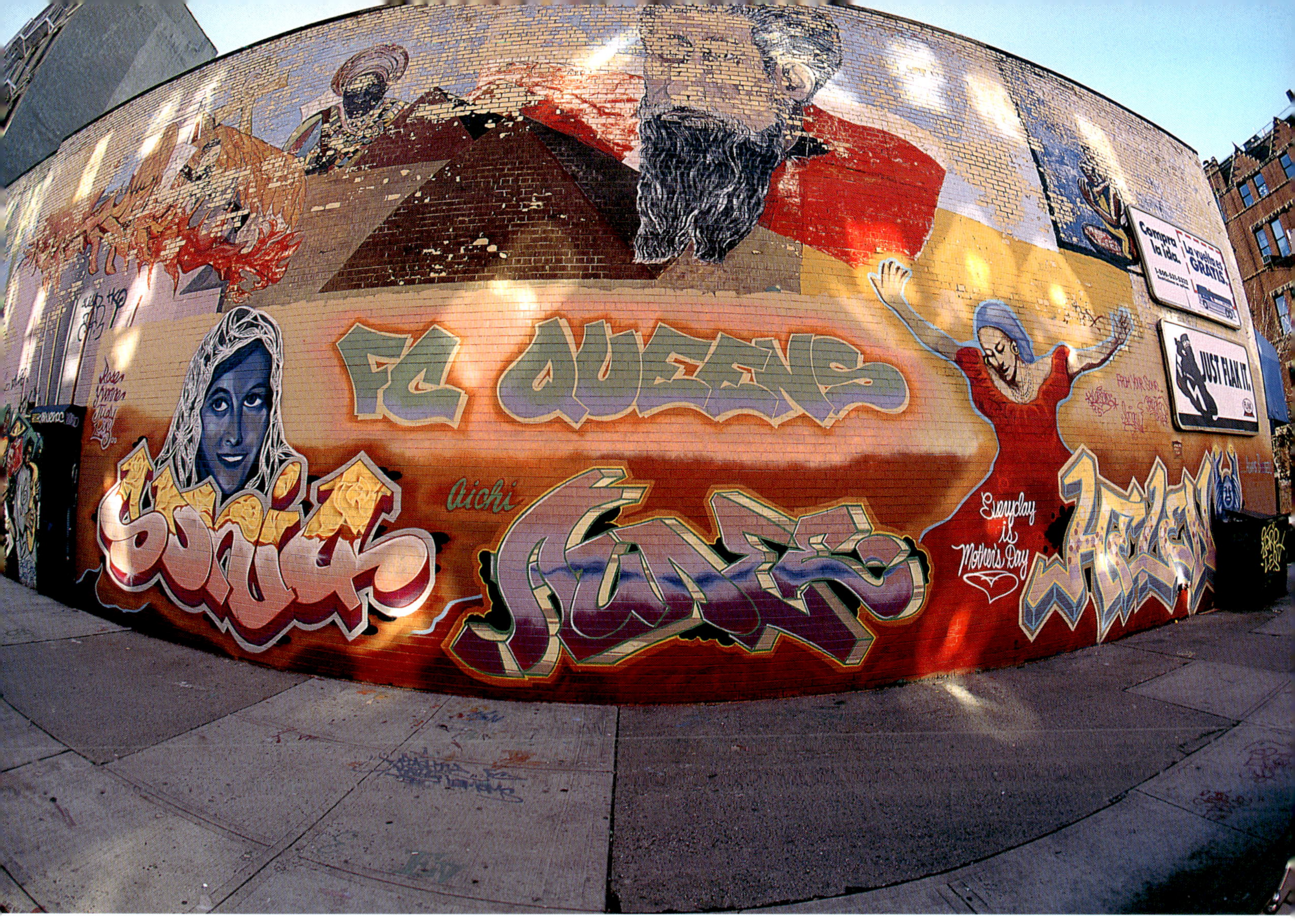

The sunny position of this decorative mural in the East Village by FCQUEENS and SONIC bring out its beautiful use of color.

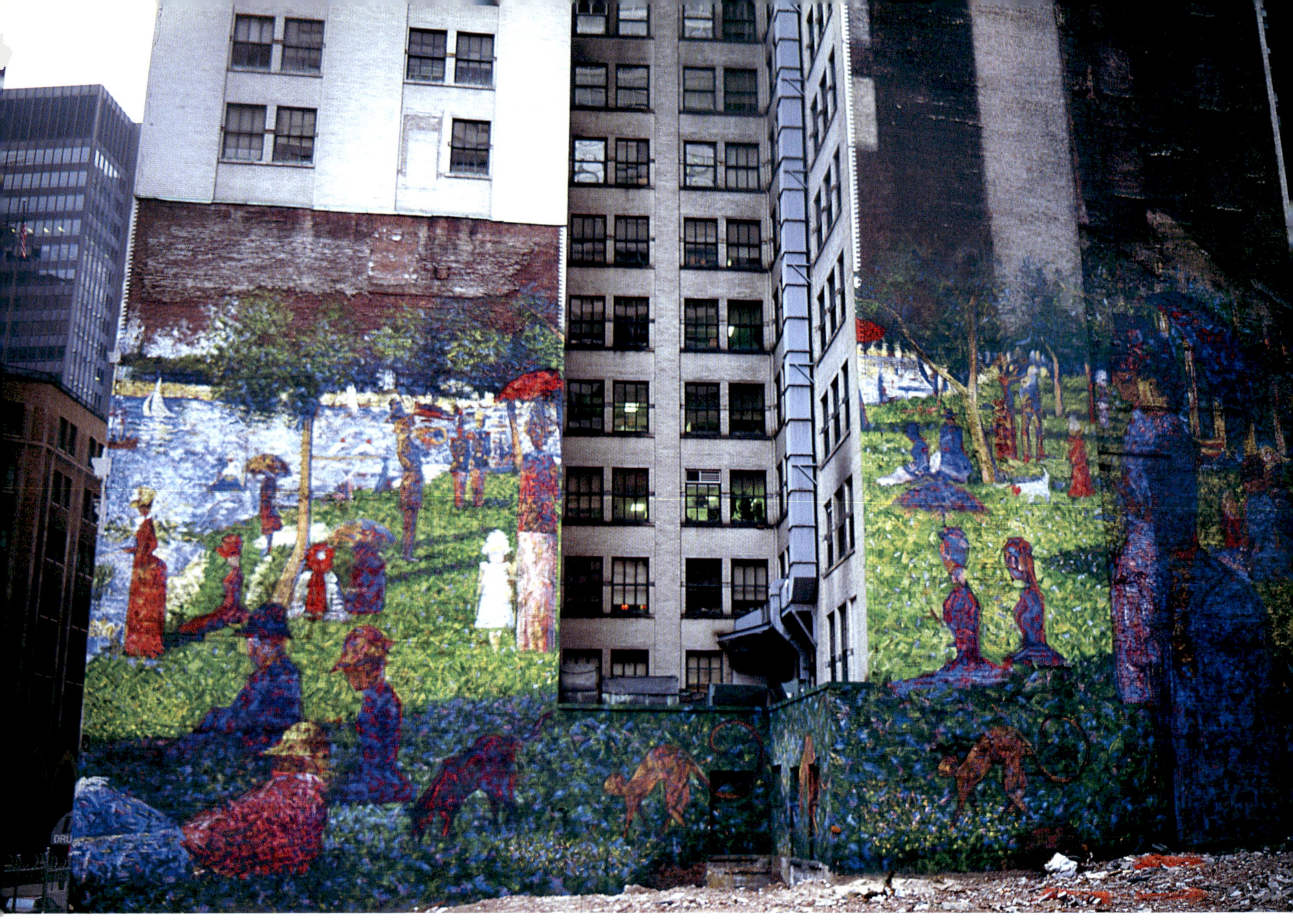

Georges Seurat's famous *Sunday on the Grand Jatte* is copied onto buildings around lower Manhattan's South Street Seaport to soften a hard urban setting.

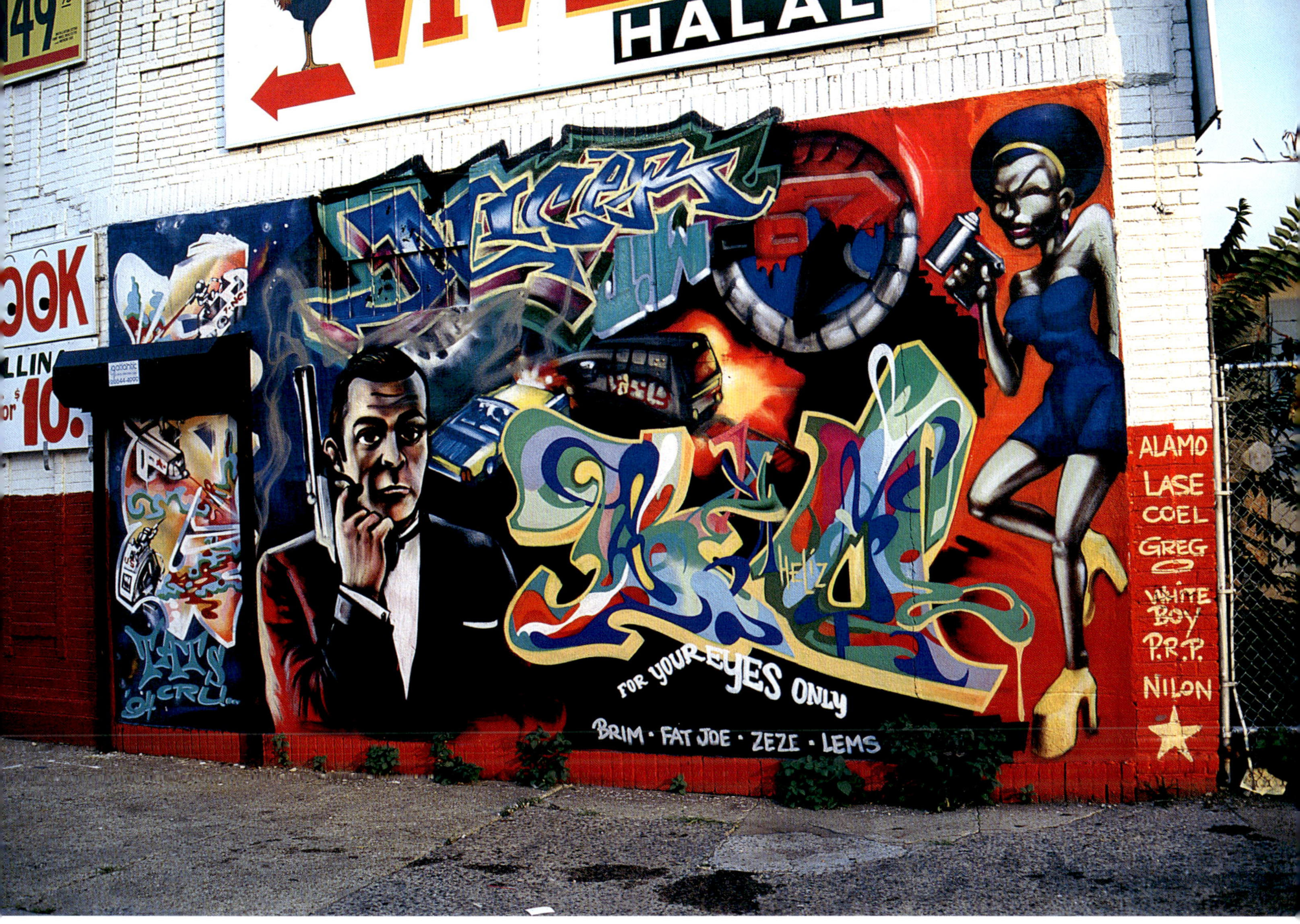

In the Hunts Point area of the Bronx, TATS CRU artist NICER creates a collage of decorative images with a prominent James Bond theme. WHITE BOY may have contributed to the painting of this mural, as his name appears with the credits.

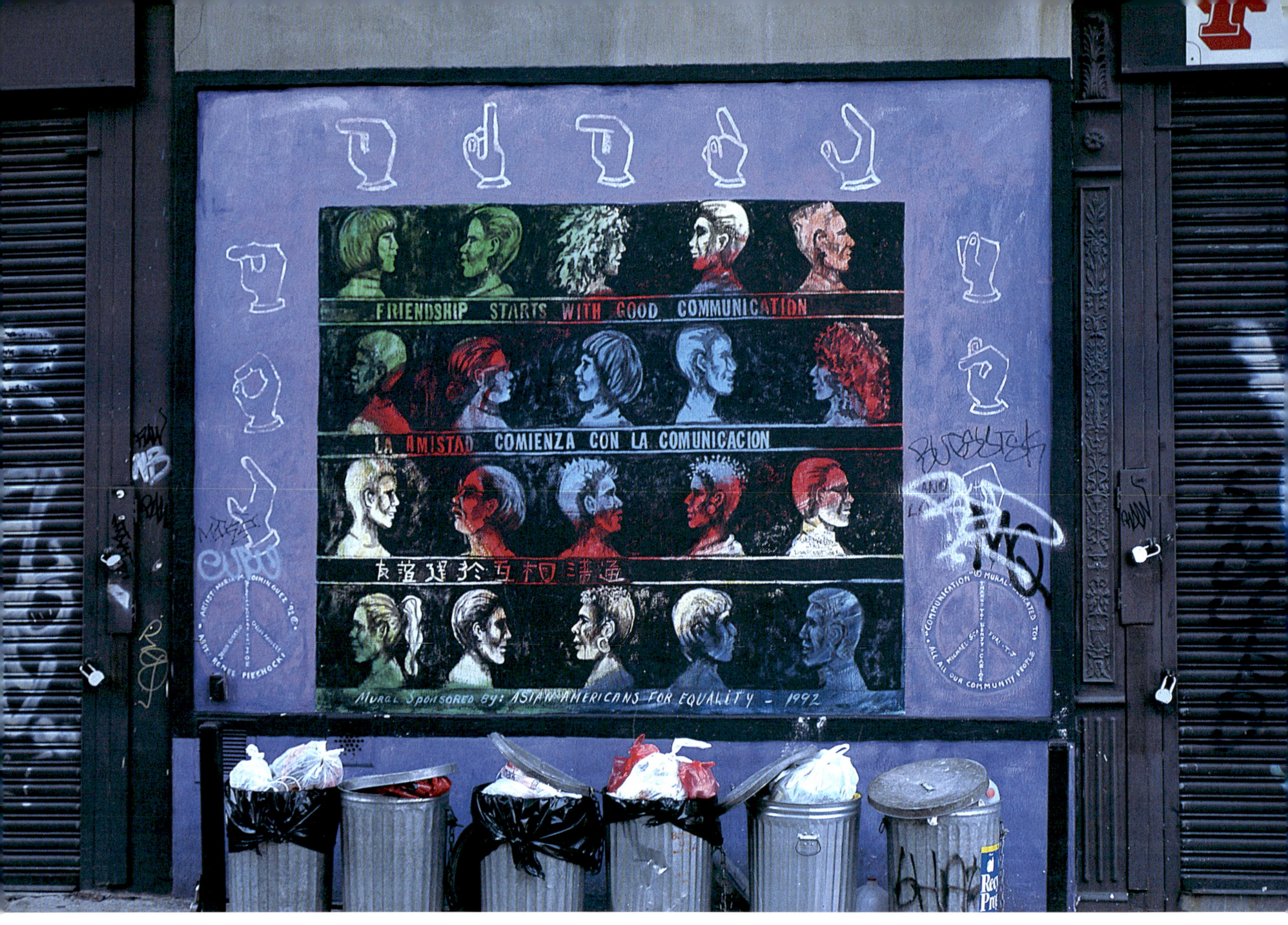

This beautiful Lower East Side mural, with sophisticated color and composition, conveys a gentle message of communication by Asian Americans for Equality.

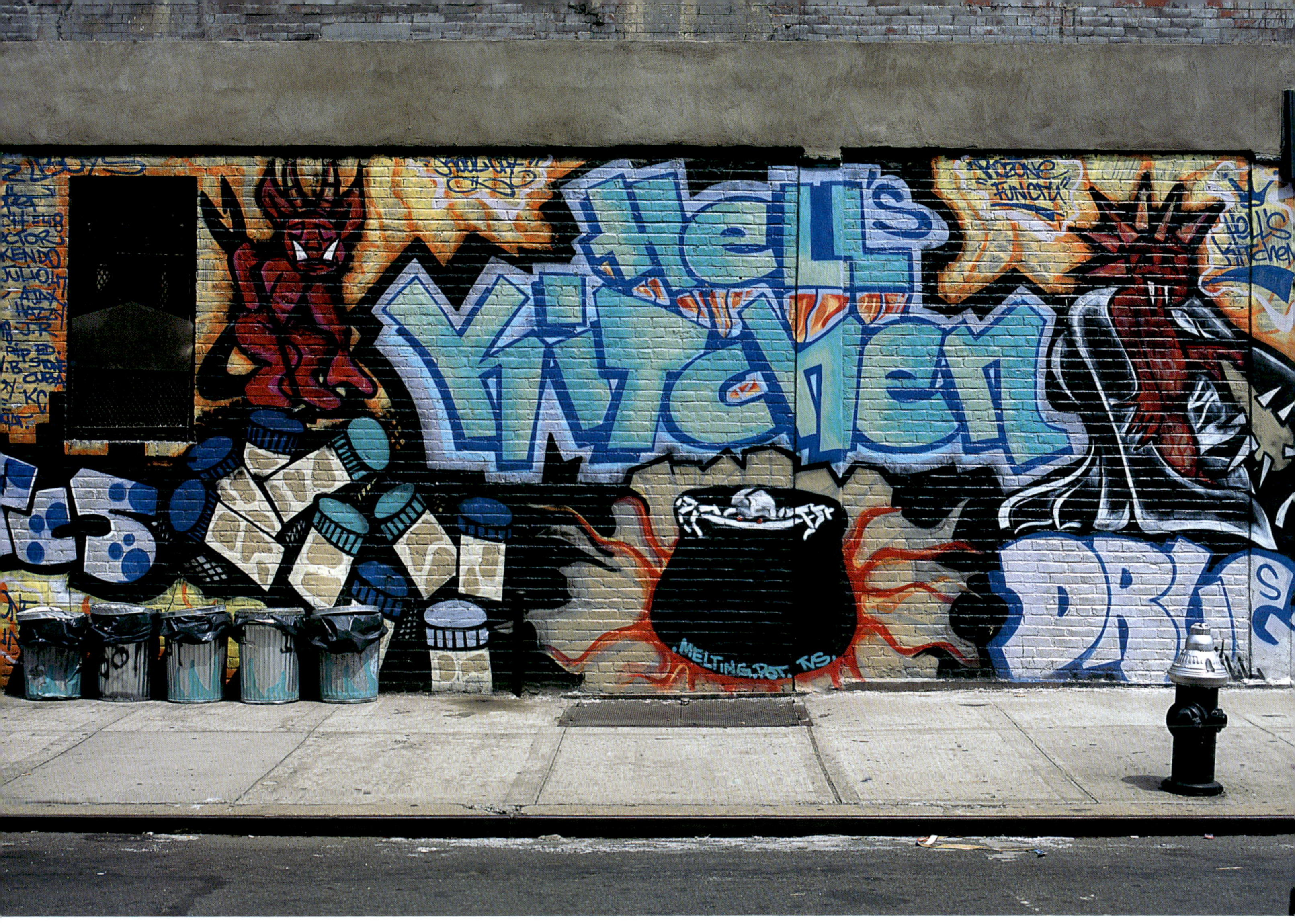

A reminder of the bygone days of the rapidly gentrifying Manhattan neighborhood familiarly known as Hell's Kitchen. The scene of Leonard Bernstein's *West Side Story,* it is now referred to as the Clinton area.

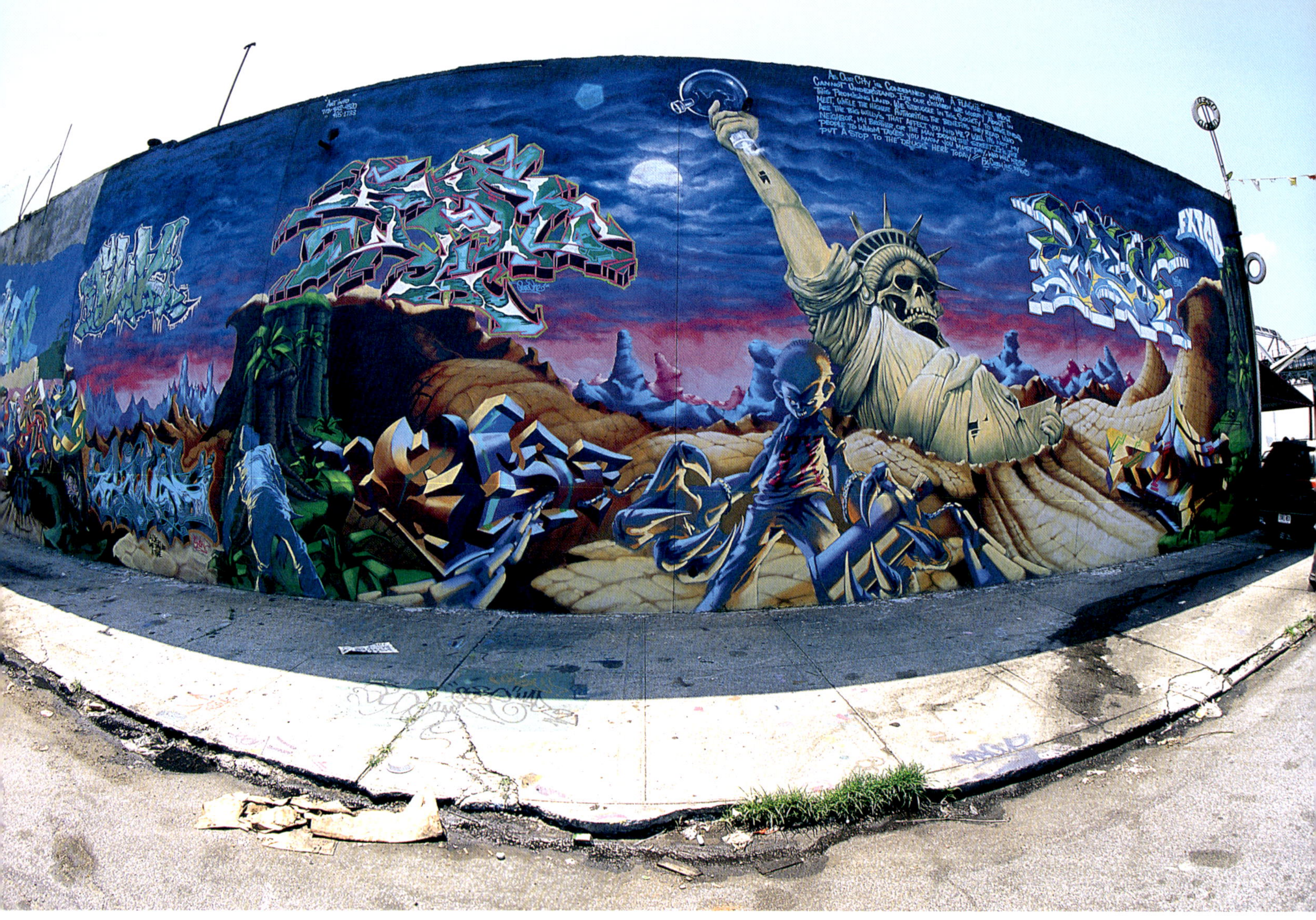

TATS CRU's arresting image of the Statue of Liberty holding a crack vial conveys a powerful statement about the mockery that drugs make of freedom.

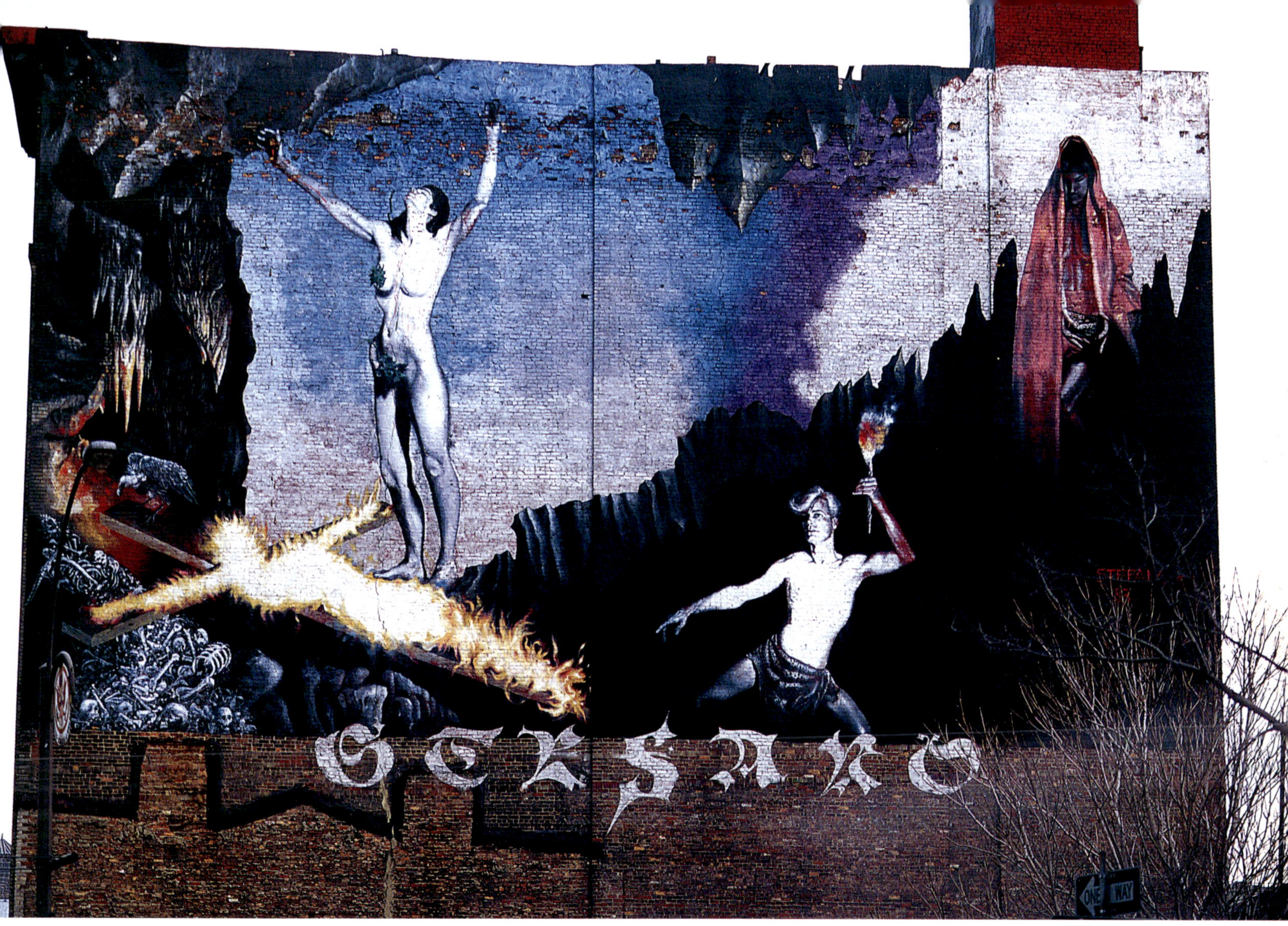

Downtown muralist STEFANO (aka Stefano Castronovo) employs mystical old continent images in this religious-themed mural in Manhattan.

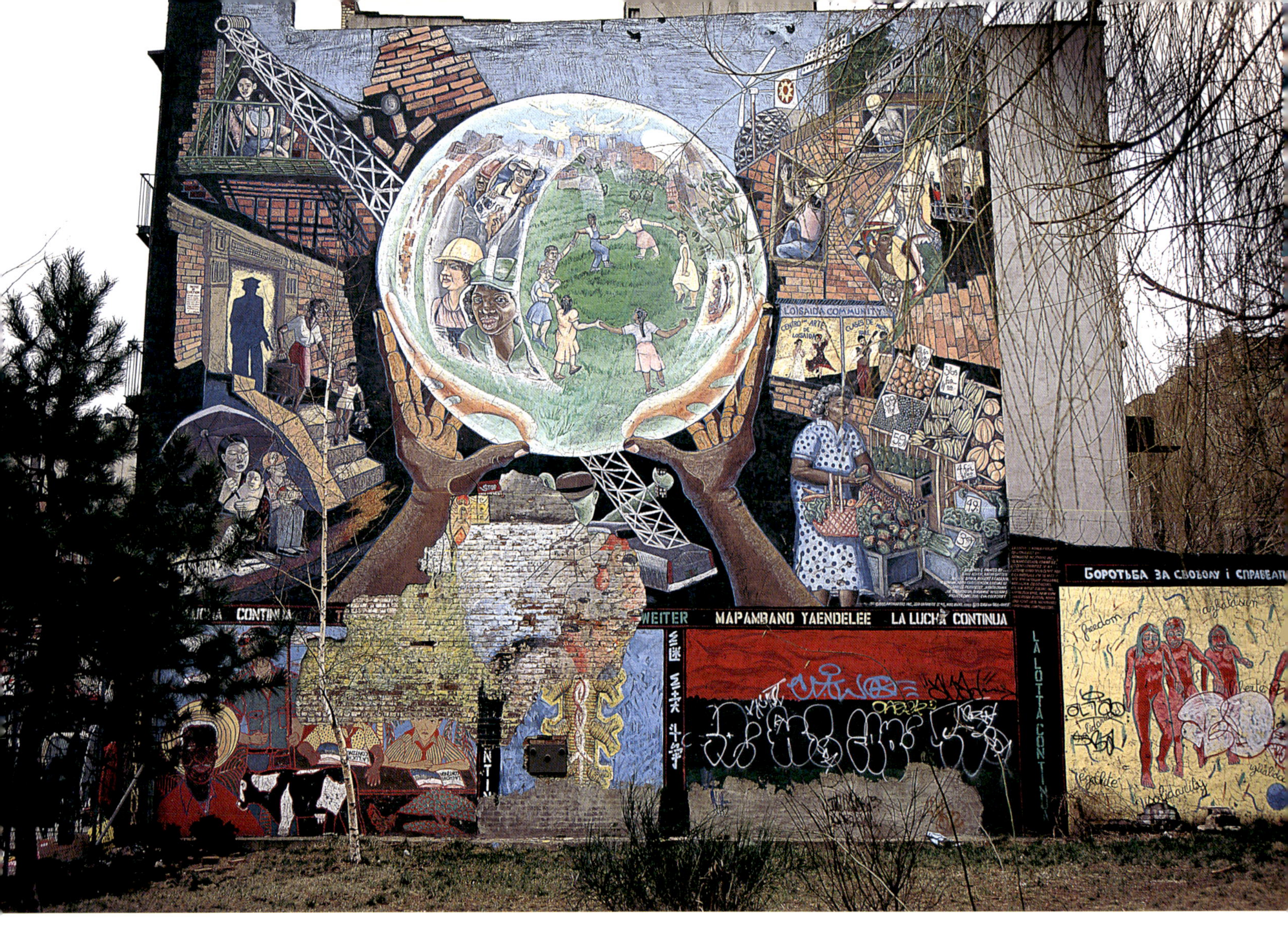

A local artist's somewhat overdone mural in the East Village makes use of decorative Latin American imagery.

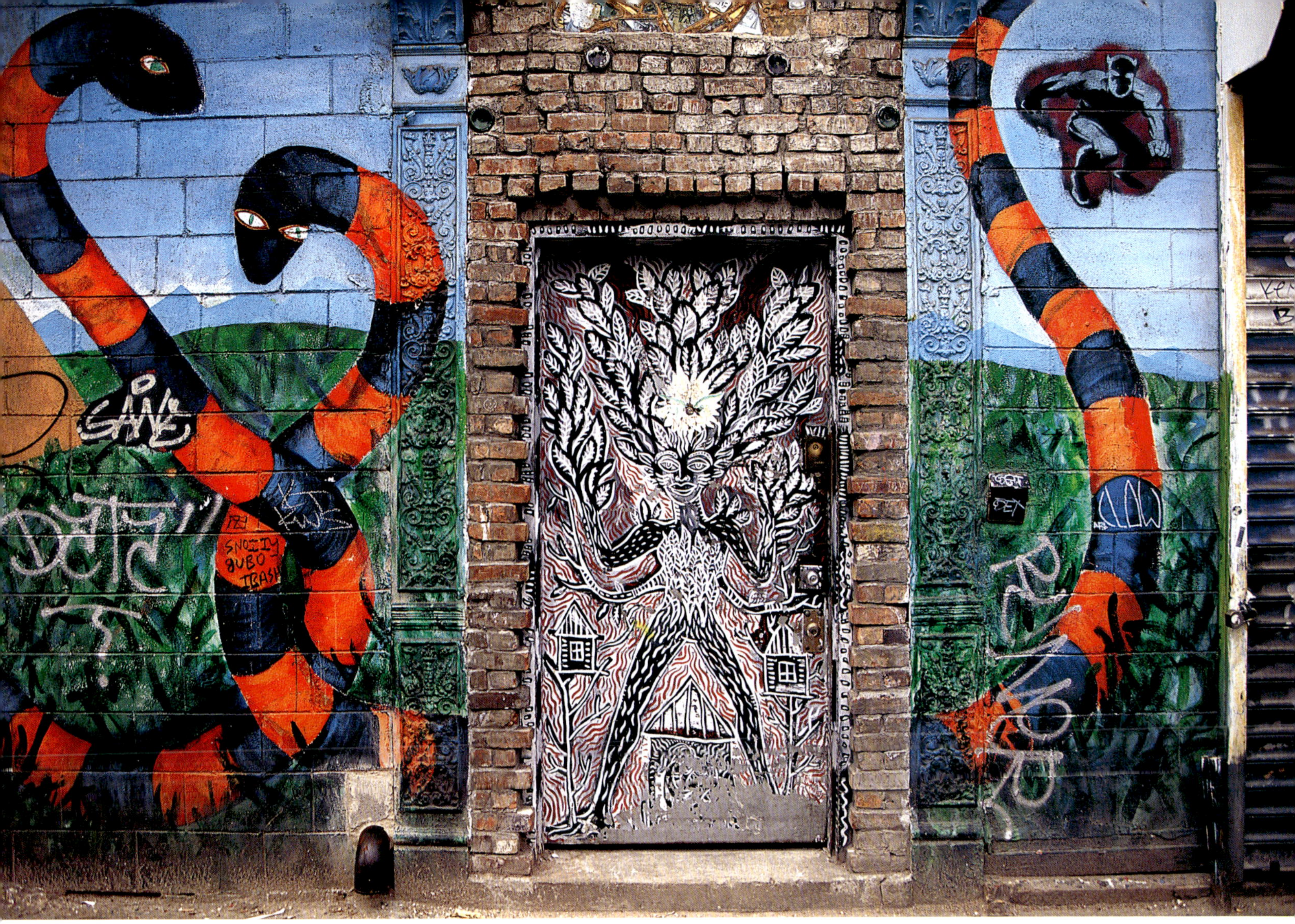

A local artist on the Lower East Side makes an apparent nod to the style of Nikki de St. Phalle, who created snake sculpture, but the significance of the mysterious central figure is unknown.

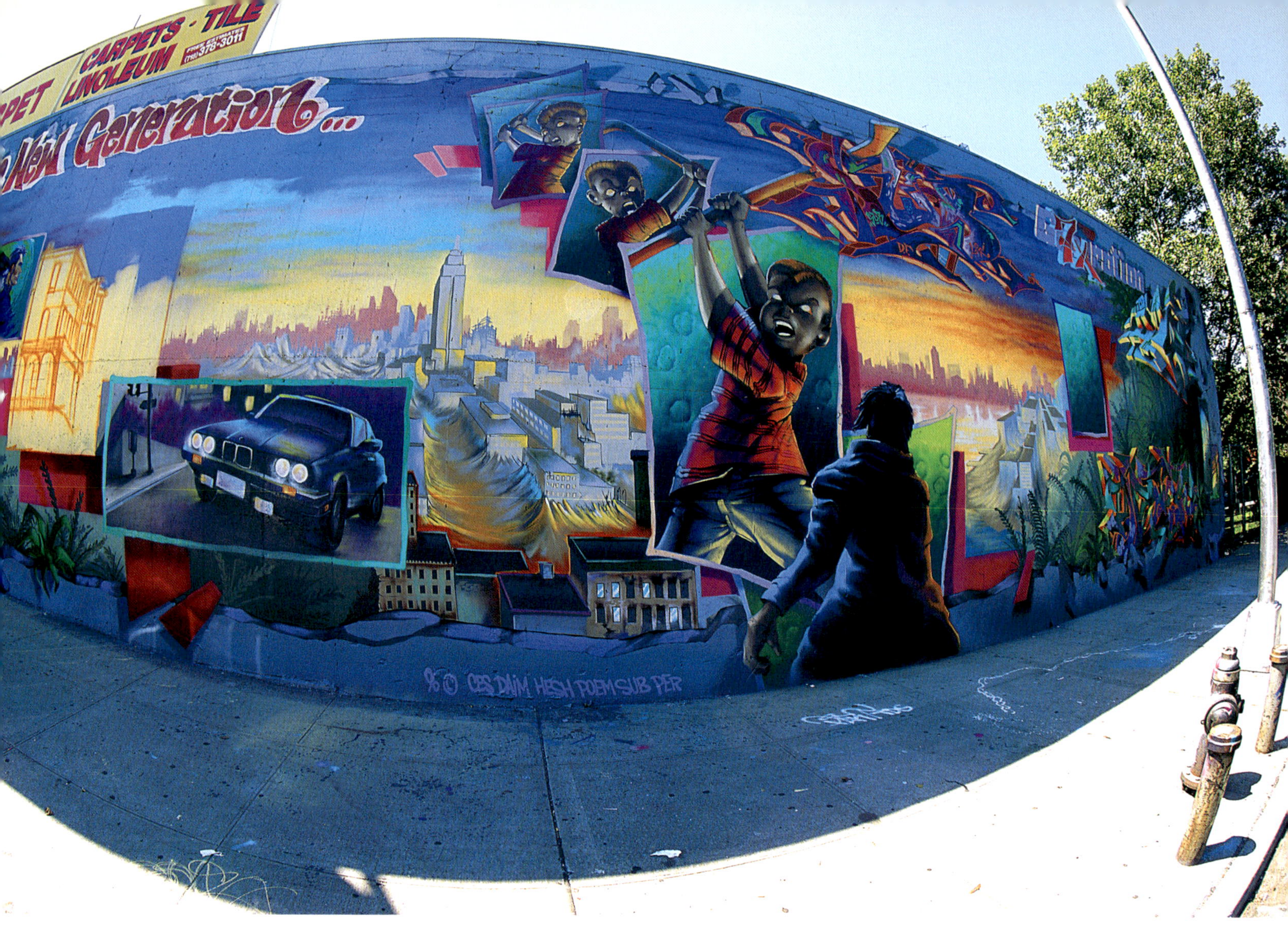

The Bronx's FX CRU makes a vividly colored mural hailing a new generation of younger aerosol artists in this decorative composition by SES, PER, and TKID.

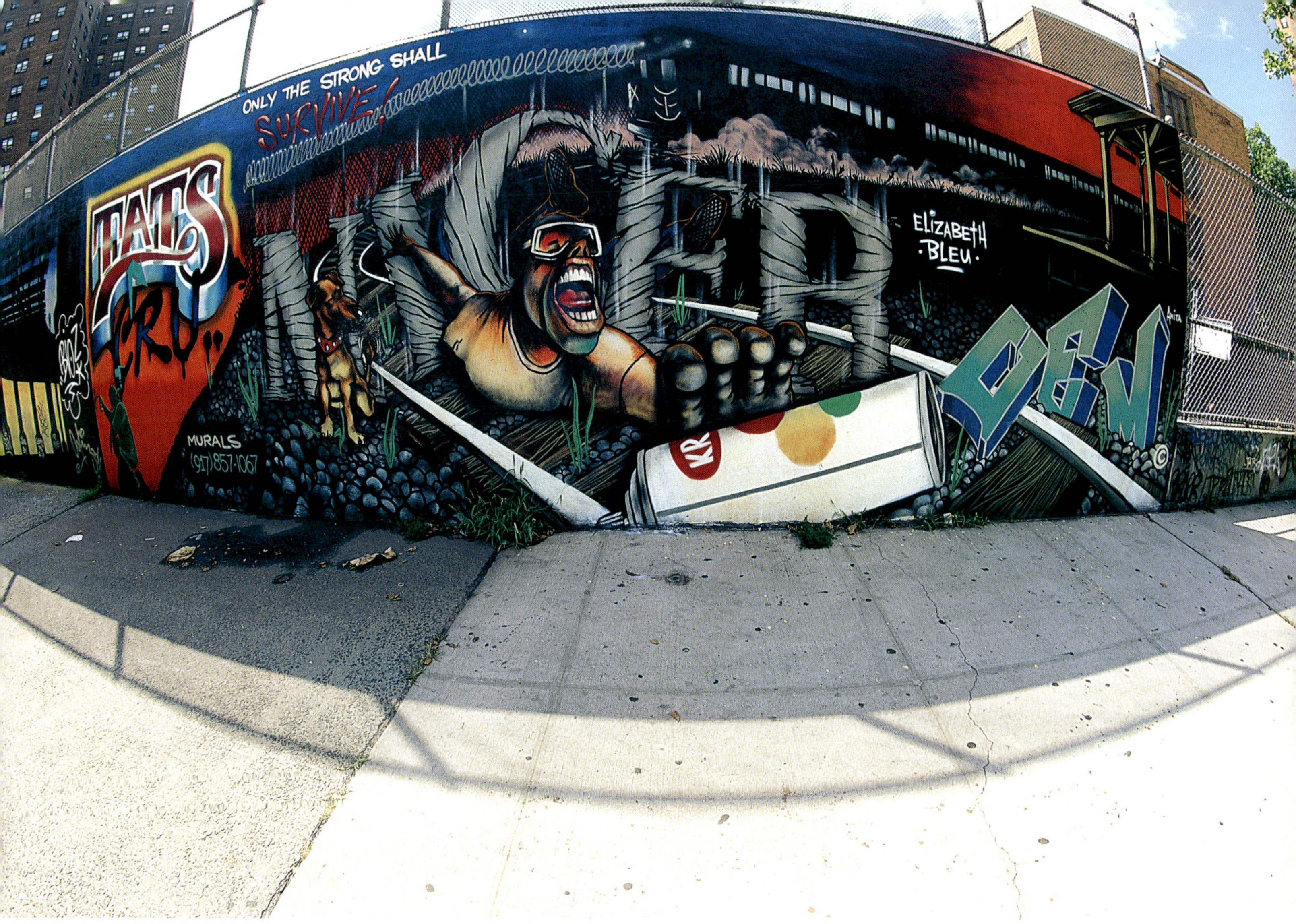

TATS CRU's NICER's homage to the boldness and survival, over the decades, of graffiti artists who encountered many perils spray-painting subway cars in the train yards throughout the 1970s.

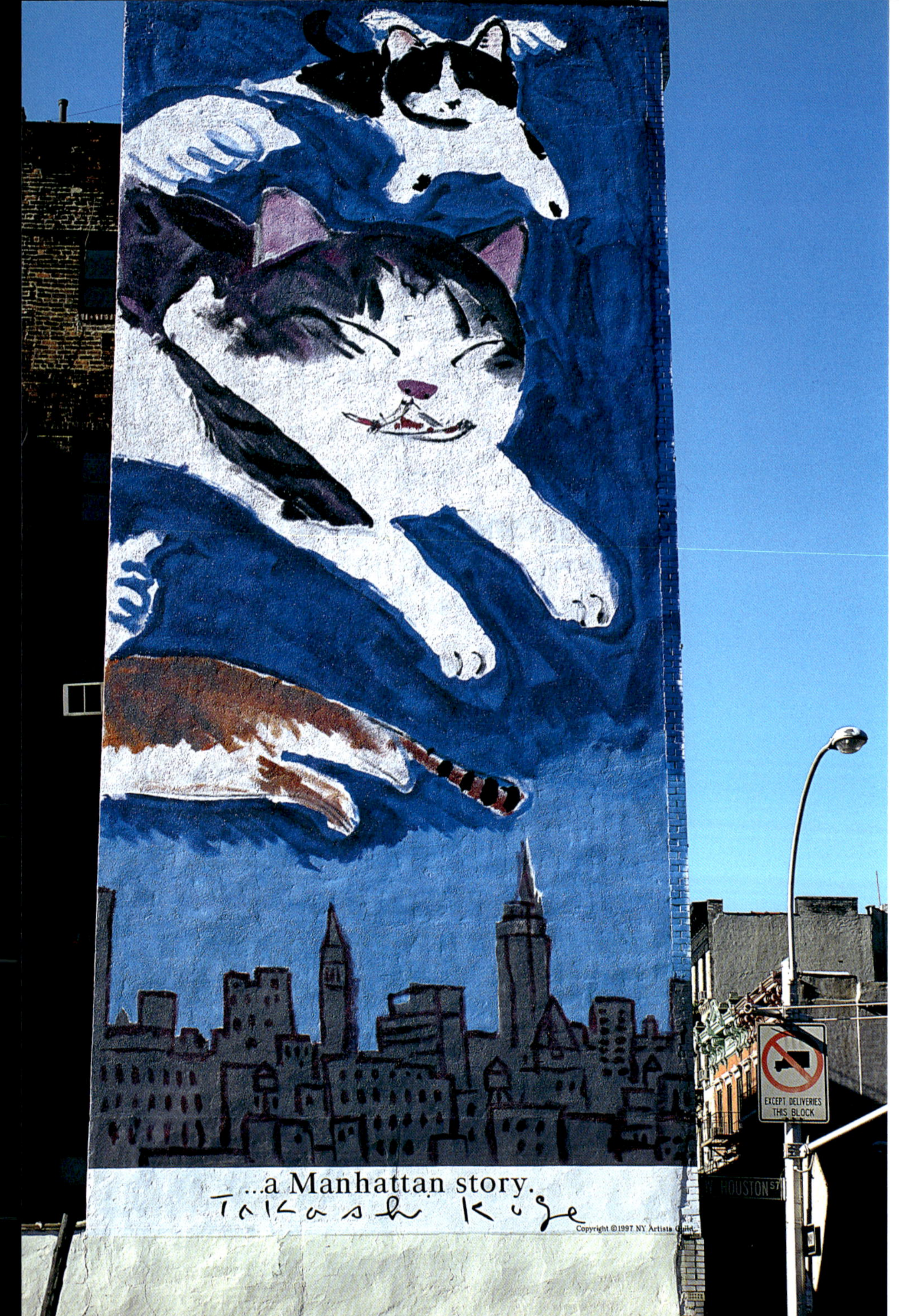

A delightful gallery-sponsored mural in Soho that makes bold use of popular Japanese cat motifs.

A decorative gallery-sponsored mural in Soho with an idealized cityscape theme.

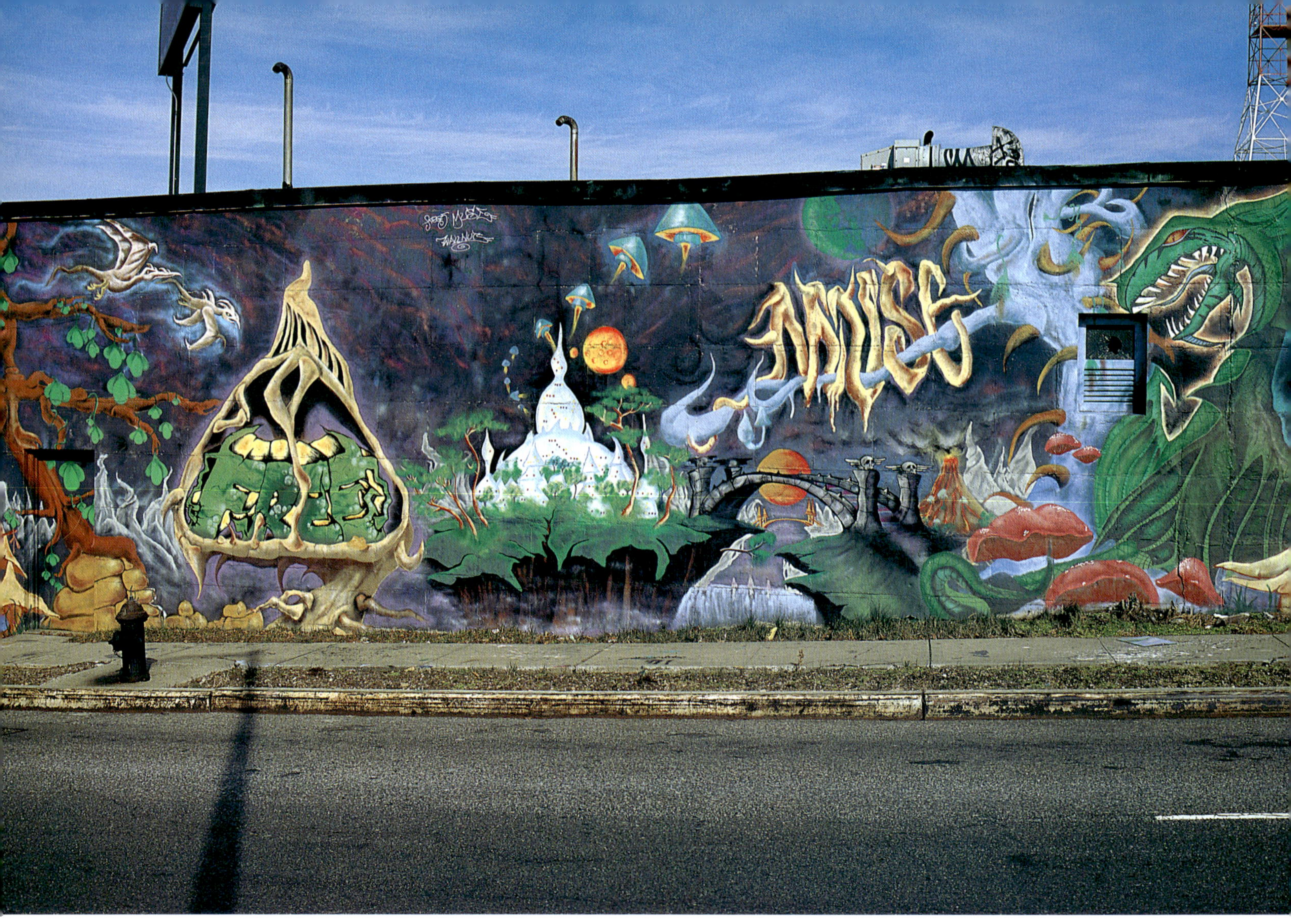

Two views of the range of talent displayed at the Long Island City entrance ramp.

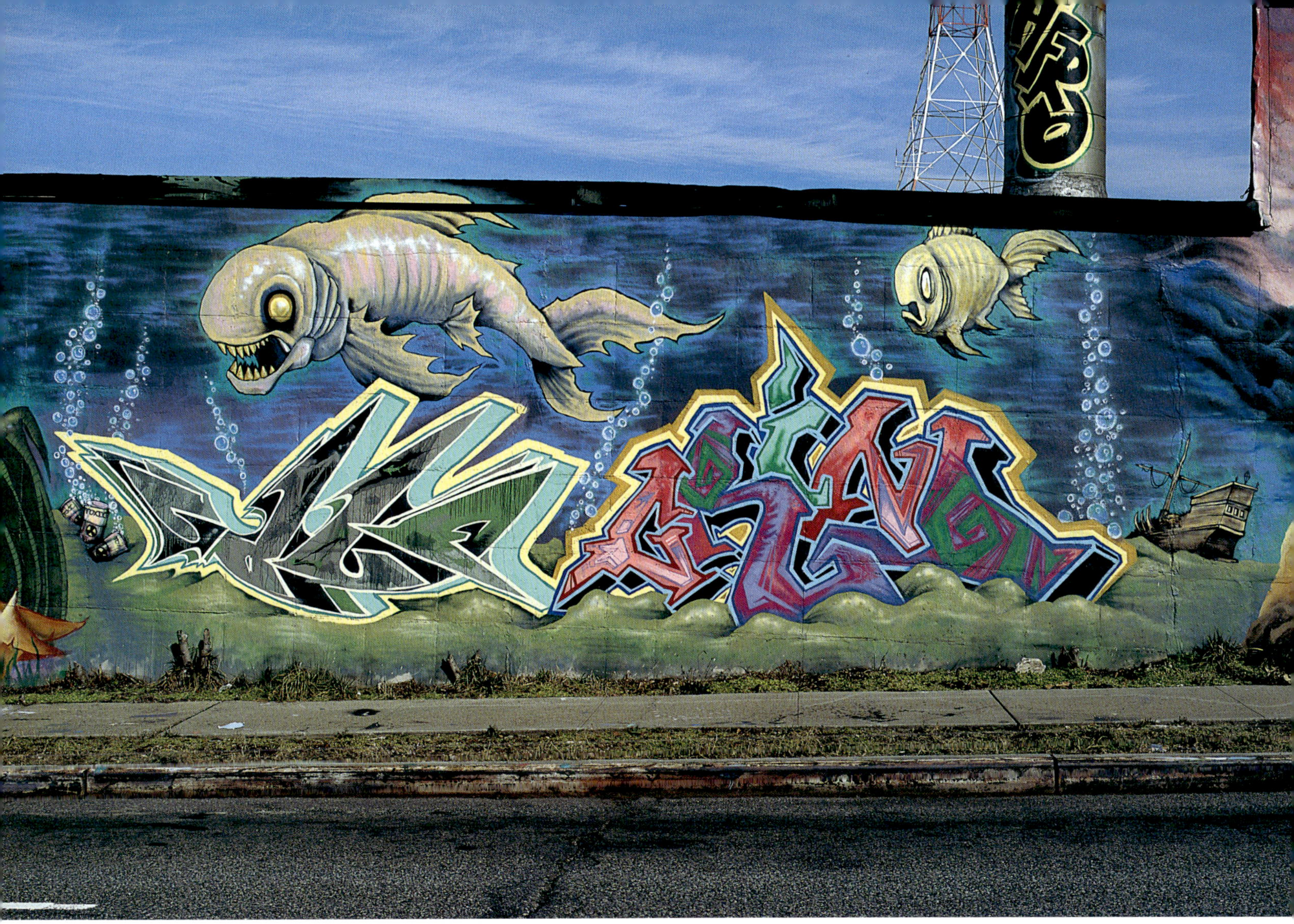

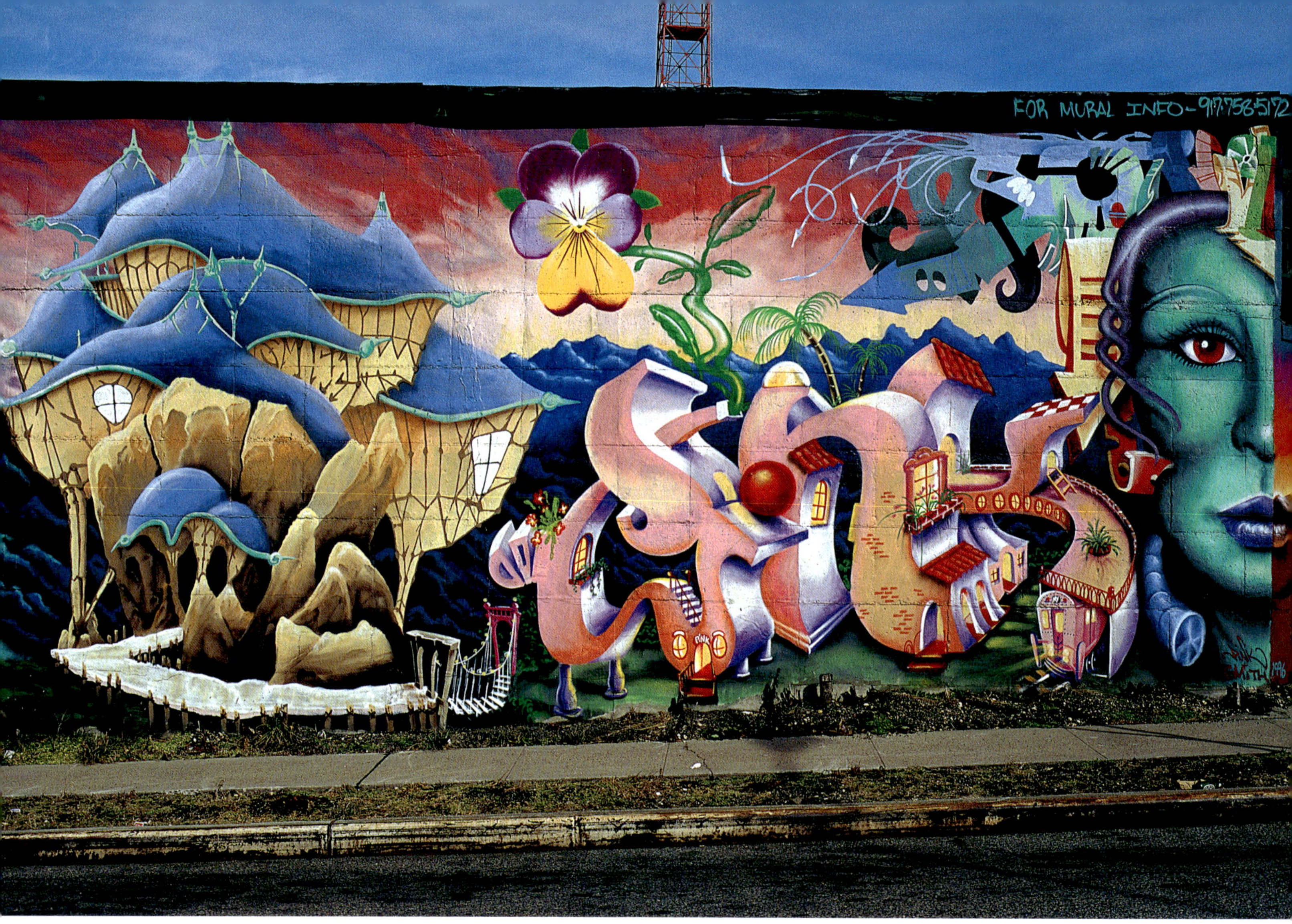

LADY PINK makes a distinctive statement at the Long Island City on-ramp.

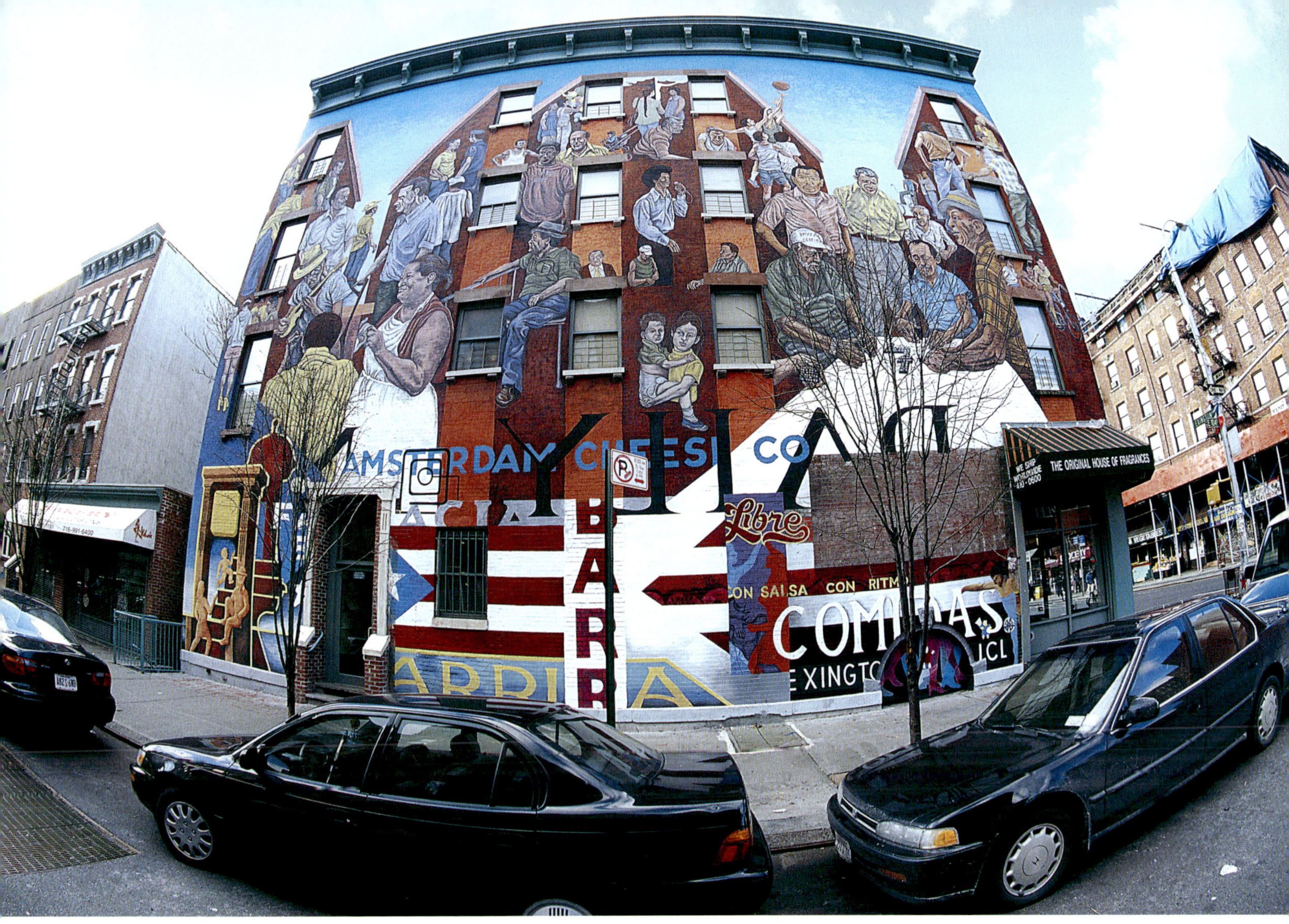

An intriguing composition by a local artist pays tribute to organized labor and daily neighborhood life in Spanish Harlem.

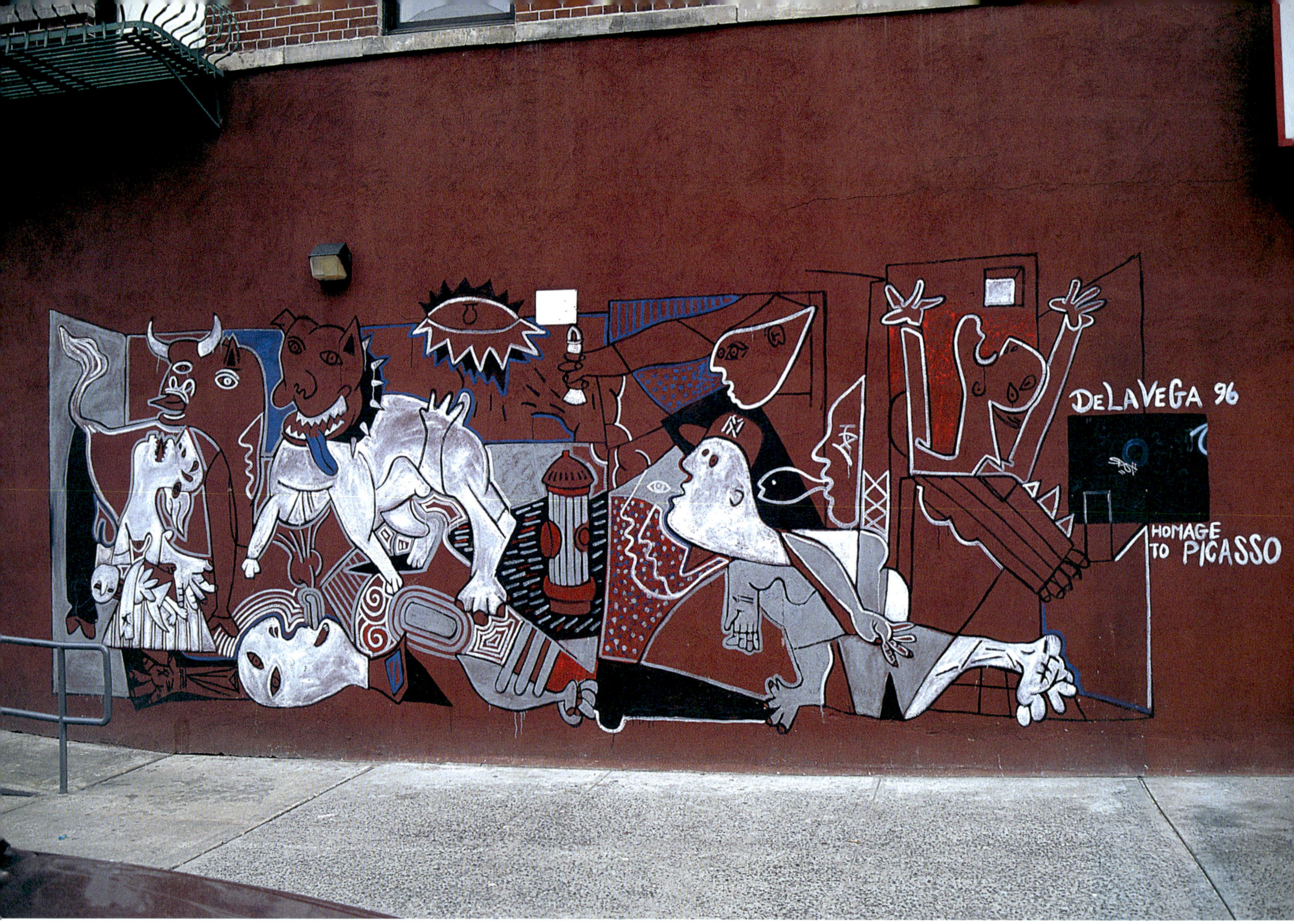

DE LA VEGA salutes Pablo Picasso's masterpiece *Guernica* in this decorative mural on 104th Street and Lexington Avenue.

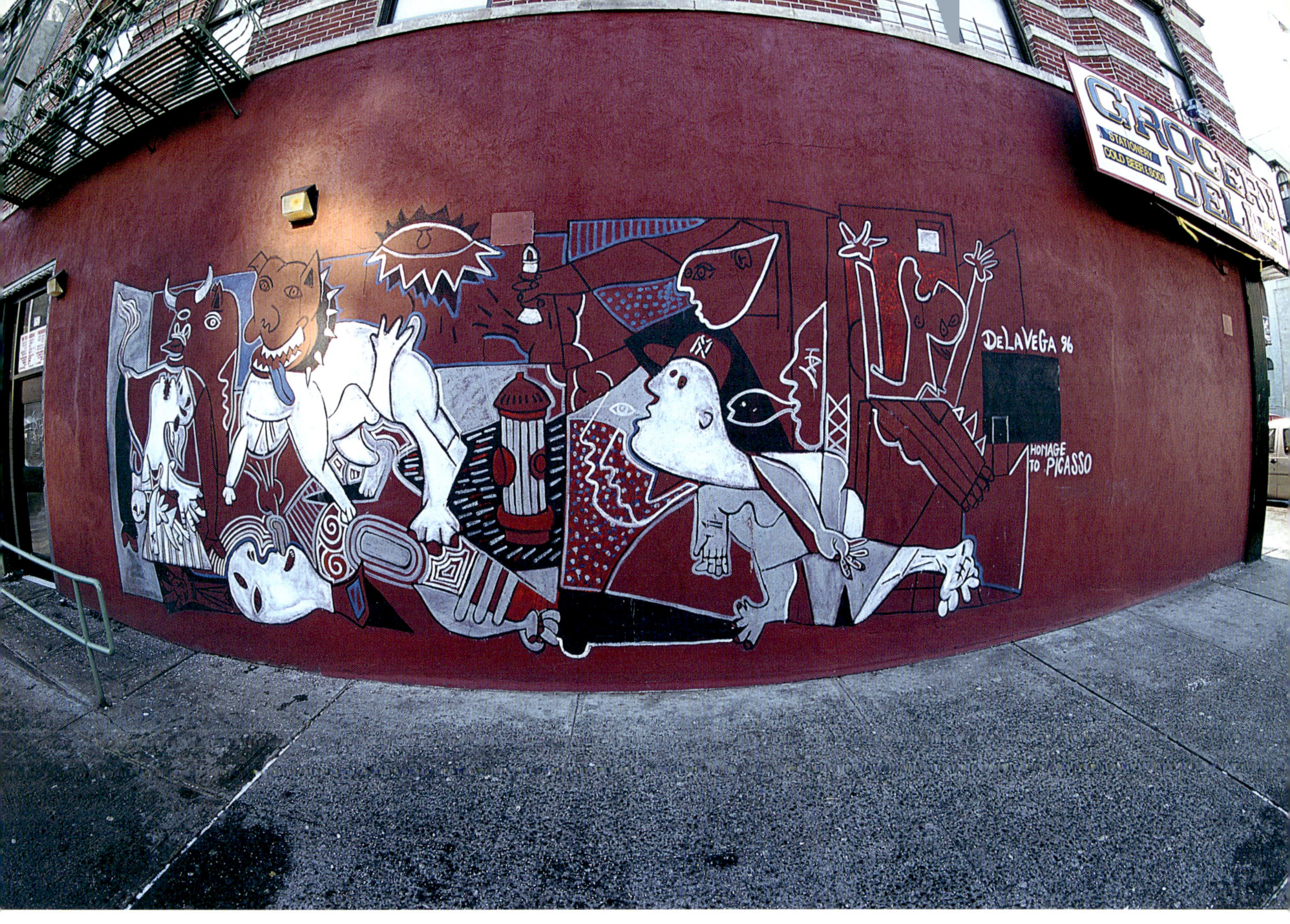
GROCERY
STATIONERY
COLD BEER & SODA
DELI
DeLaVega 96
HOMAGE
TO PICASSO

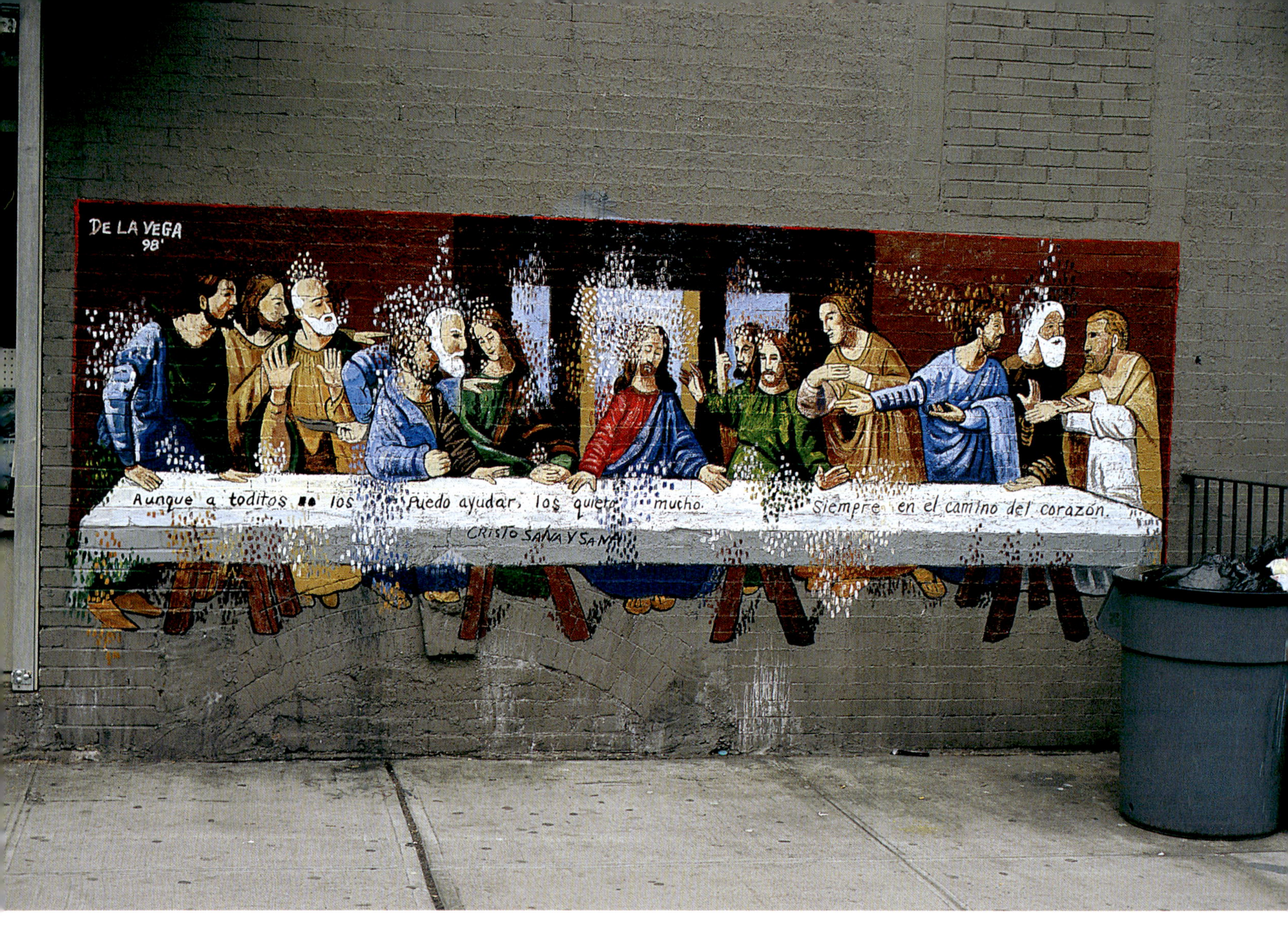

DE LA VEGA creates his interpretation of Leonardo da Vinci's *Last Supper* near 110th Street and Lexington Avenue.

Cats form a decorative motif in this gallery-sponsored mural on Houston Street.

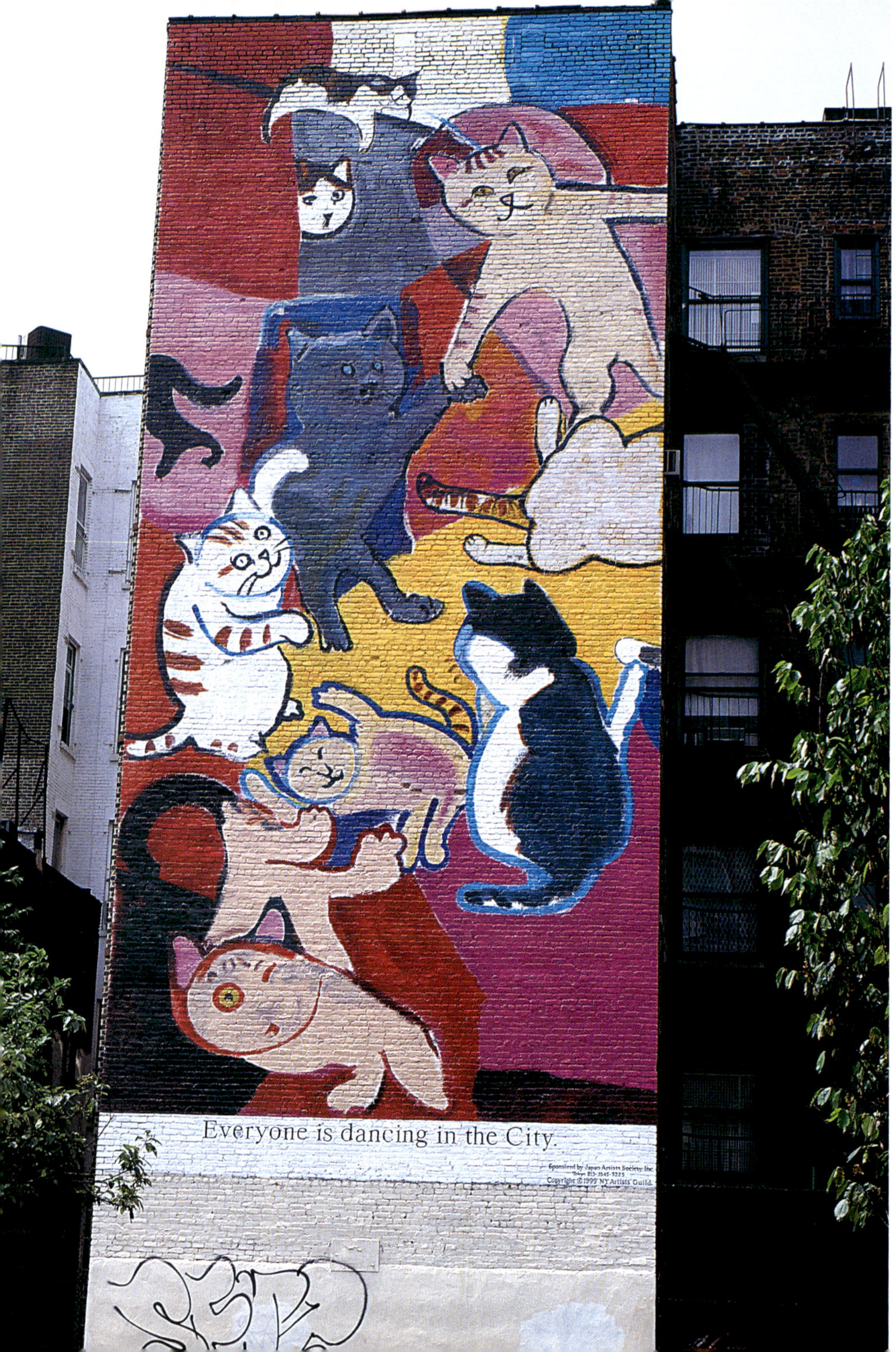

Cats gaze furtively in this gallery-sponsored decorative mural on Houston Street in Manhattan's trendy Soho.

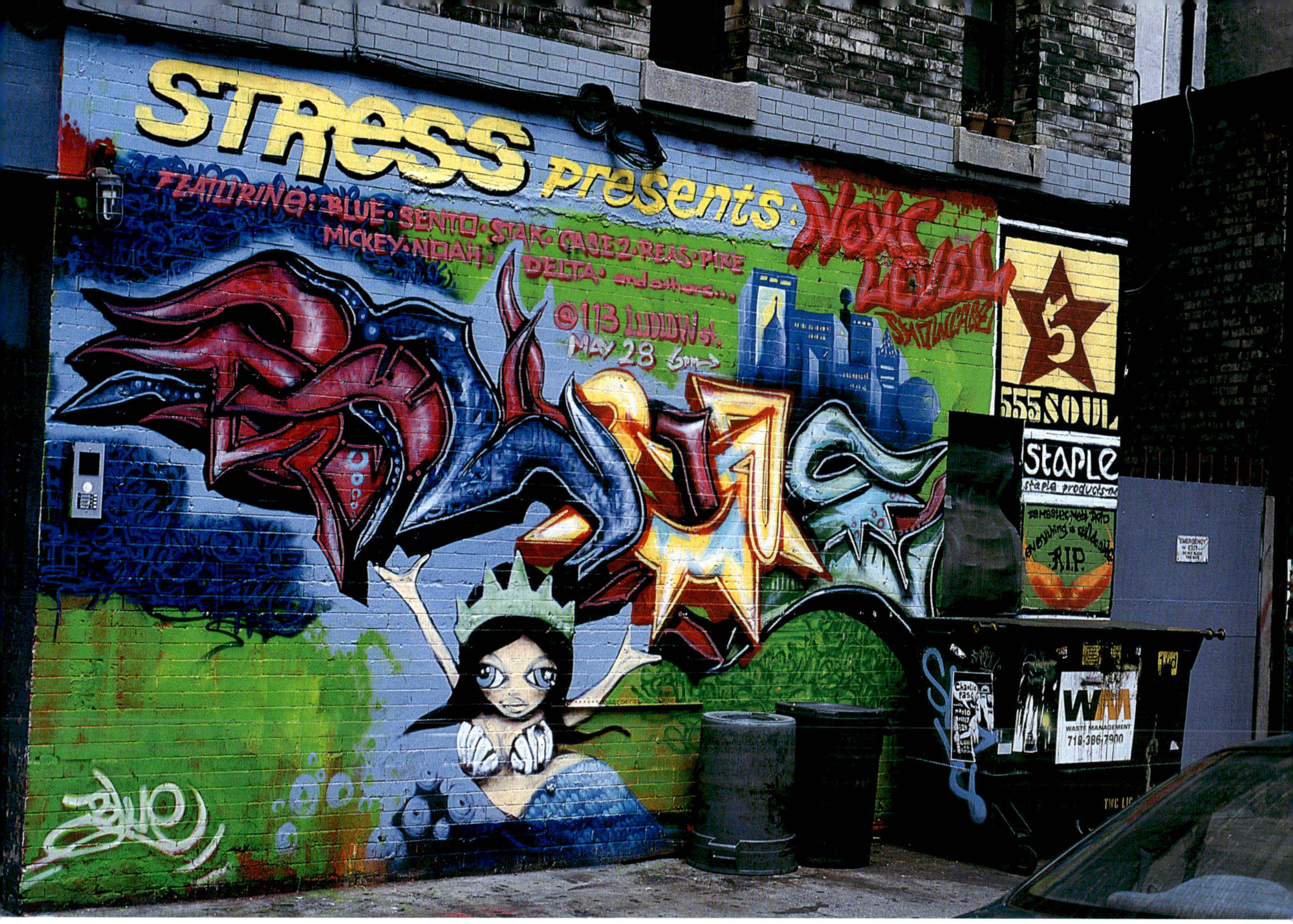

The decorative mural, by a local artist, on the Upper East Side of Manhattan is also an advertisement for *Stress* magazine, which has since folded.

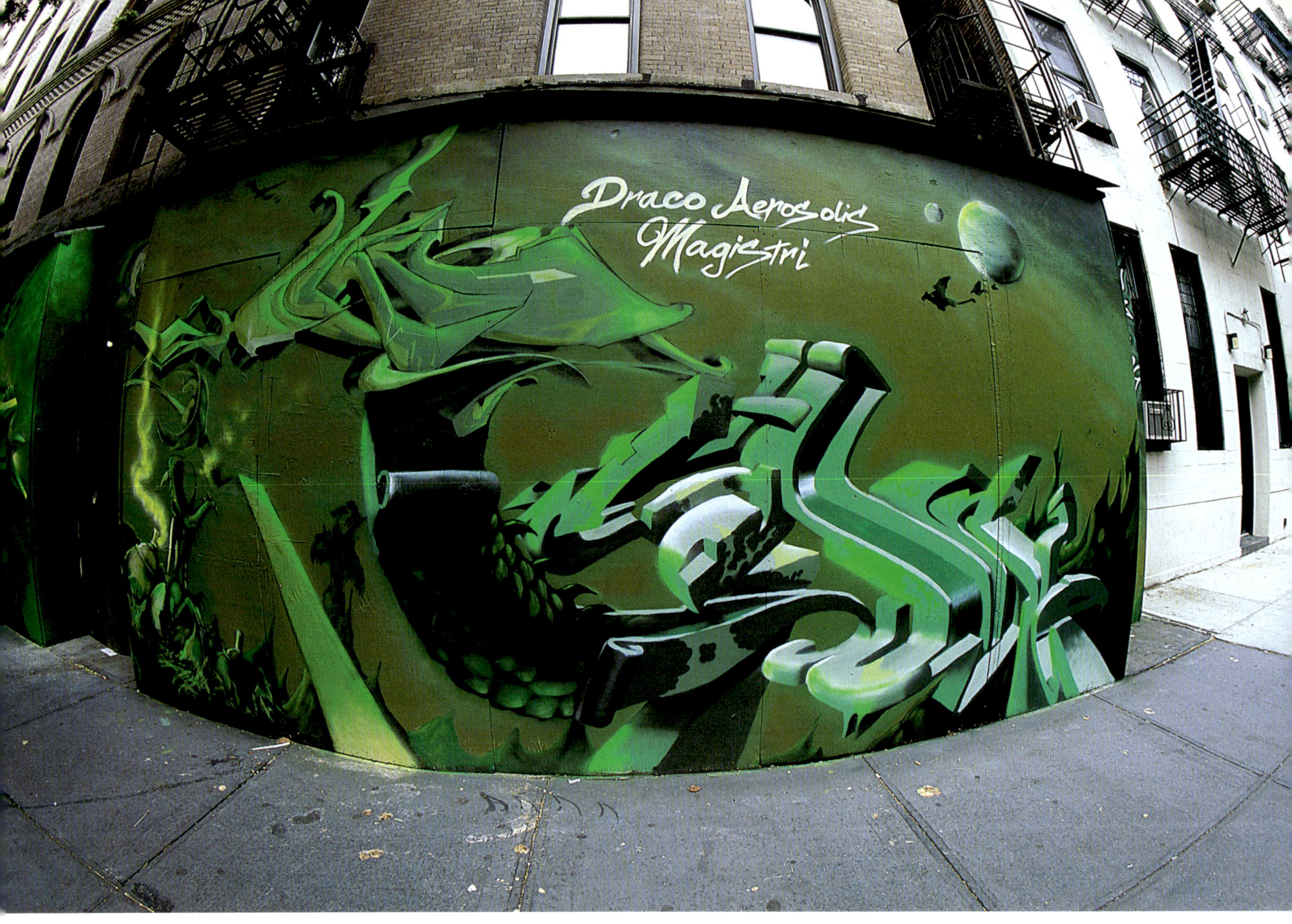

A decorative mural by a local artist in Manhattan's trendy Upper East Side with an attention-getting all-green color scheme camouflages a construction site.

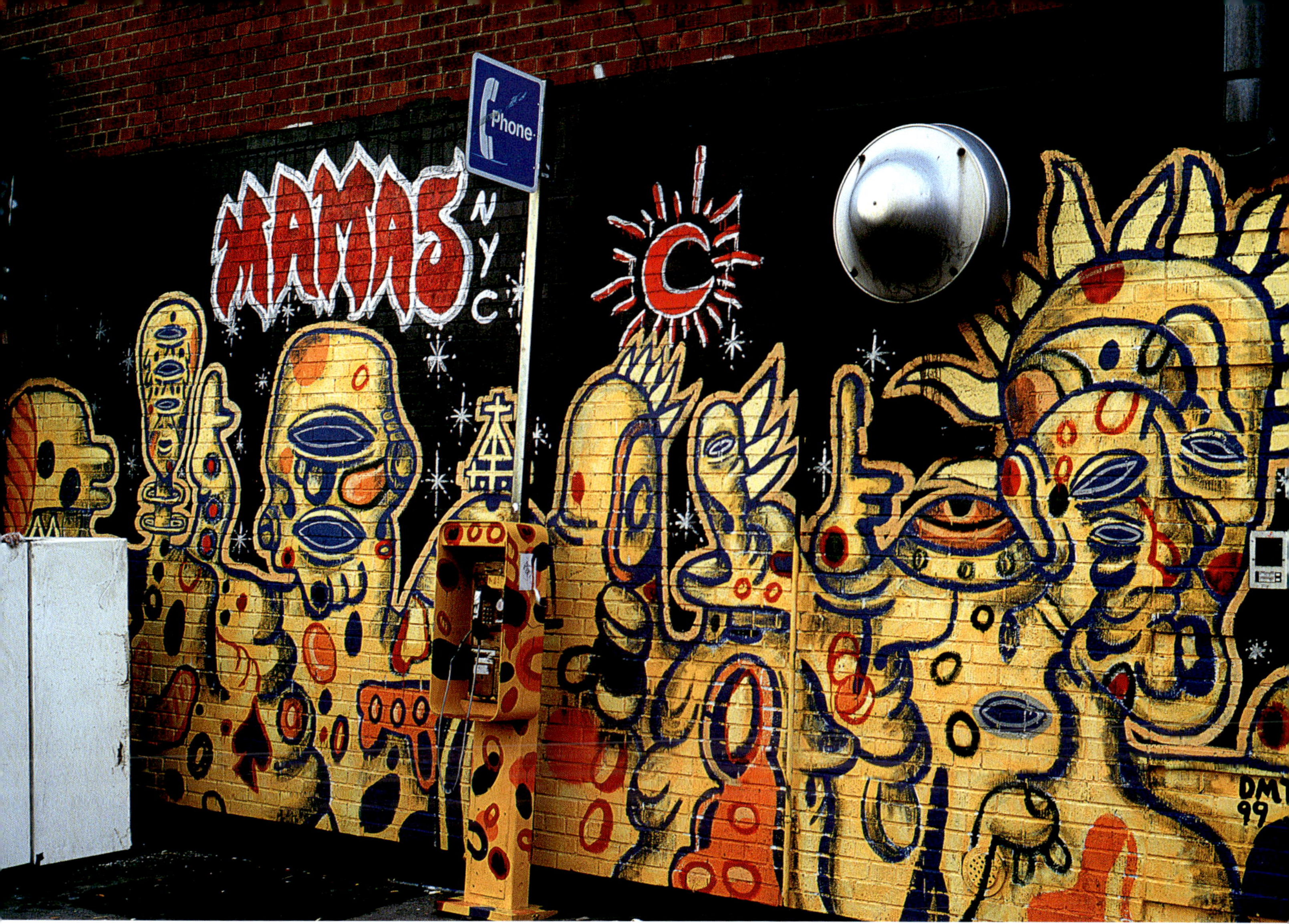

An original instance of an artist altering the external surroundings to harmonize with the art. This East 4th Street artist paints a public phone to match the rich textile-like gold and black pattern of the vibrant decorative mural.

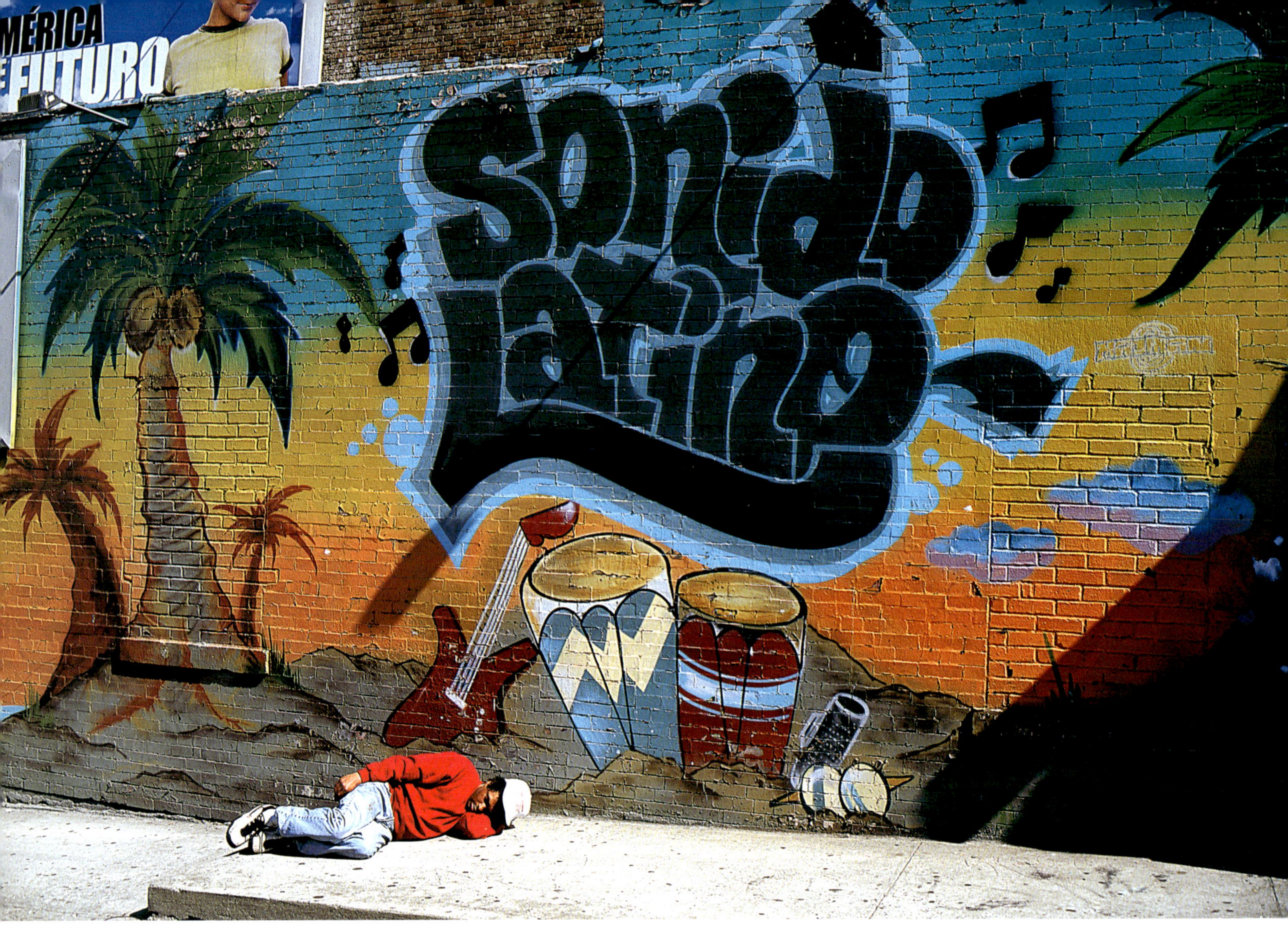

A local Brooklyn artist's decorative mural expressing the tropical color of the Caribbean and the musical sound of Latin America.

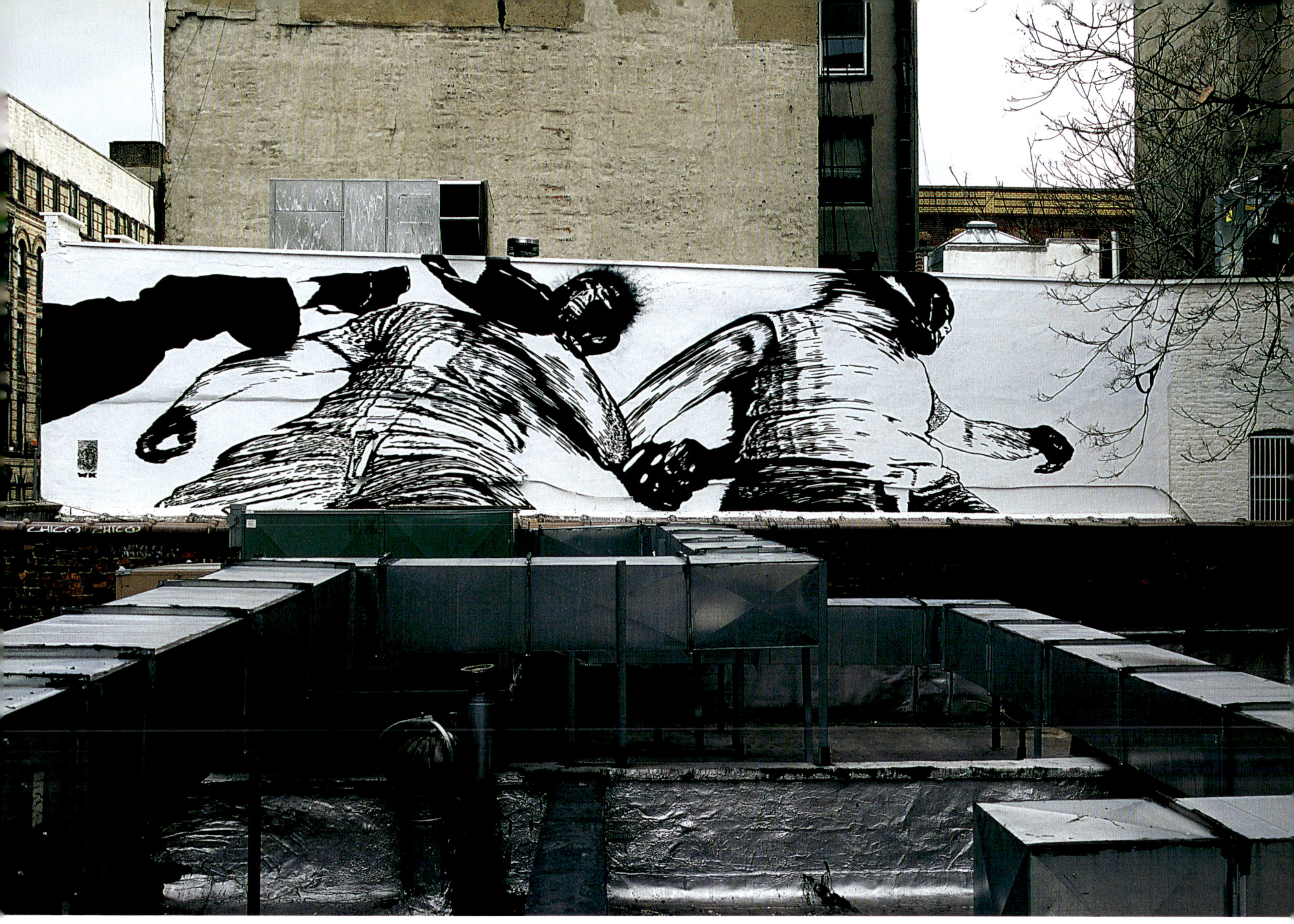

A local Manhattan artist's ink-like technique produces powerful if somewhat somber murals on Manhattan's Lower East Side. After the wall has been painted white, the image is beamed onto the surface with a slide projector and traced over.

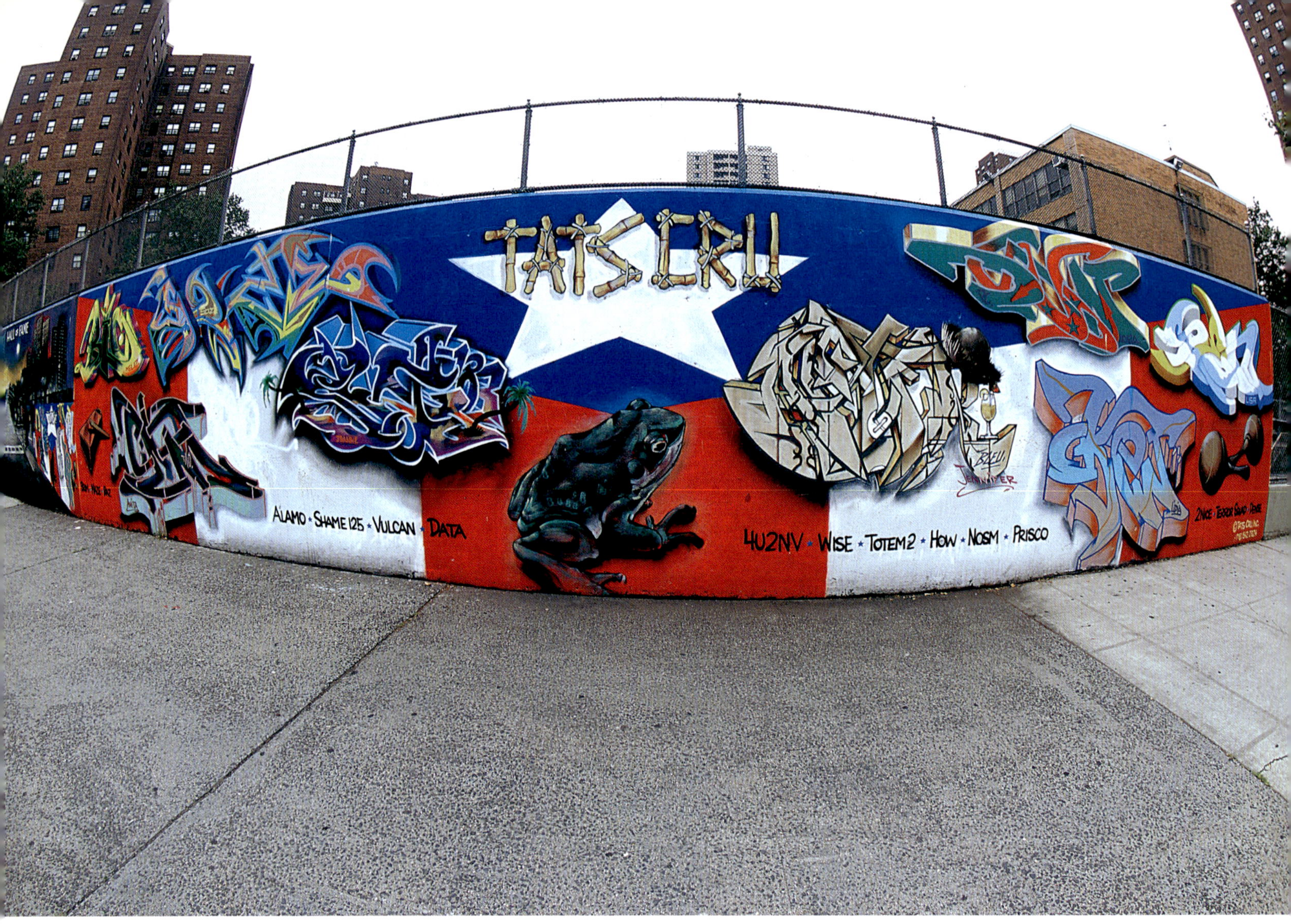

BG 183, BIO, and NICER of TATS CRU make a decorative statement in several styles to express the astounding variety of Latin American culture in this late-nineties Pride of Heritage mural on 106th Street and Park Avenue in Spanish Harlem, the Graffiti Hall of Fame.

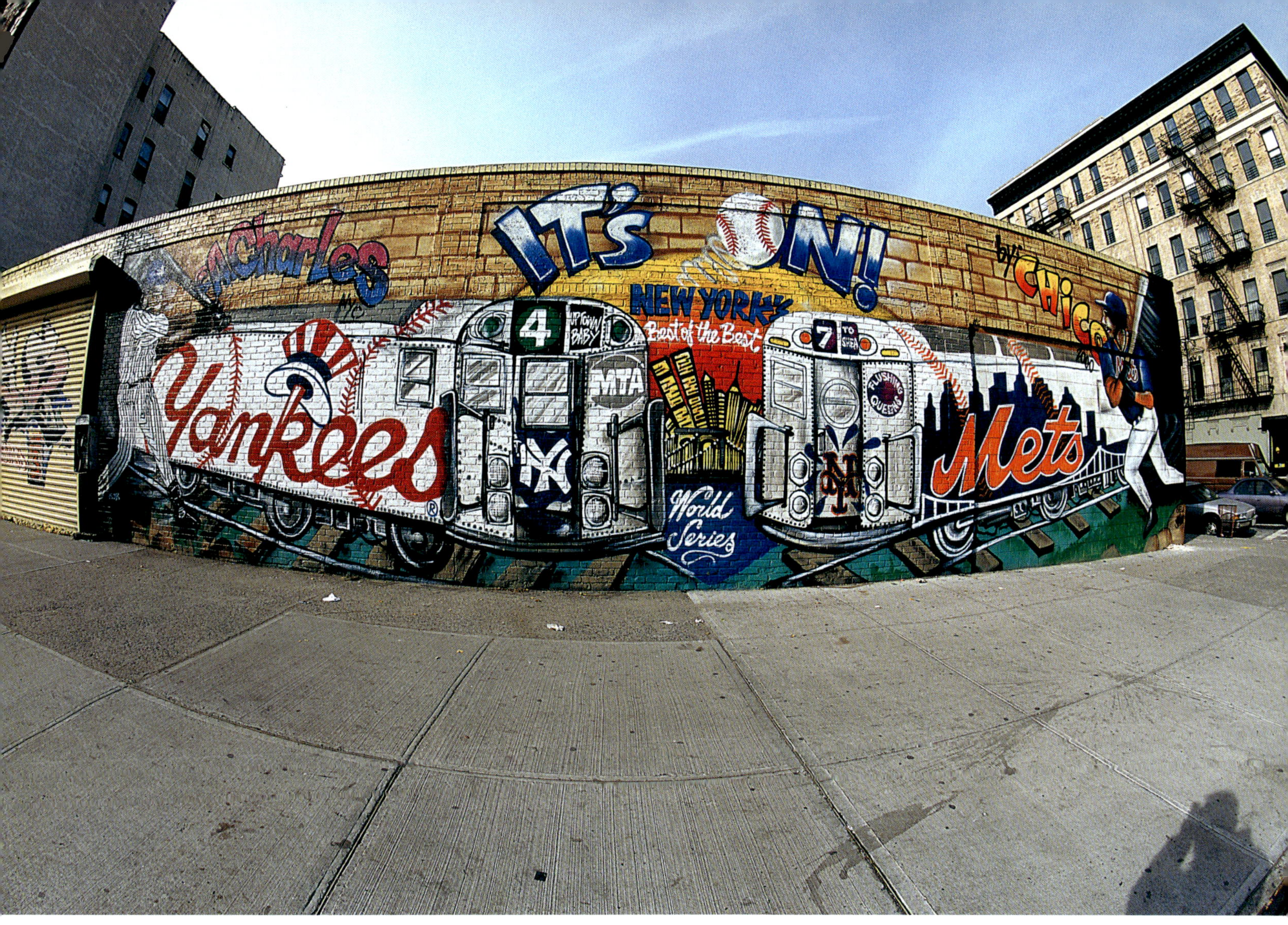

Andre Charles's and CHICO's mural in the Lower East Side is a joint creation after their rivalry over turf in lower Manhattan was settled. It is a popular commemoration of the year 2000, when the Yankees played the Mets in the subway World Series. The 4 and 7 are the subway lines to the teams' stadiums.

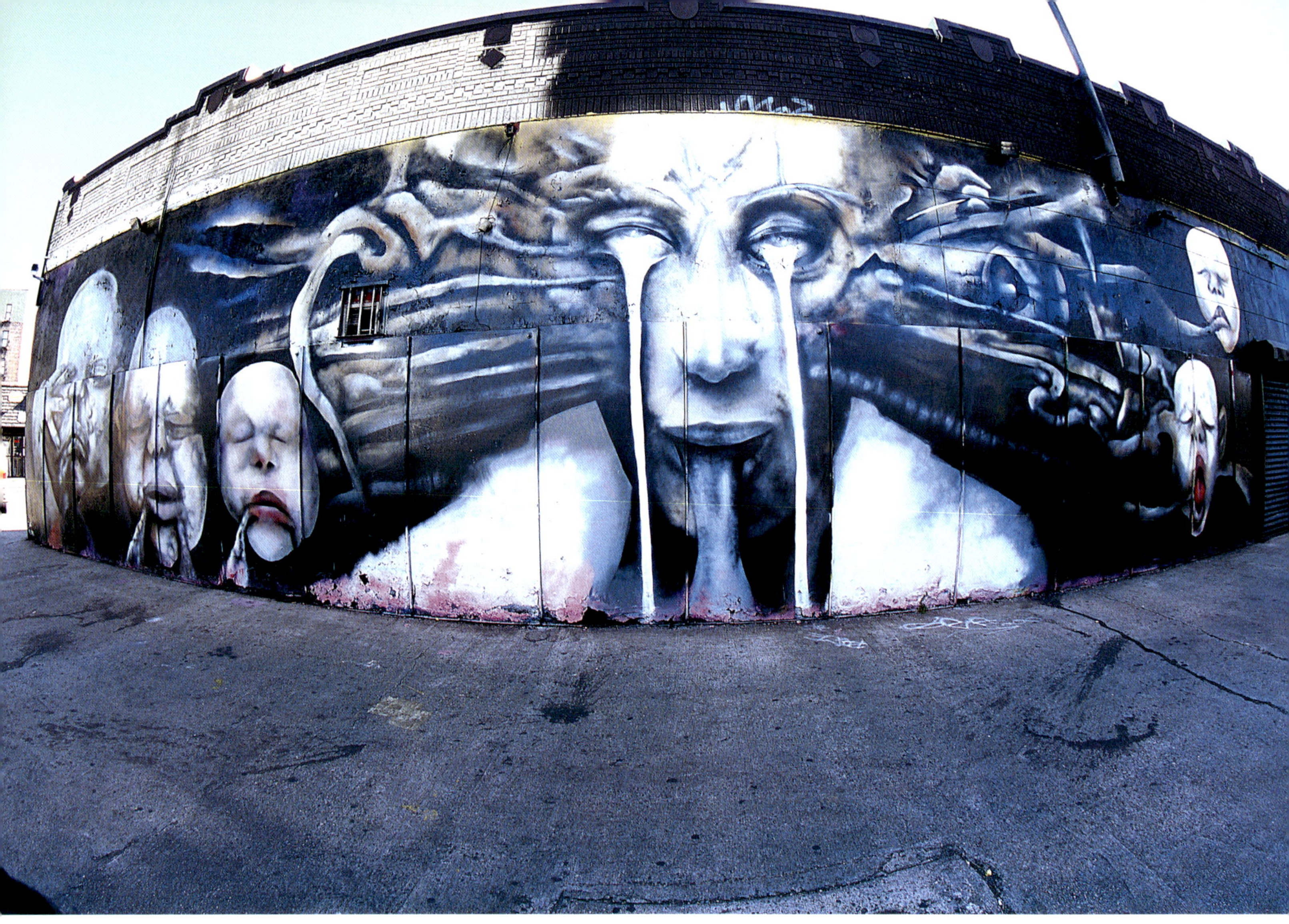

TATS CRU borrows from *Alien* artist H. R. Geiger in this decorative mural near Hunts Point in the Bronx.

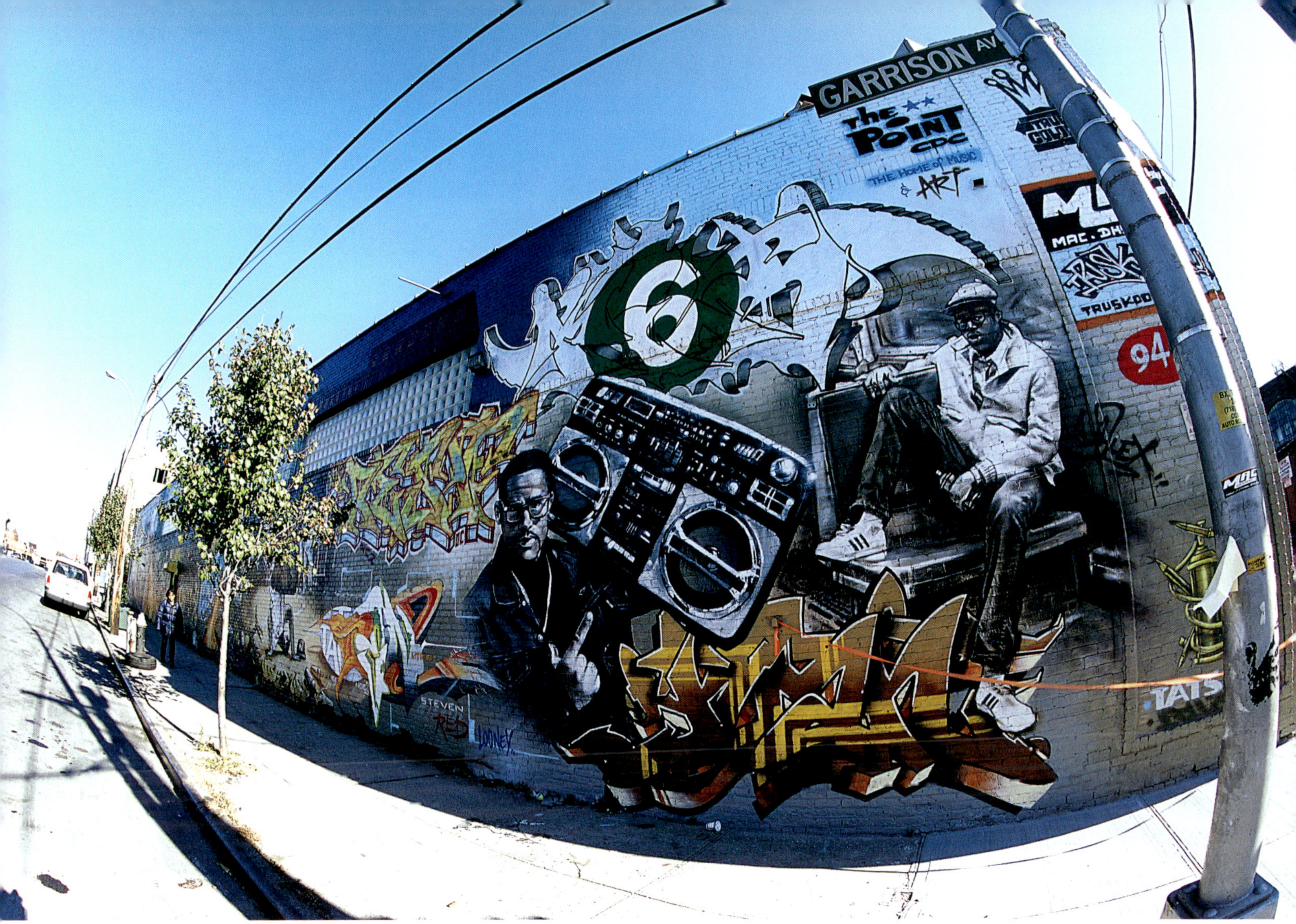

Some murals are done as commercial advertisements but are effective organic messengers of the inner city. TATS CRU departs from its usual style to create an ad for a rap group. The 6 is a nod to a subway line through the South Bronx.

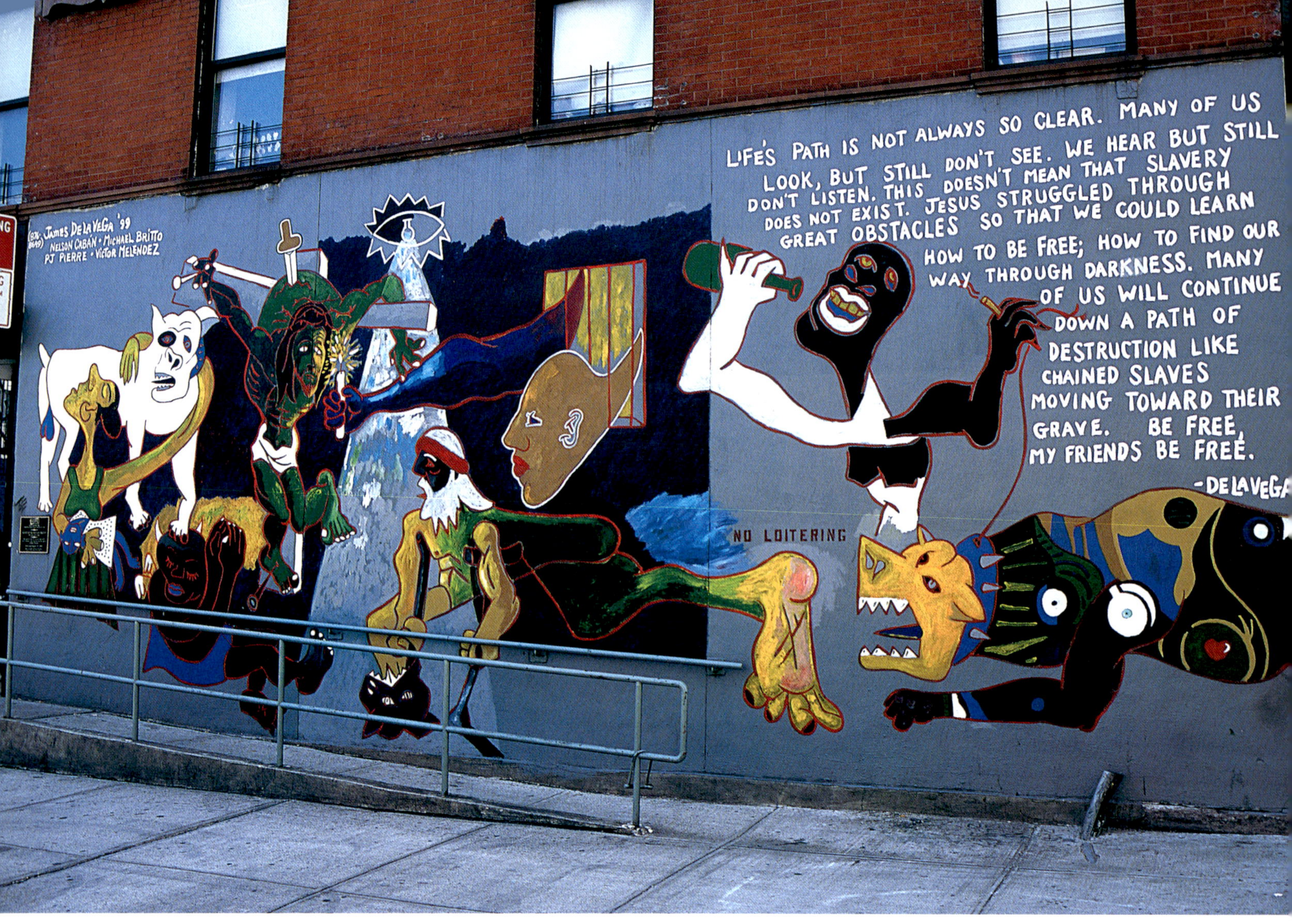

DE LA VEGA's obsession with Picasso influences yet another of his Spanish Harlem murals.

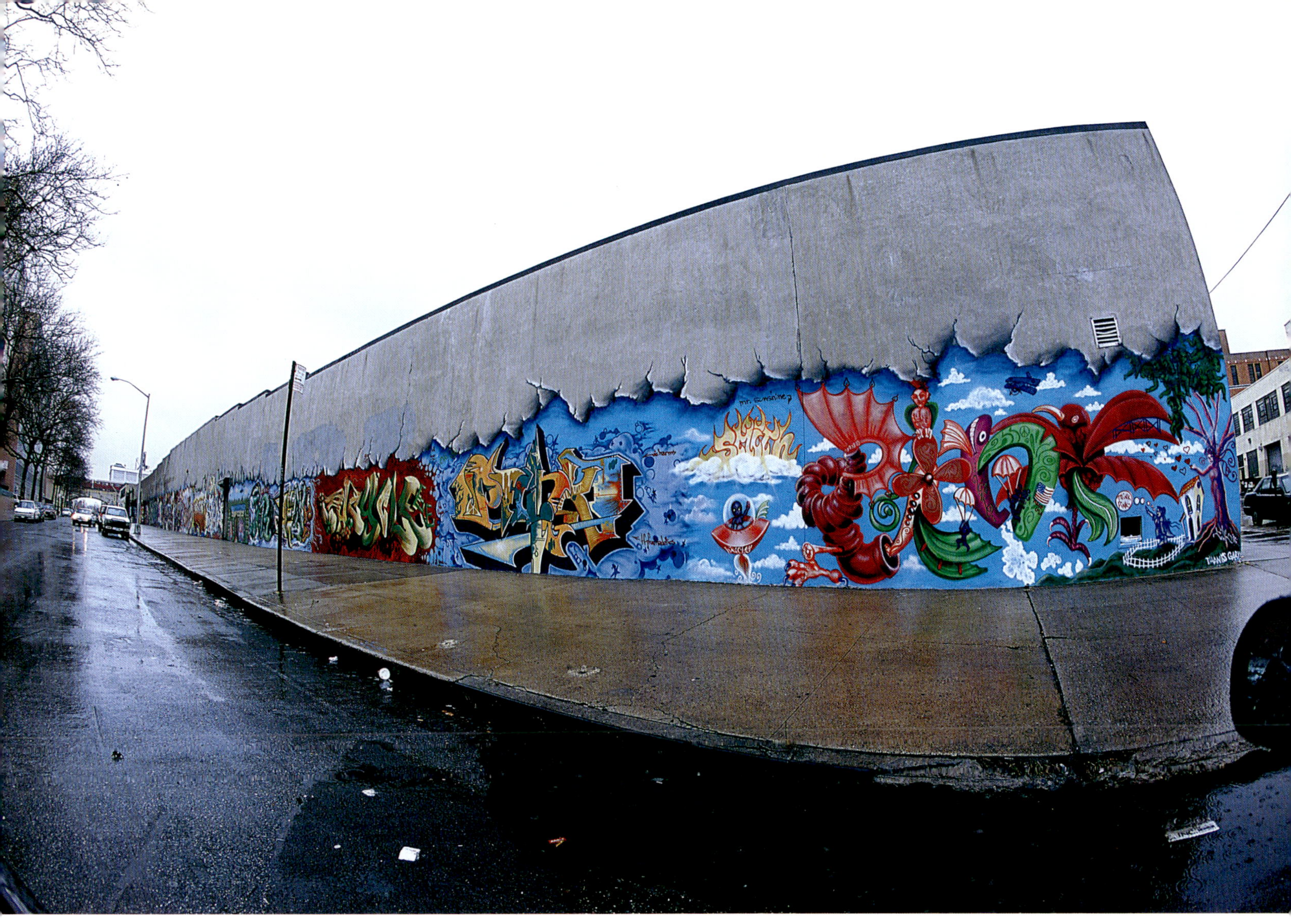

Long Island City's long monotonous walls are broken up by many artists' renditions.
Page 104 by REVOLT, page 105 by MARK BODE, page 106 by PEYTON and MAZE, page 107 by WARM and EZO, page 108 by IZTHEWIZ, page 109 by FREE5, page 110 by CYCLE, page 111 by PFUNK, SMITH, and LADY PINK.

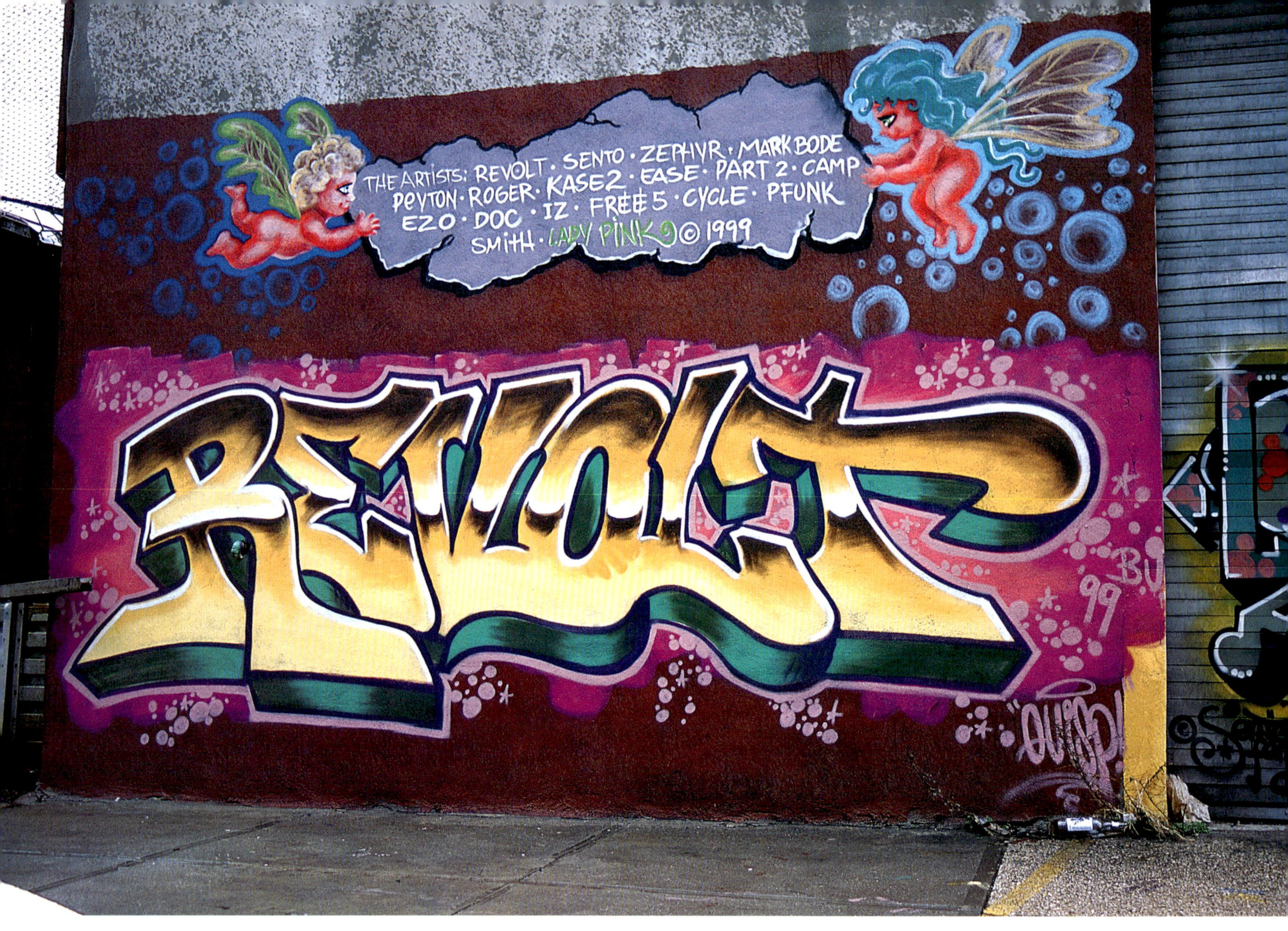
THE ARTISTS: REVOLT · SENTO · ZEPHYR · MARK BODE
PEYTON · ROGER · KASE2 · EASE · PART 2 · CAMP
EZO · DOC · IZ · FREE 5 · CYCLE · PFUNK
SMITH · LADY PINK © 1999
REVOLT

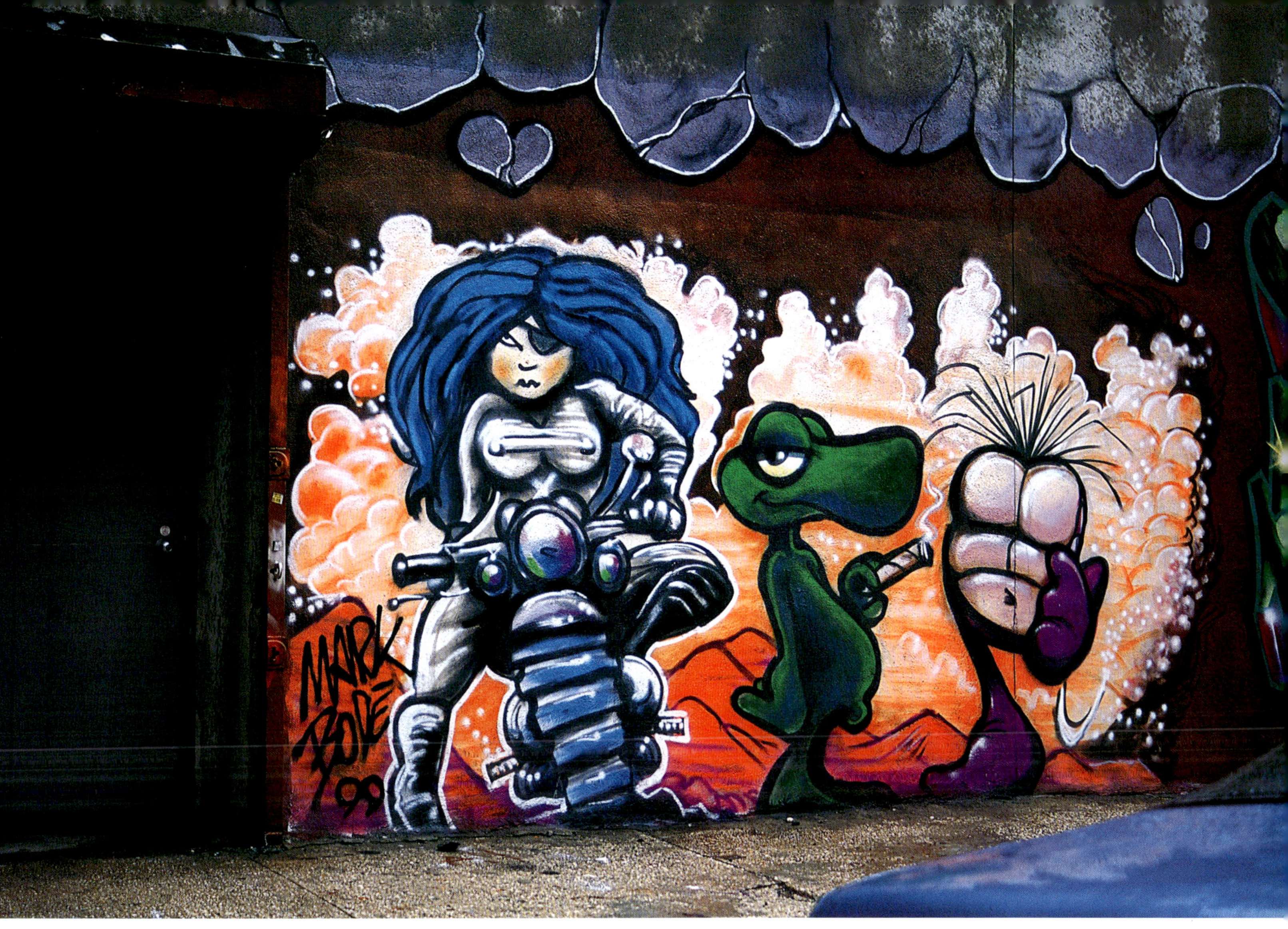
MARK BODÉ
'99

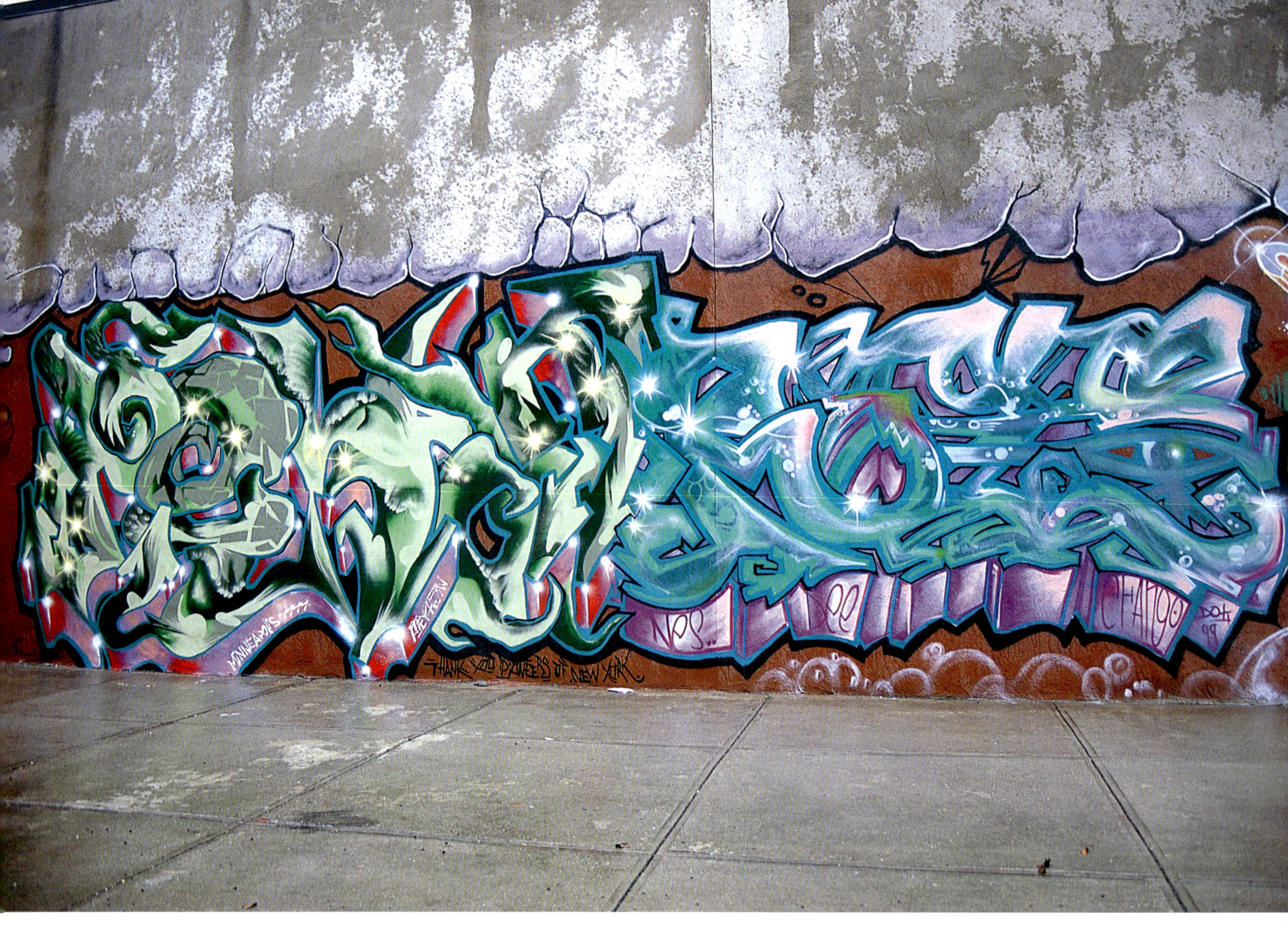
MINNEAPOLIS
THANK YOU PIONEERS OF NEW YORK

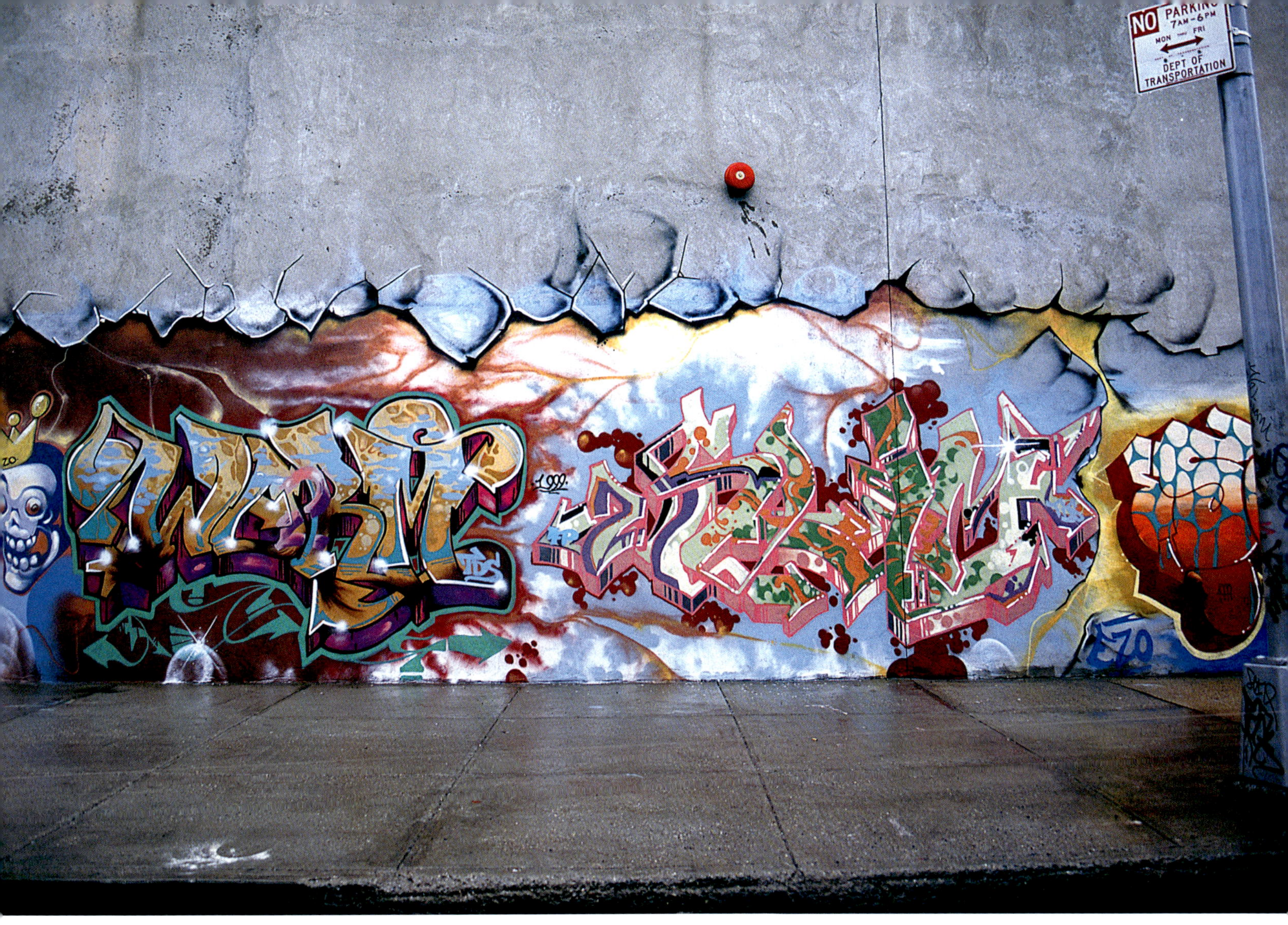
NO
7AM-6PM
MON FRI
DEPT OF
TRANSPORTATION

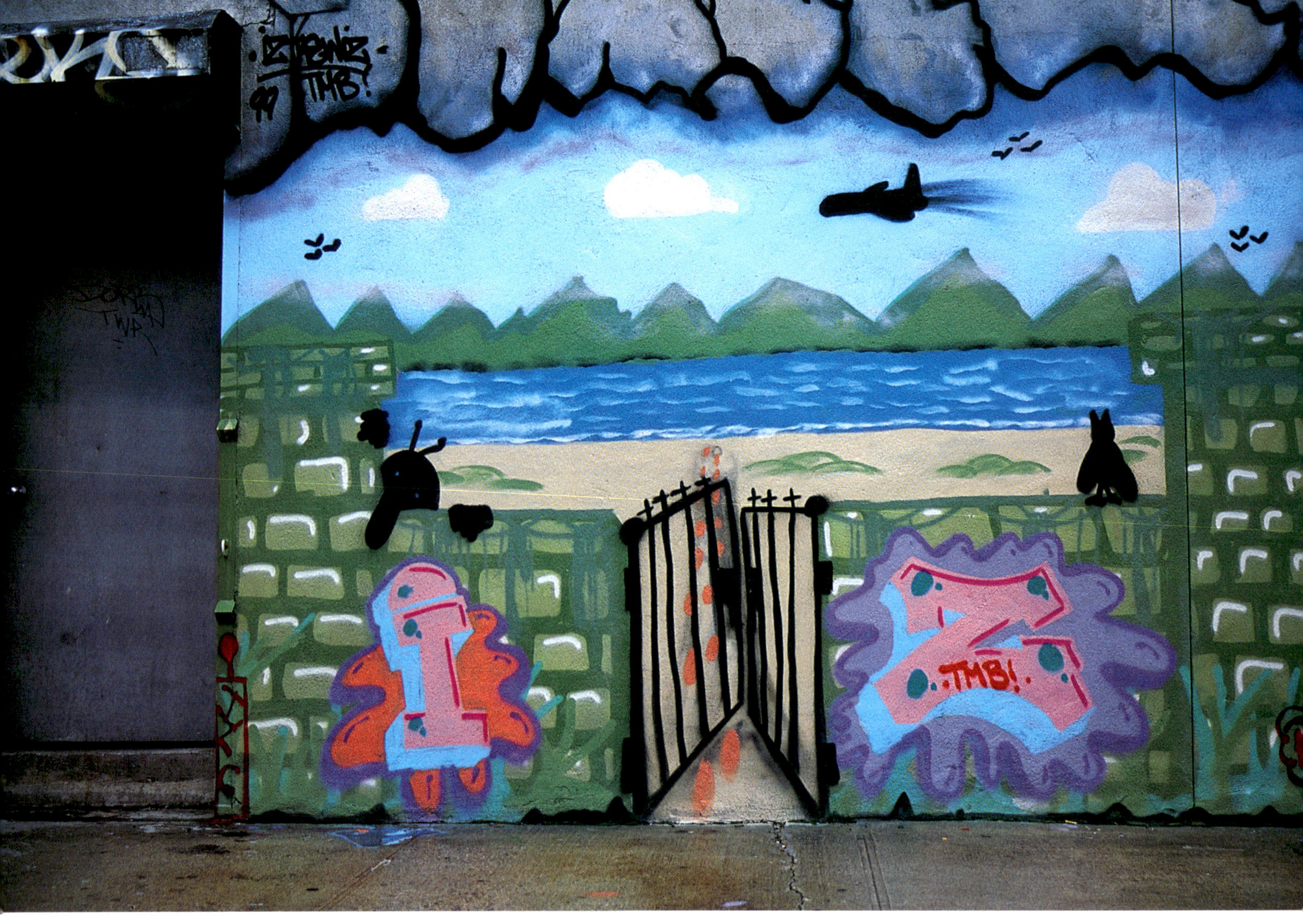
TMB!
.TMB!.

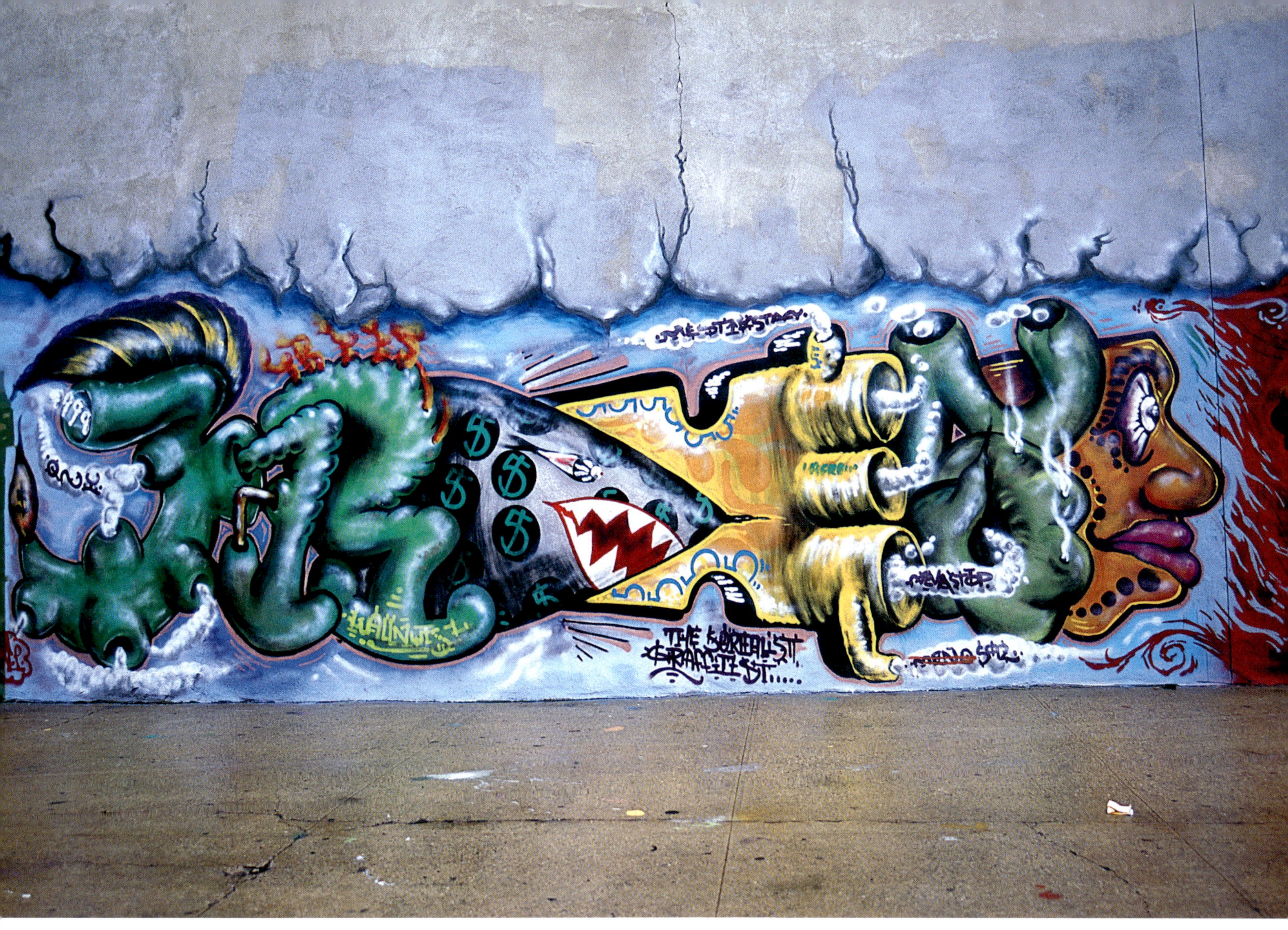
THE SURREALIST
GRAFFITIST.....

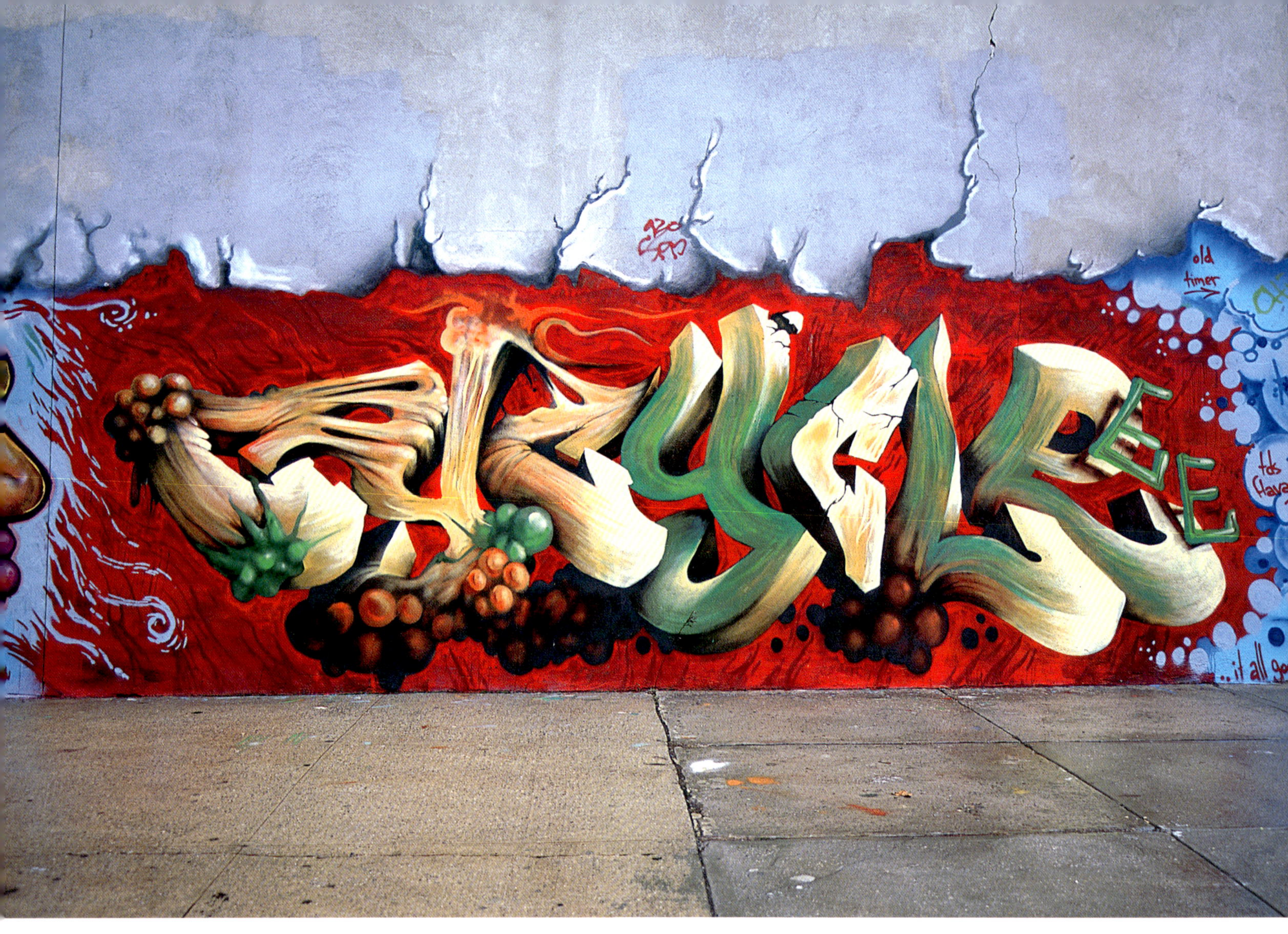
old
timer

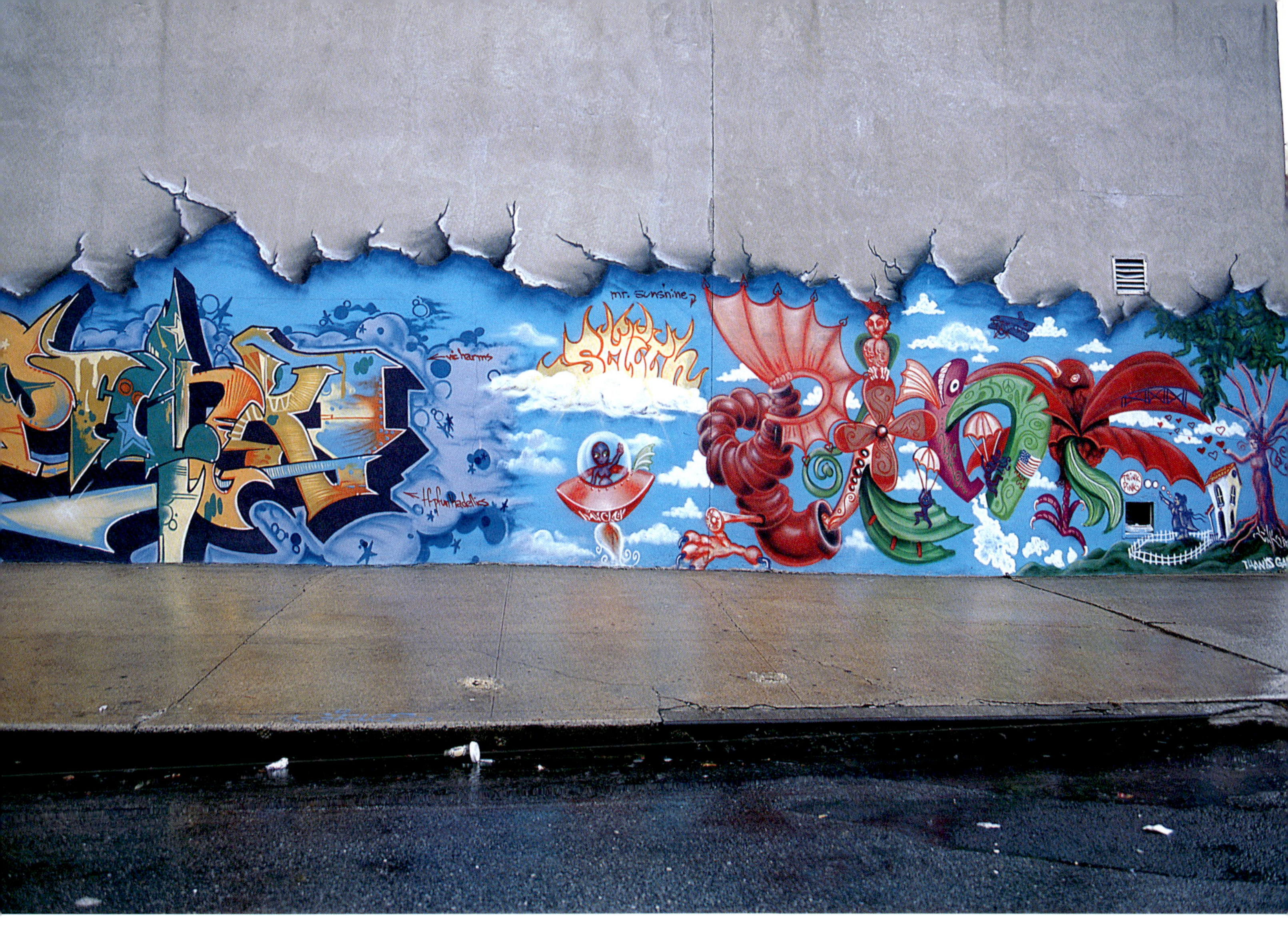
mr. sunshine

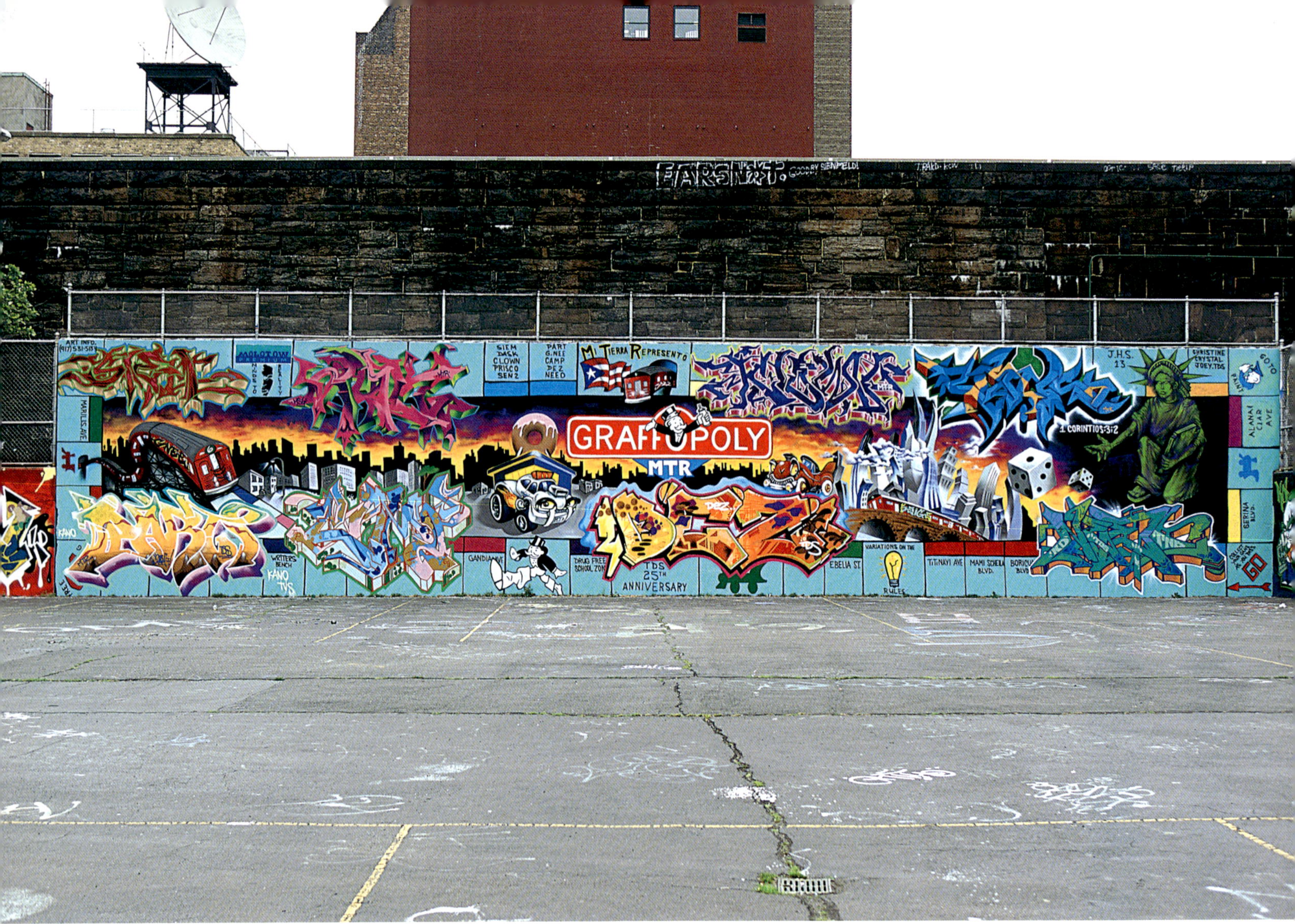

The DEATH SQUAD's inside wall at the Graffiti Hall of Fame depicts chance and the role of the ups and downs of success in the scheme of life. A takeoff on the board game Monopoly is renamed Graffopoly by this famous and respected group.

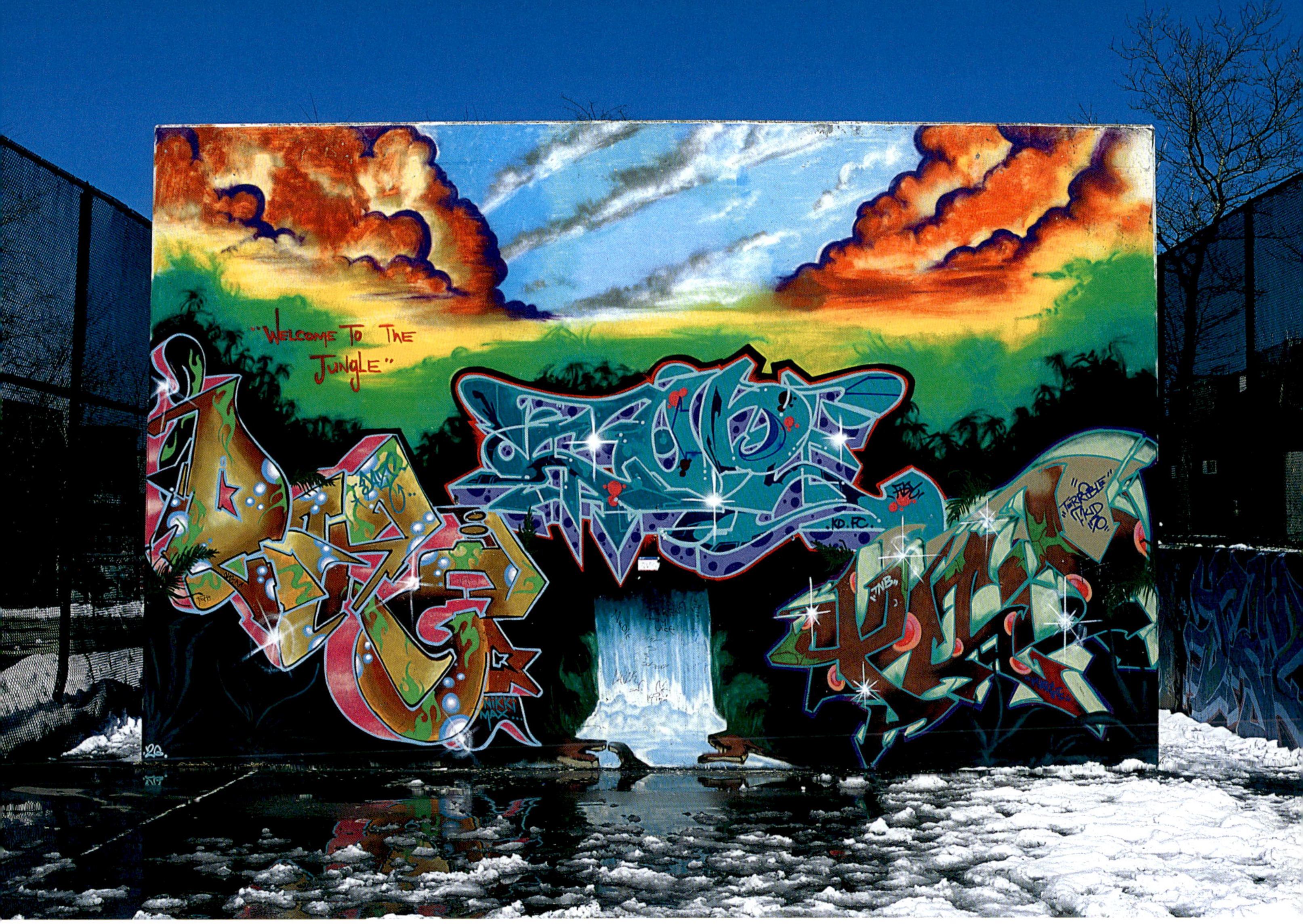

Decorative wall in a handball court in the Bronx painted by DAZE, COPE, and TKID.

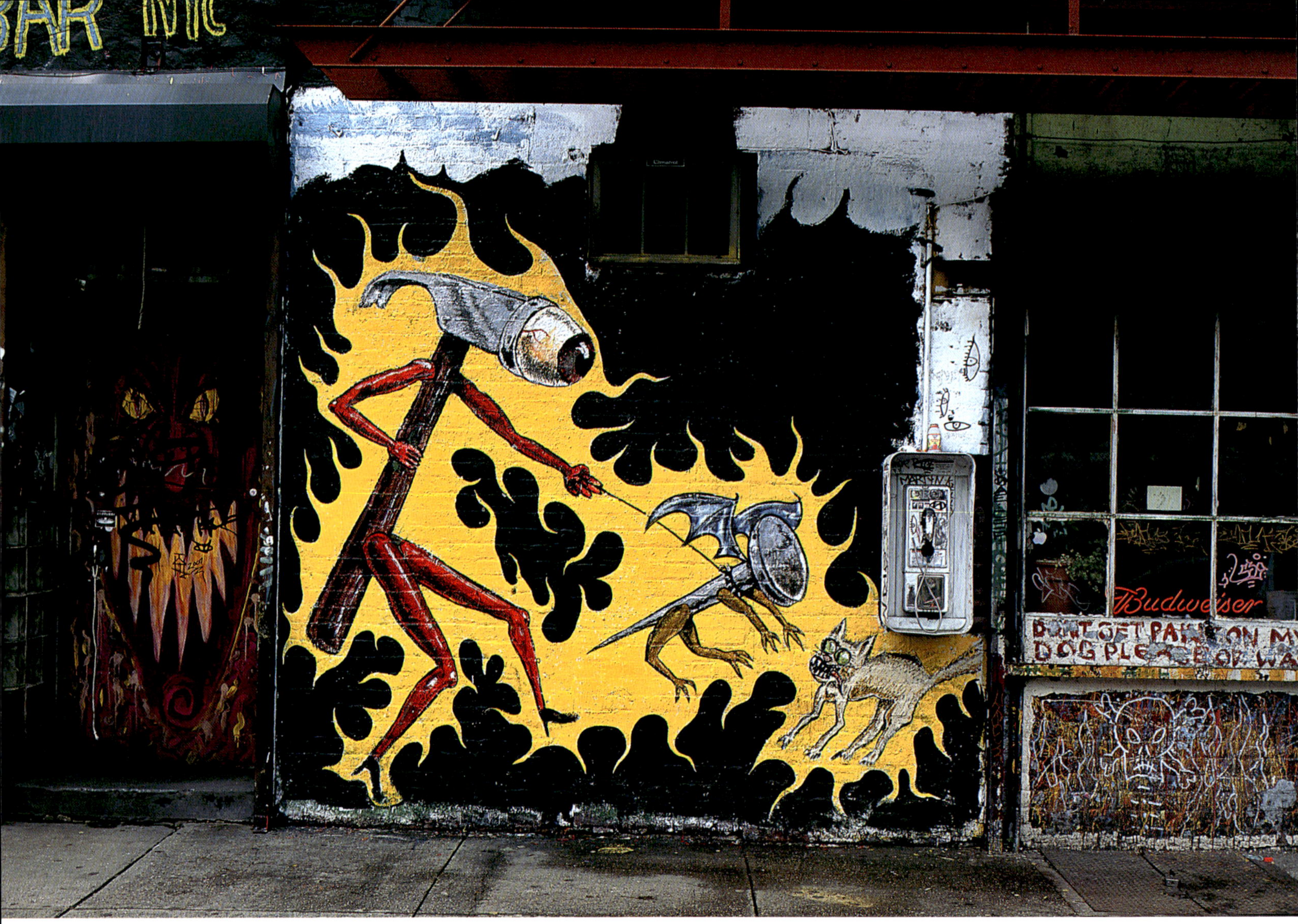

A local Lower East Side artist brightens a grim urban wall with a decorative mural at the entrance of the legendary Mars Bar.

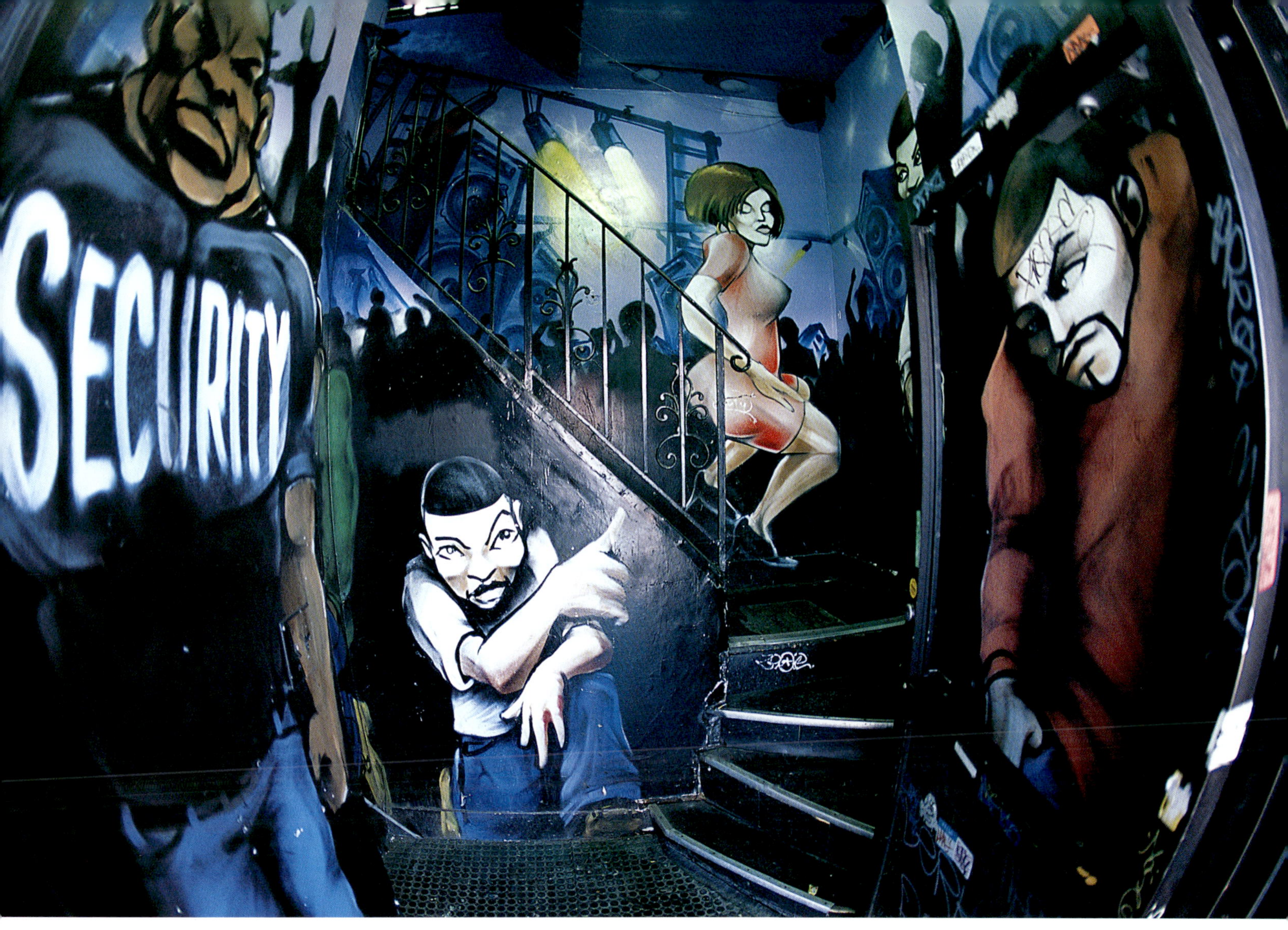

The concentrated energy, forceful color, and bold images of this composition by PCKIDONE (Greg Sessoms) create a powerful and intriguing mural in an urban building lobby in Queens. A joint effort with TATS CRU's NICER offers a theme party for a record shop.

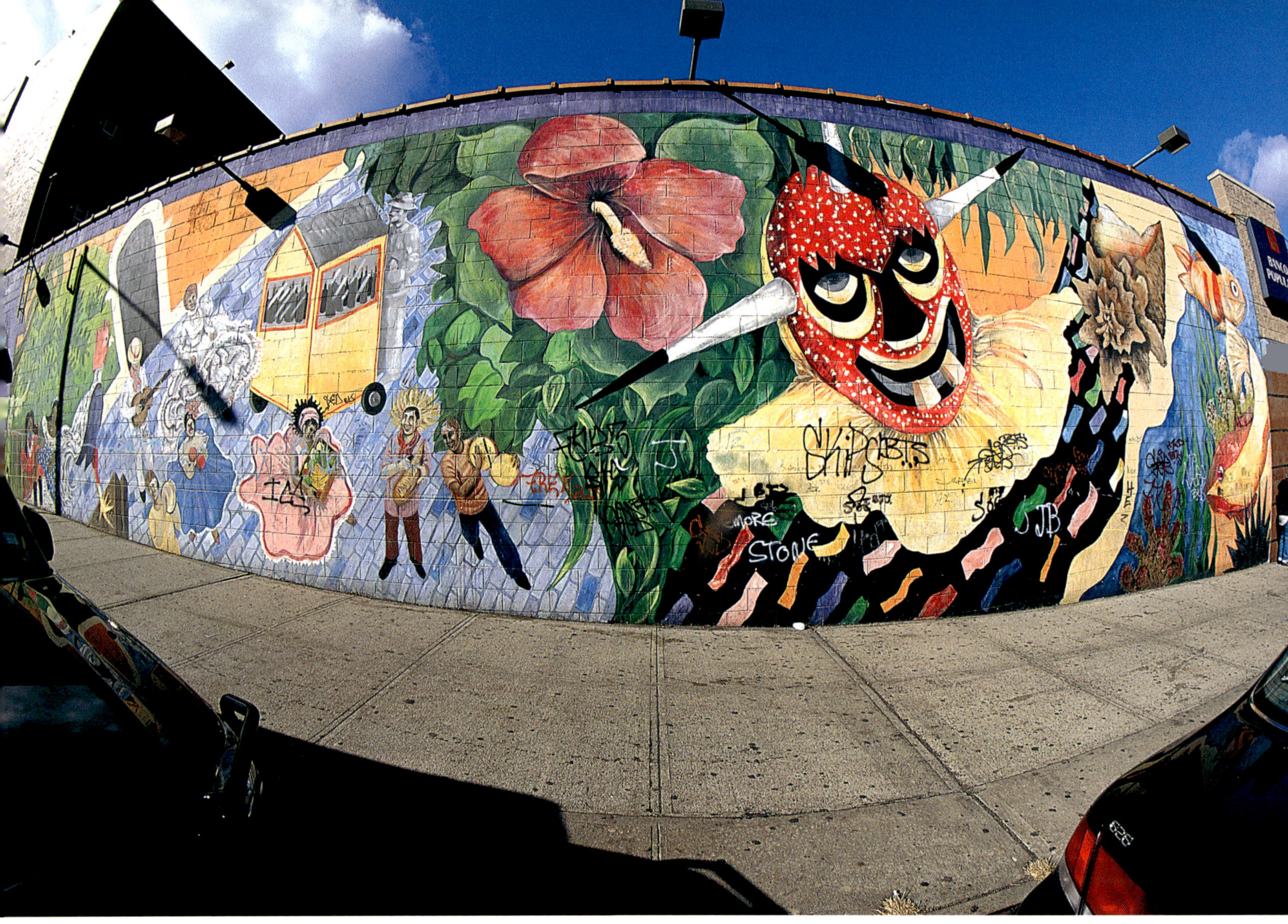

An Afro-Caribbean theme from a local artist adds to the ambience in Manhattan.

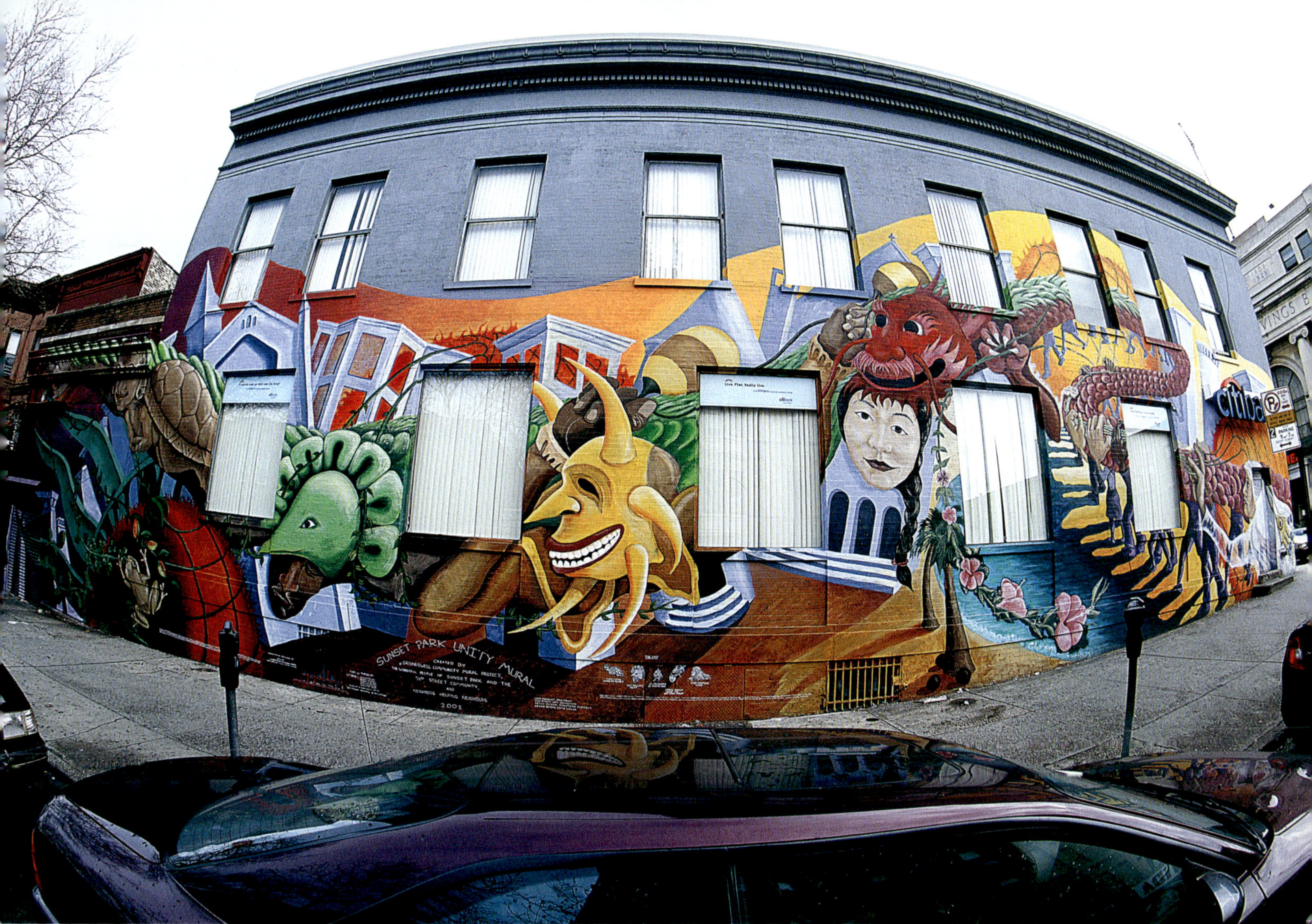

Middle-class Sunset Park in Brooklyn harbors decorative murals that make vivid use of color and lack the artistic energy conflict of their Bronx counterparts. The colorful community wall by local artists is titled "The Sunset Park Unity Mural."

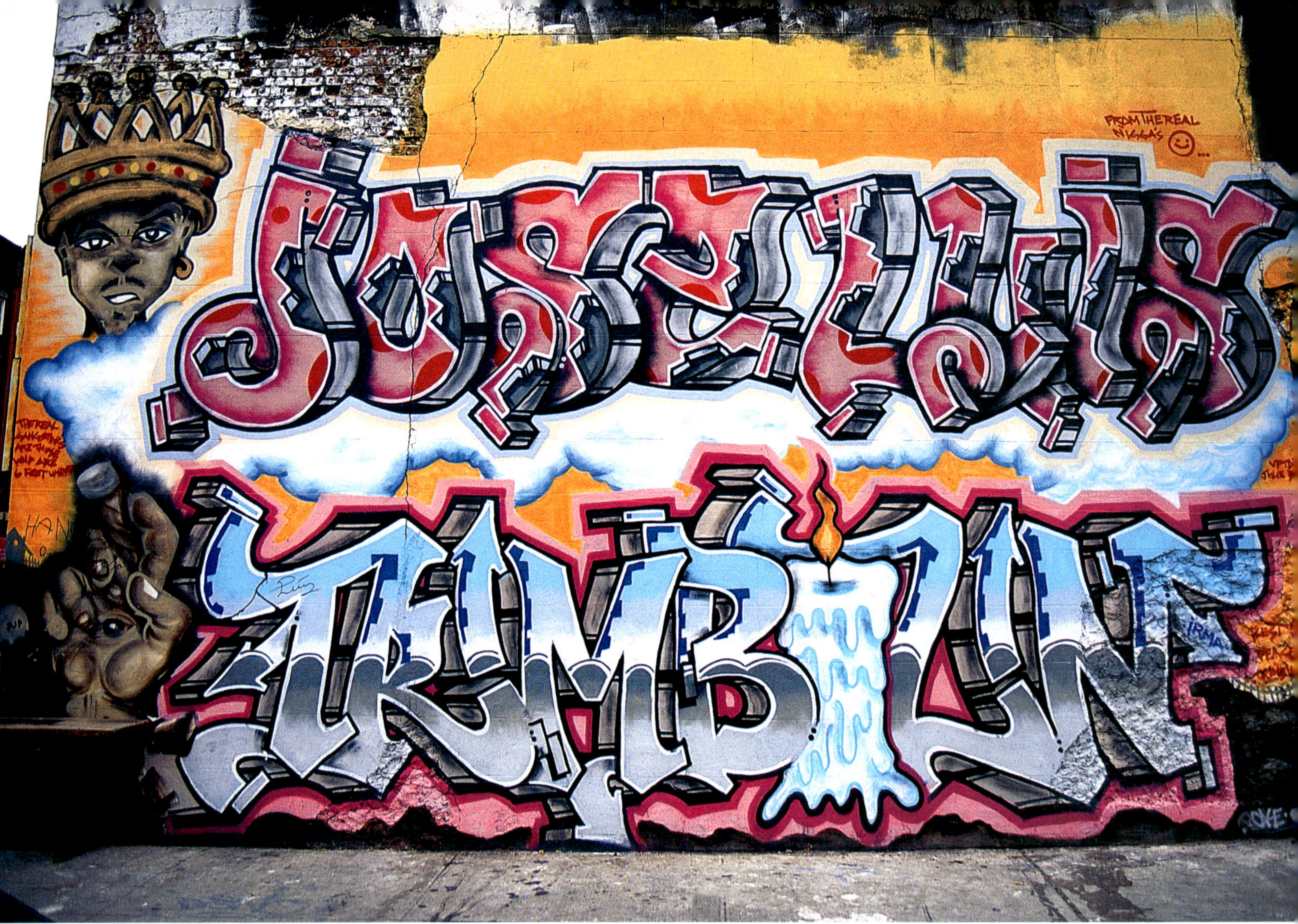

In East Harlem, the writing on the wall is a rest-in-peace tribute to a member of the Latin Kings gang in Los Angeles. Also, it alerts police officers who patrol the public housing that gangs inhabit the area.

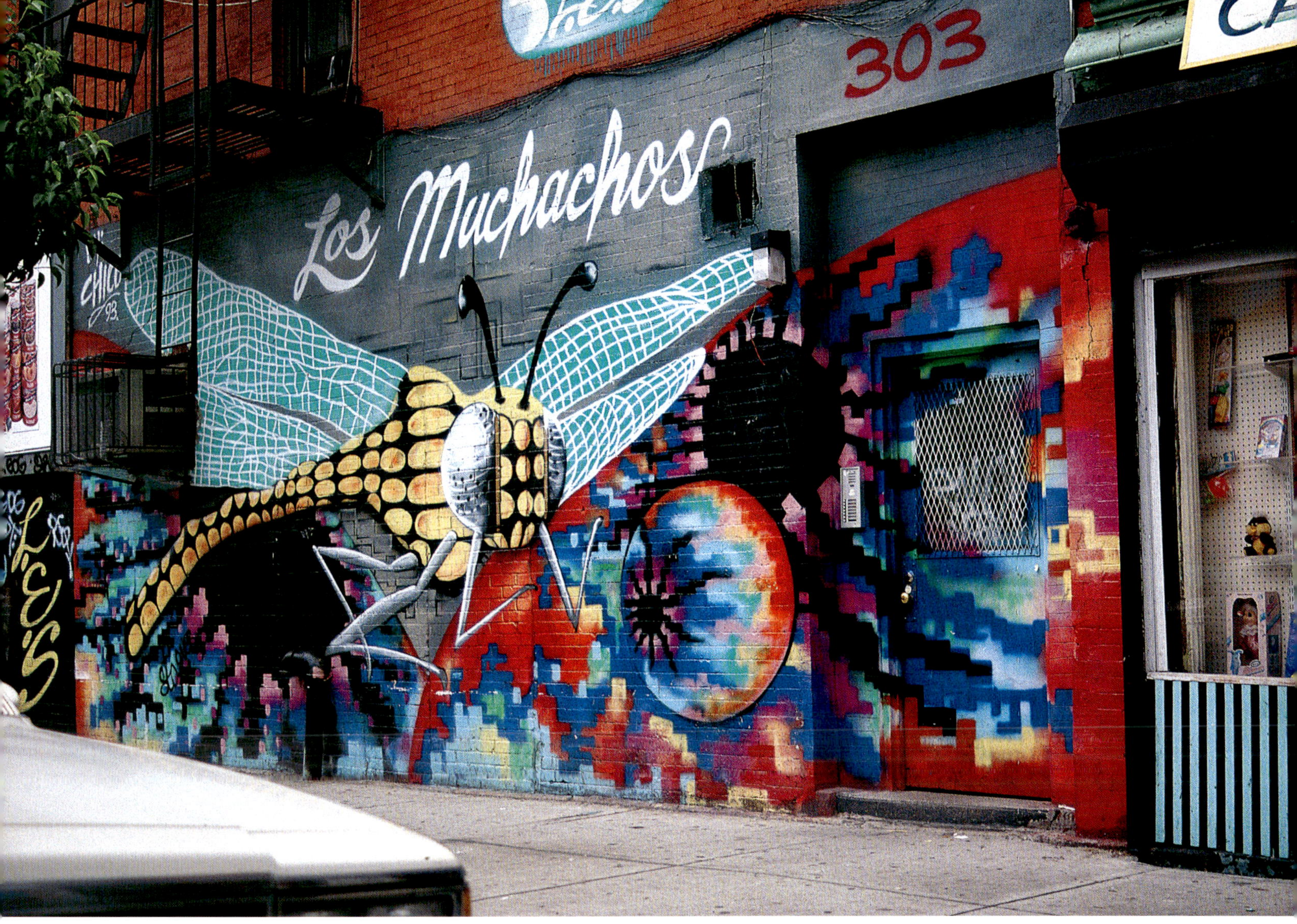

A local East Village artist's buzzing statement about "Los muchachos," presumably the area's homeboys.

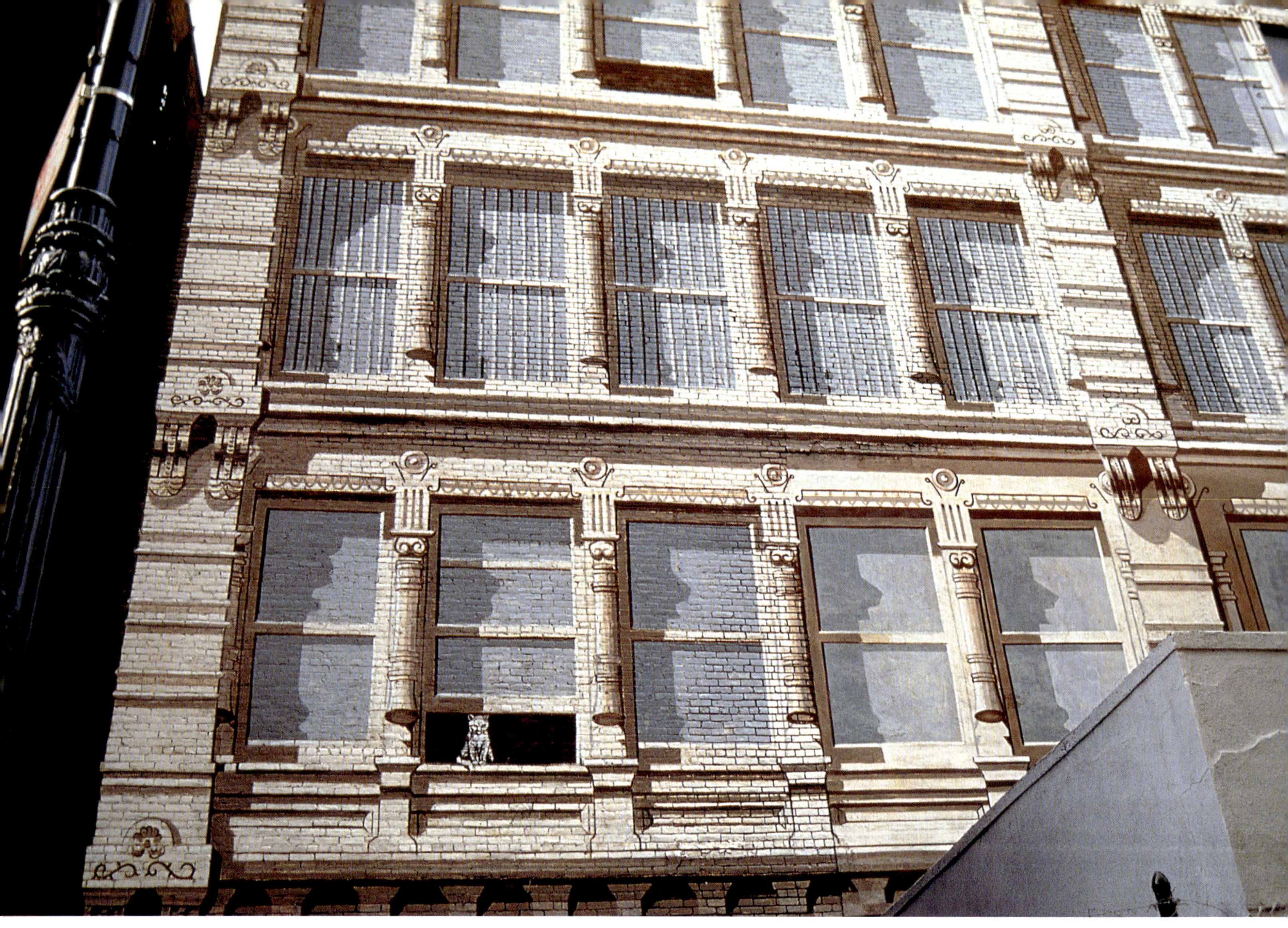

A strong example of trompe l'oeil by well-known muralist Richard Haas. This design represents his first exterior project, in 1975, located at 112 Prince Street in Soho.

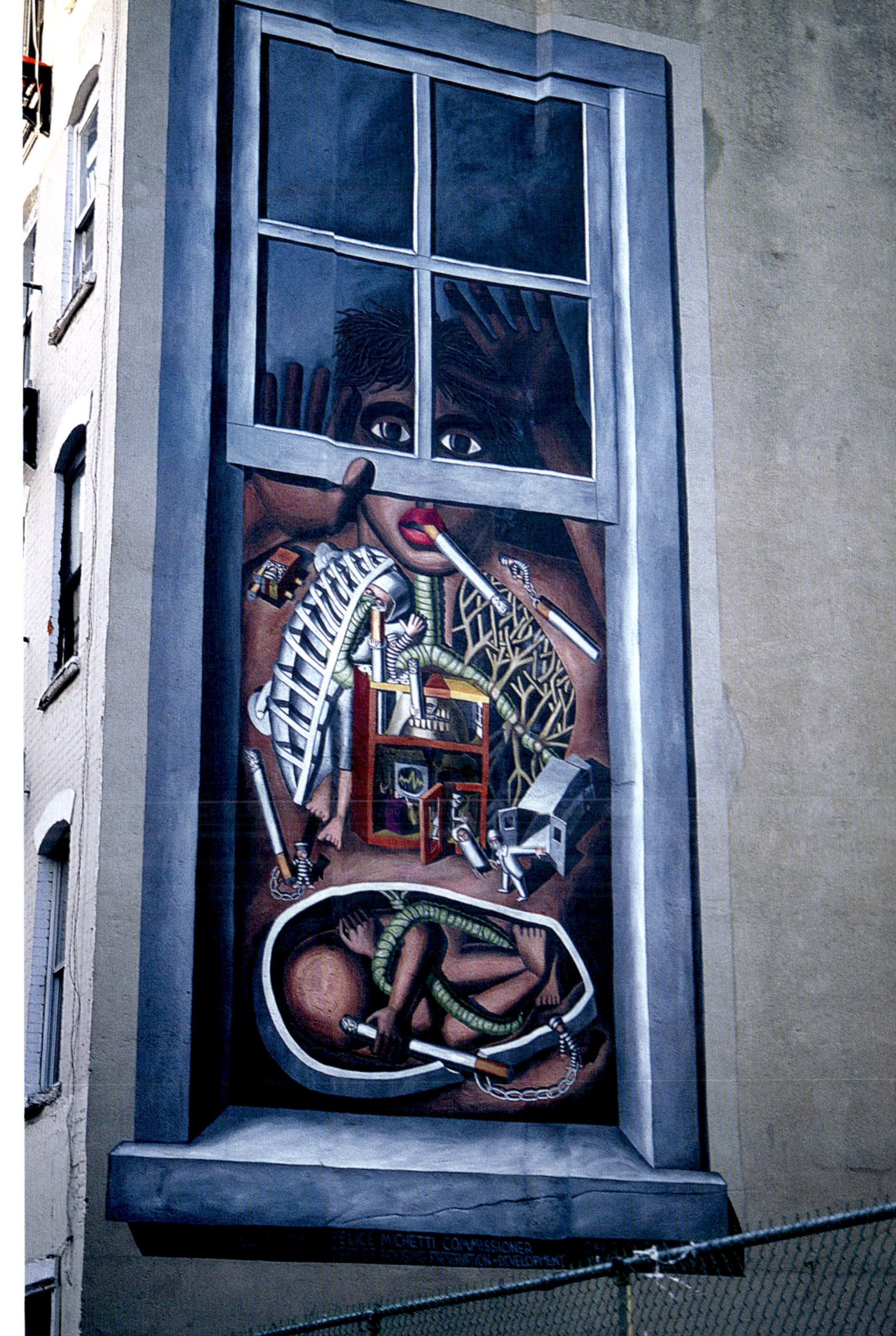

A surrealist trompe l'oeil by a local East Village artist.

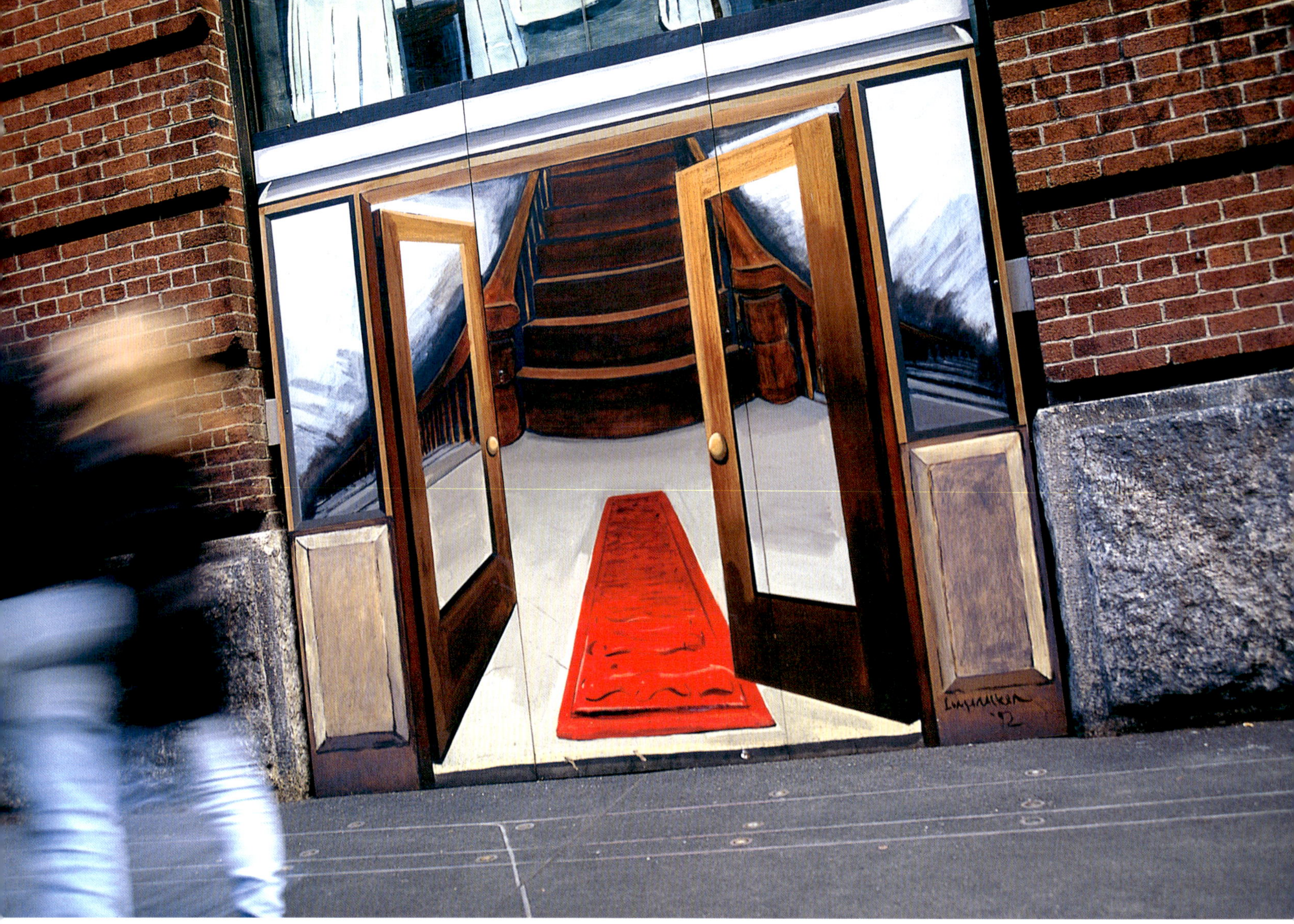

An inviting Soho trompe l'oeil.

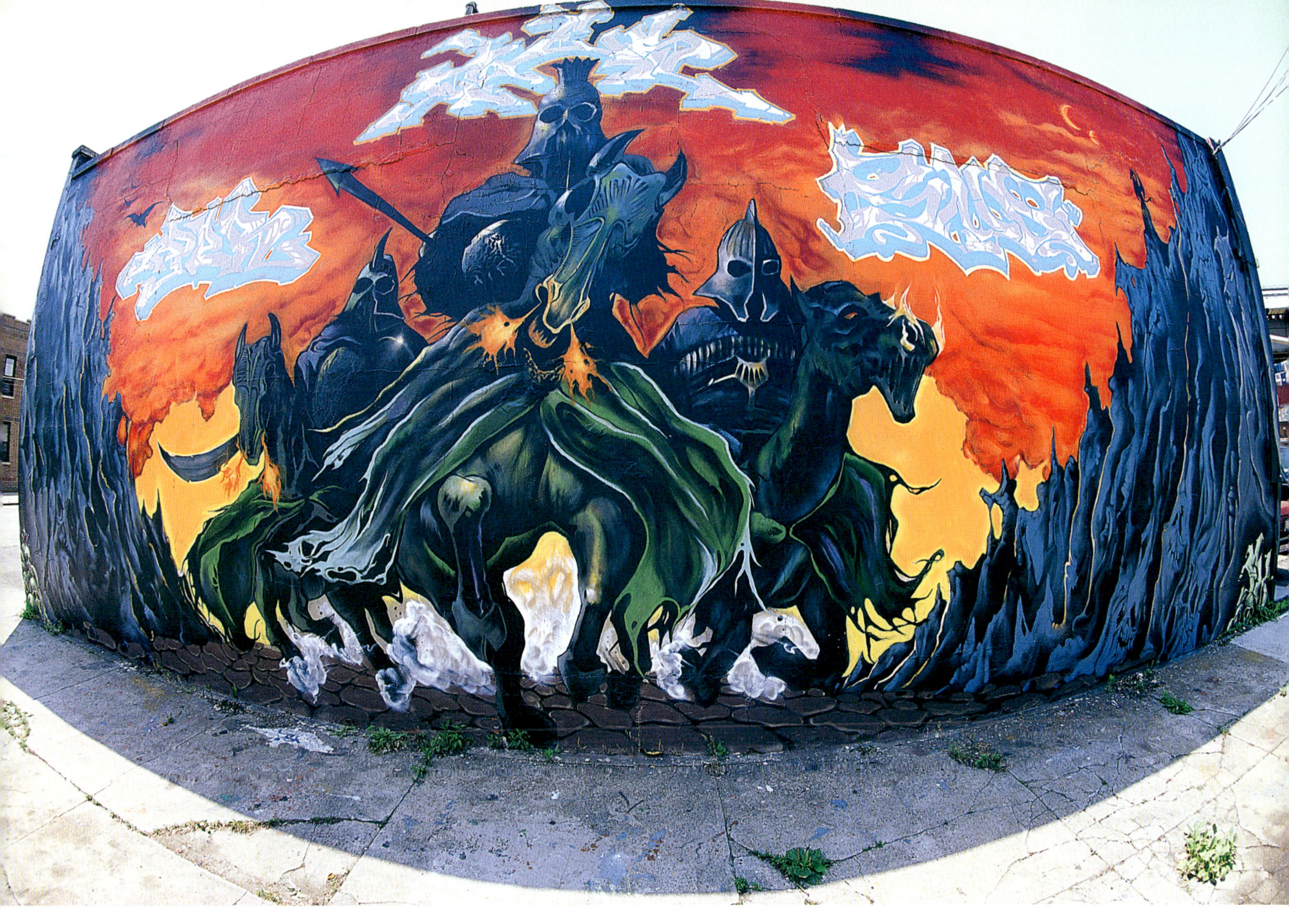

These Bronx apocalyptic masked riders were inspired by comic book characters and can be attributed to FX CRU.

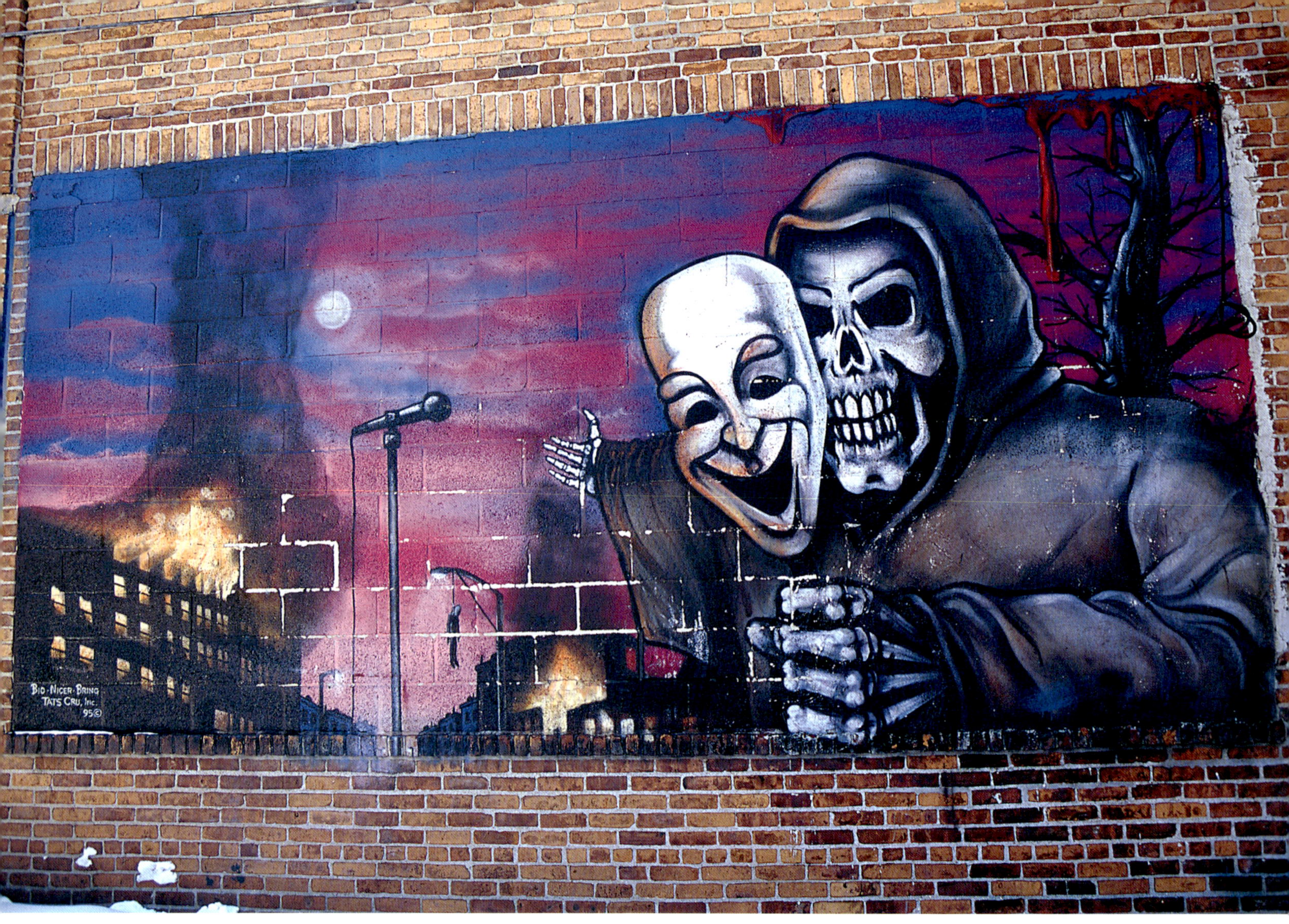

The Grim Reaper on Devil's Night is an omen of mayhem and chaos before Halloween in this mural in the Hunts Point section of the Bronx.

An unusual composition in the East Village features an abstract Pollock-like mural in this neighborhood's bohemian landscape.

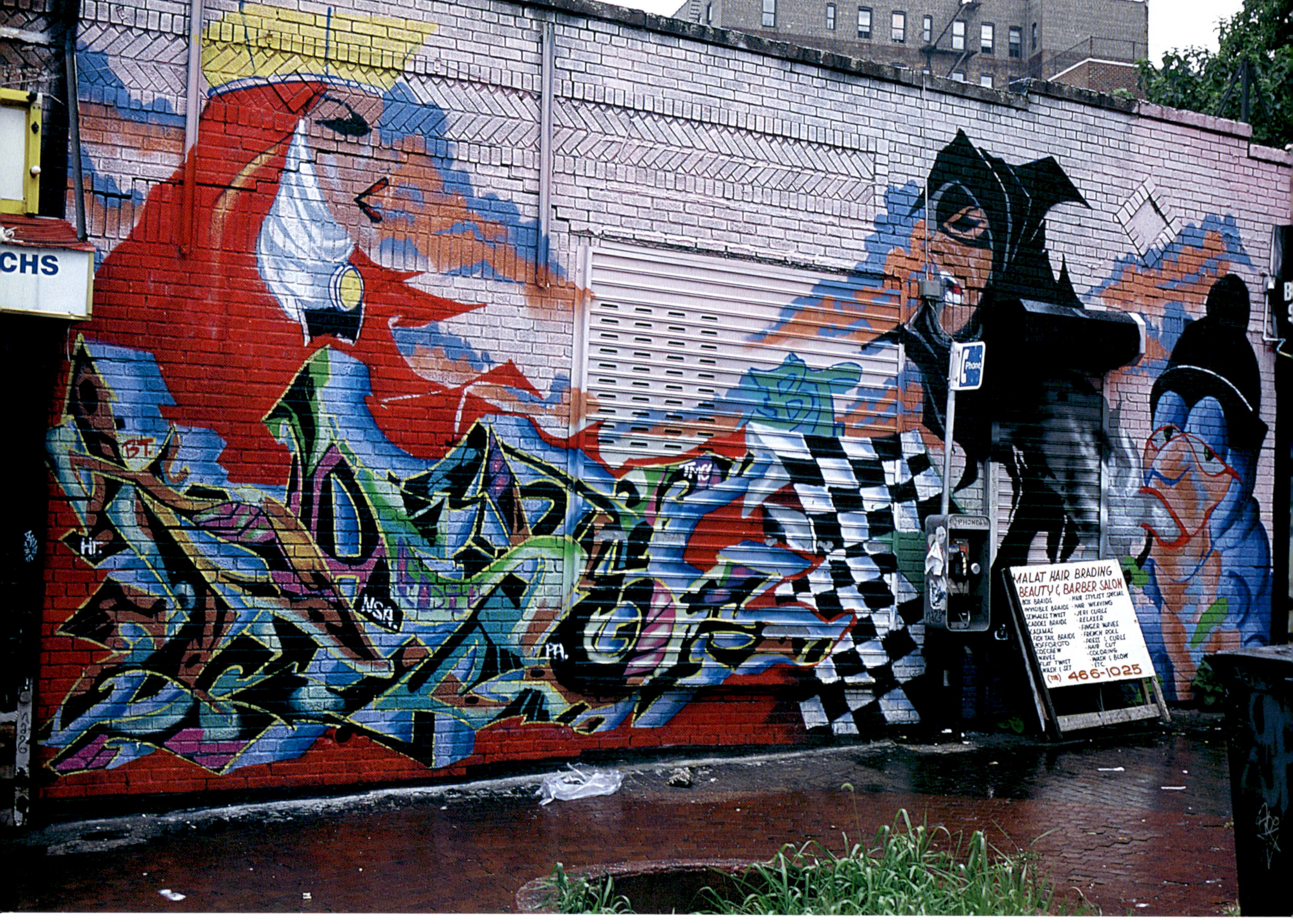

TKID's Bronx mural experiments with Wizard of Oz themes.

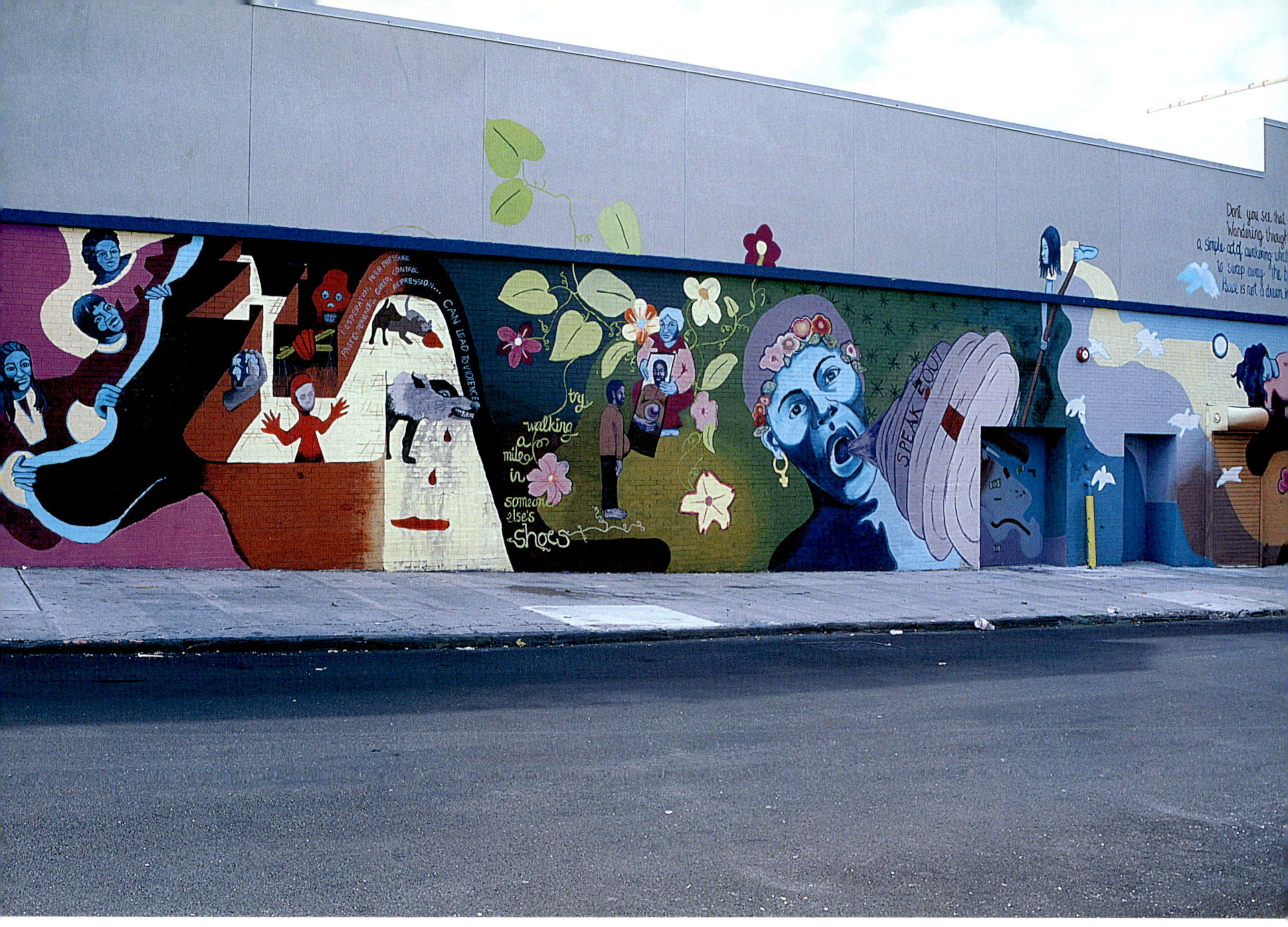

When nine teenaged girls created this mural in the Park Slope section of Brooklyn, they intended the guns and knives to speak of their fears, but other residents felt it made the upscale neighborhood too much like a ghetto, and it was removed from the large Rite Aid pharmacy exterior wall where it had appeared.

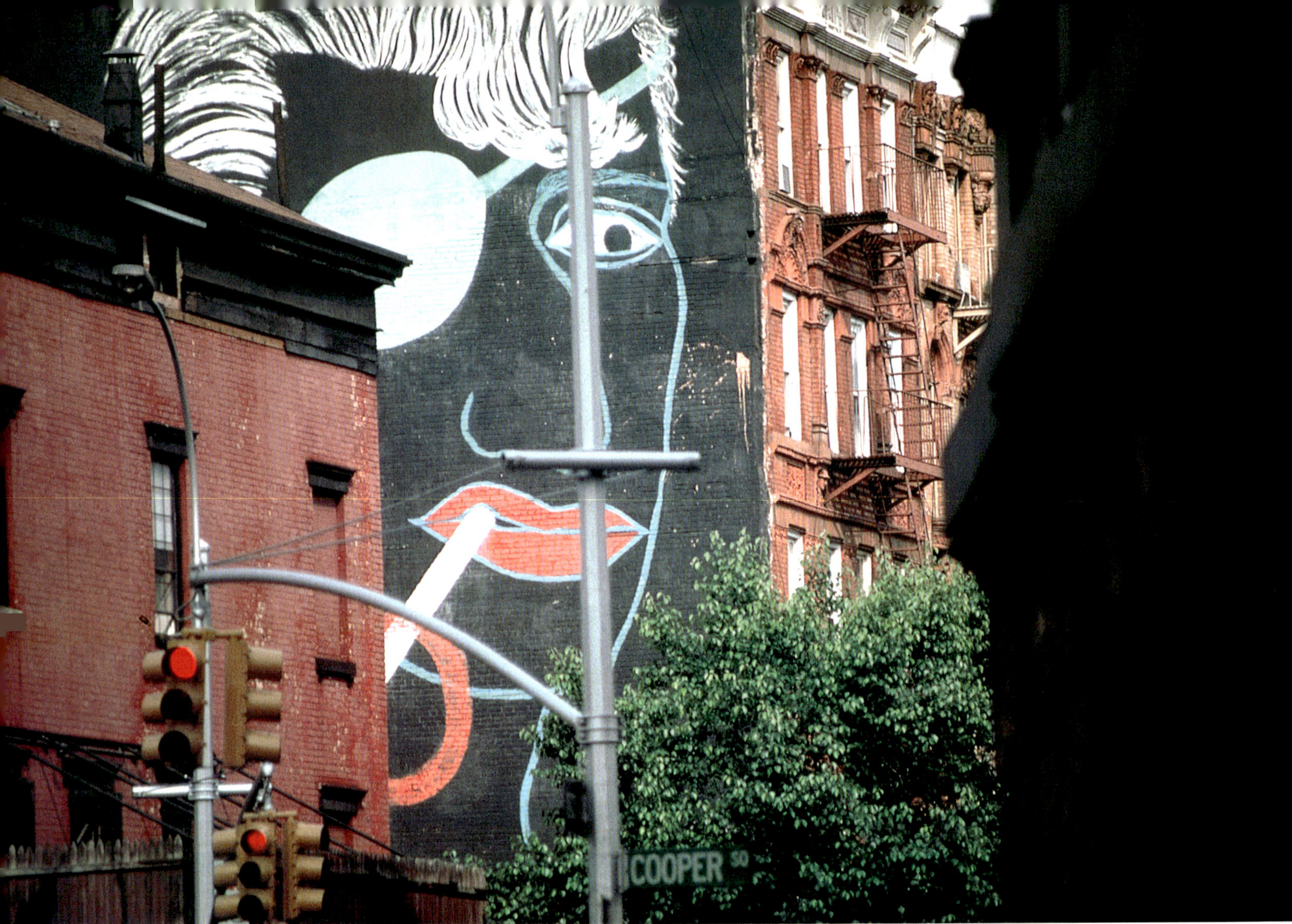

"Gringo" was a mural commissioned by a filmmaker in the mid-1980s. Artist Art Guerrero was paid five thousand dollars to paint the image of John Spacely, the subject of a documentary. Spacely was a heroin addict who died of AIDS. He had lived in the neighborhood on St. Mark's Place, in the heart of the East Village.

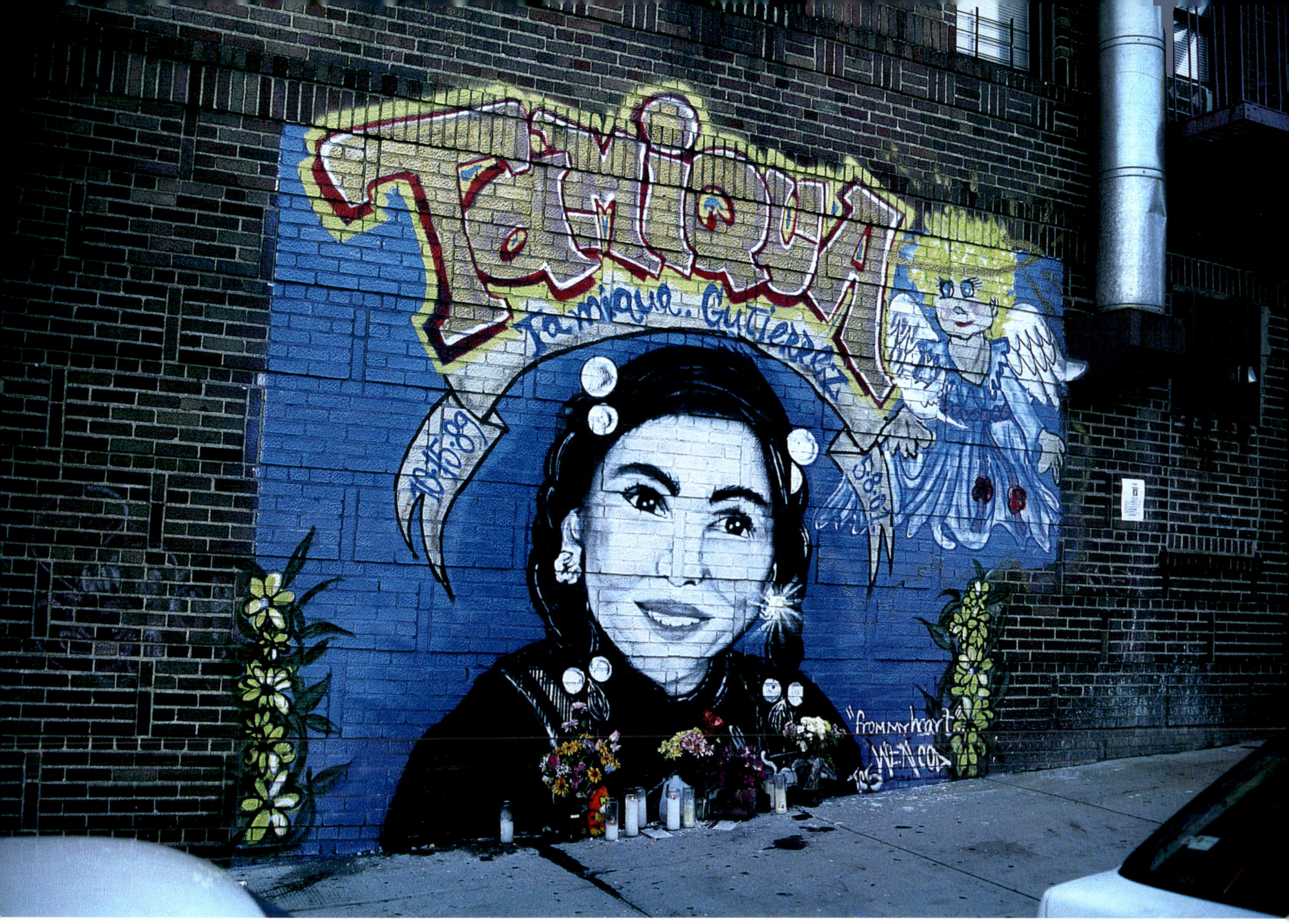

Tamiqua Gutierrez, an eleven-year-old girl, is remembered on the side of the brick wall near where she was raped and murdered in the Bronx in May 2001. A neighbor who lived two doors down the hall was accused of the crime. Though Tamiqua's family has moved away, her relatives return to attend prayer vigils, and block parties are held to raise money for the Gutierrez family. The tragedy changed the area and saw parents adjusting their work schedules to accompany their children to and from school, only a few blocks away.

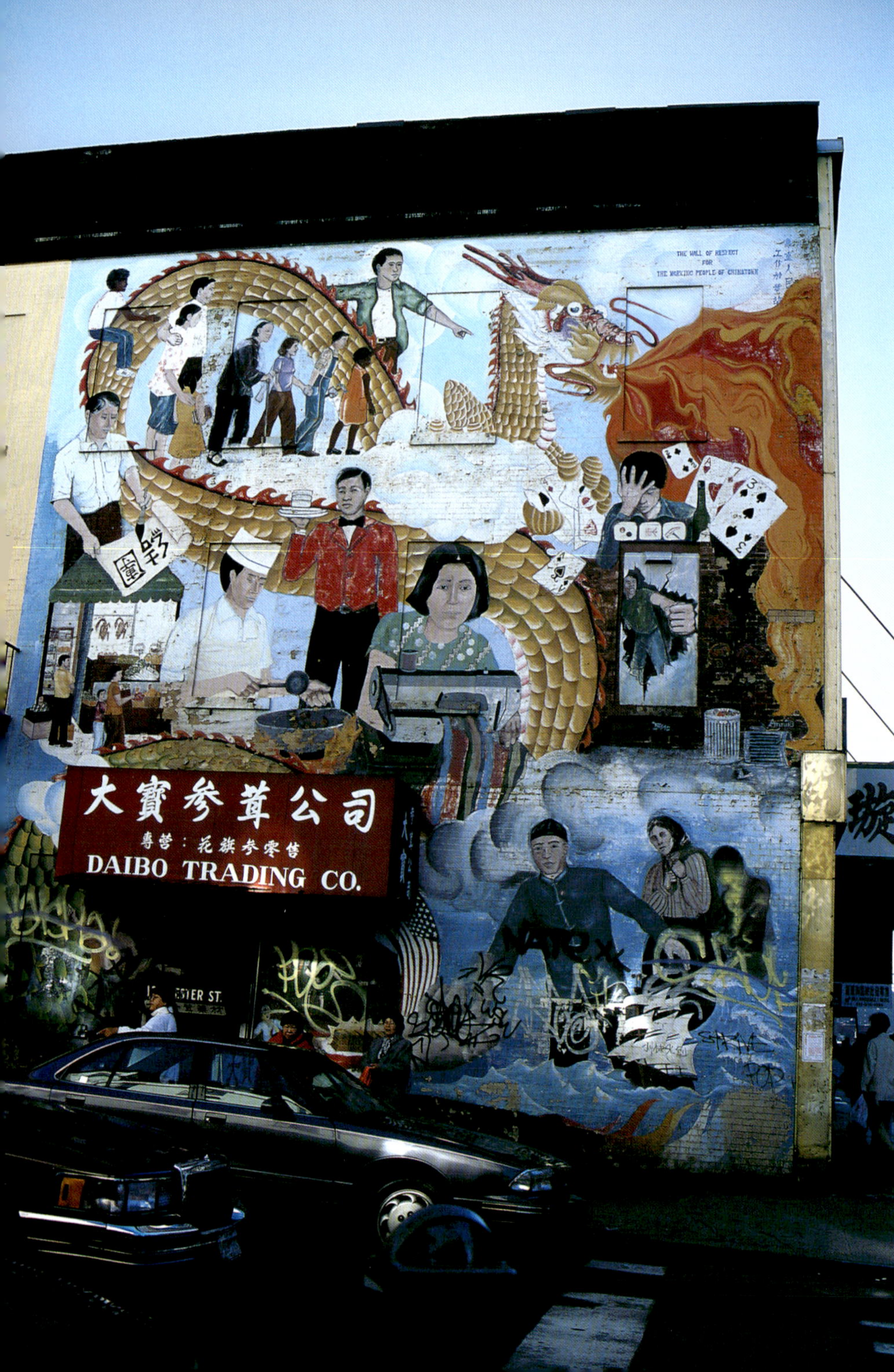

In New York's Chinatown, half a dozen murals showing political themes had survived for more than two decades, only to have all but one of them vanish under the paintbrushes wielded by new property owners. The one surviving mural, depicting cooks, garment workers, and card players—a panorama of life in this Asian neighborhood—is in danger, too. The building houses a theater that is expected to shut down due to financial problems.

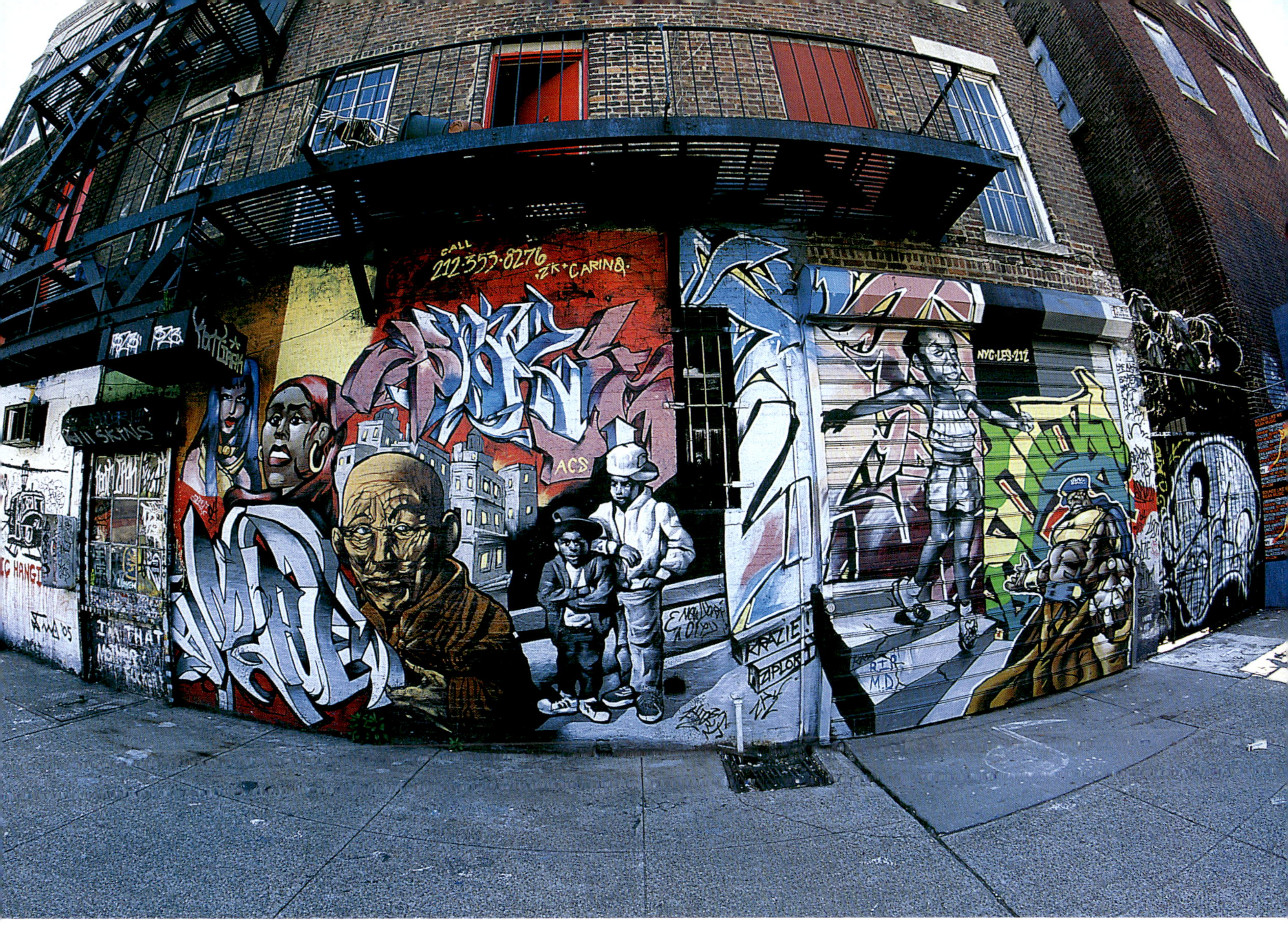

Over the years, the legendary and eclectic Mars Bar on 1st Street and 2nd Avenue, in the East Village, has proven to be a magnet for graffiti artists. Seemingly existing in its own time warp, Mars Bar lives up to its reputation as an artsy dive, inside and out.

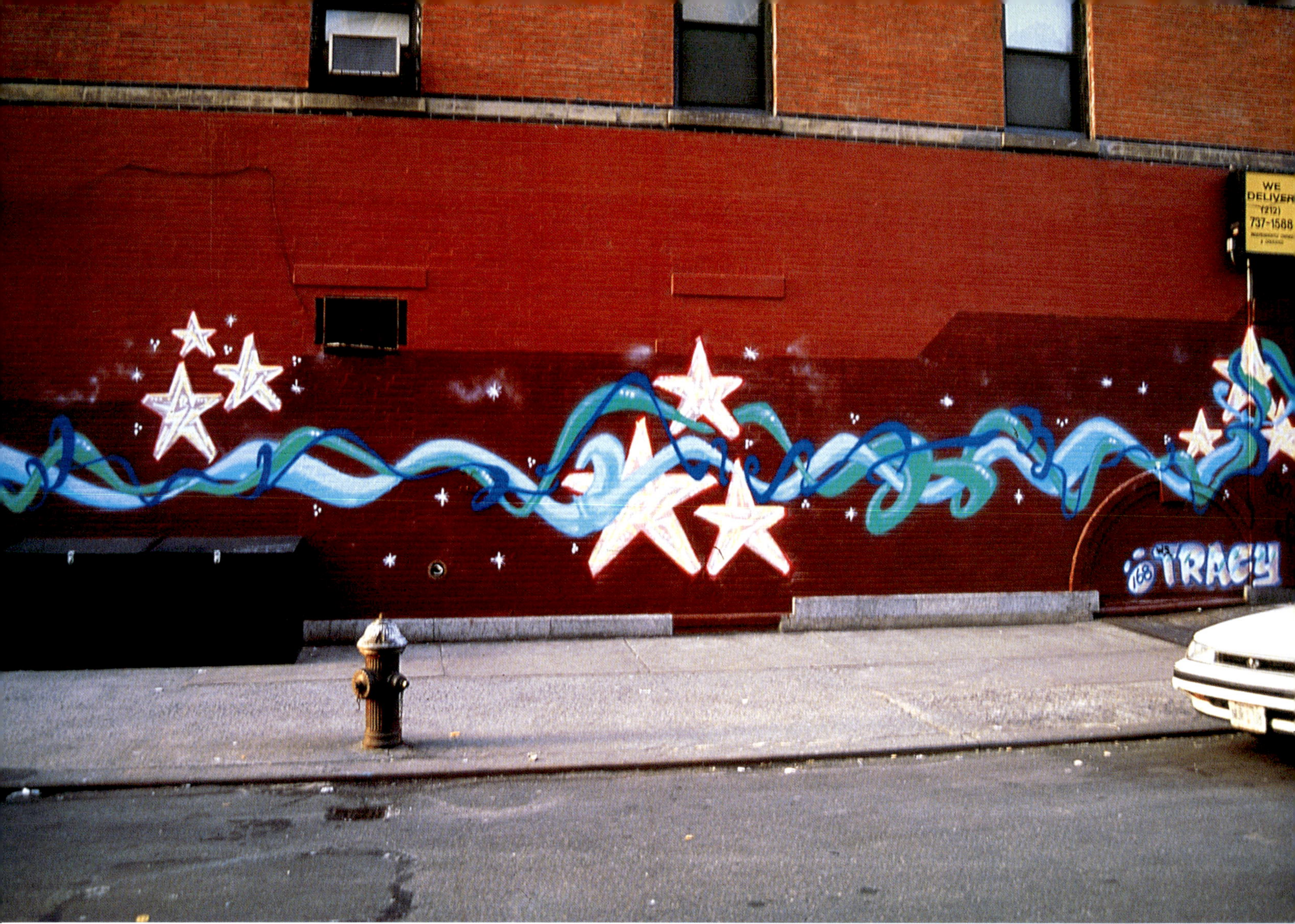

The legendary muralist Michael Tracy, TRACY 168, has been involved with aerosol expressionism for more than twenty-five years. His work has been on display in the Hip Hop Show at the Brooklyn Museum of Art, among other places. In the year 2000, he was involved in a controversy over whether a subway door he had painted belonged to him or to the museum.

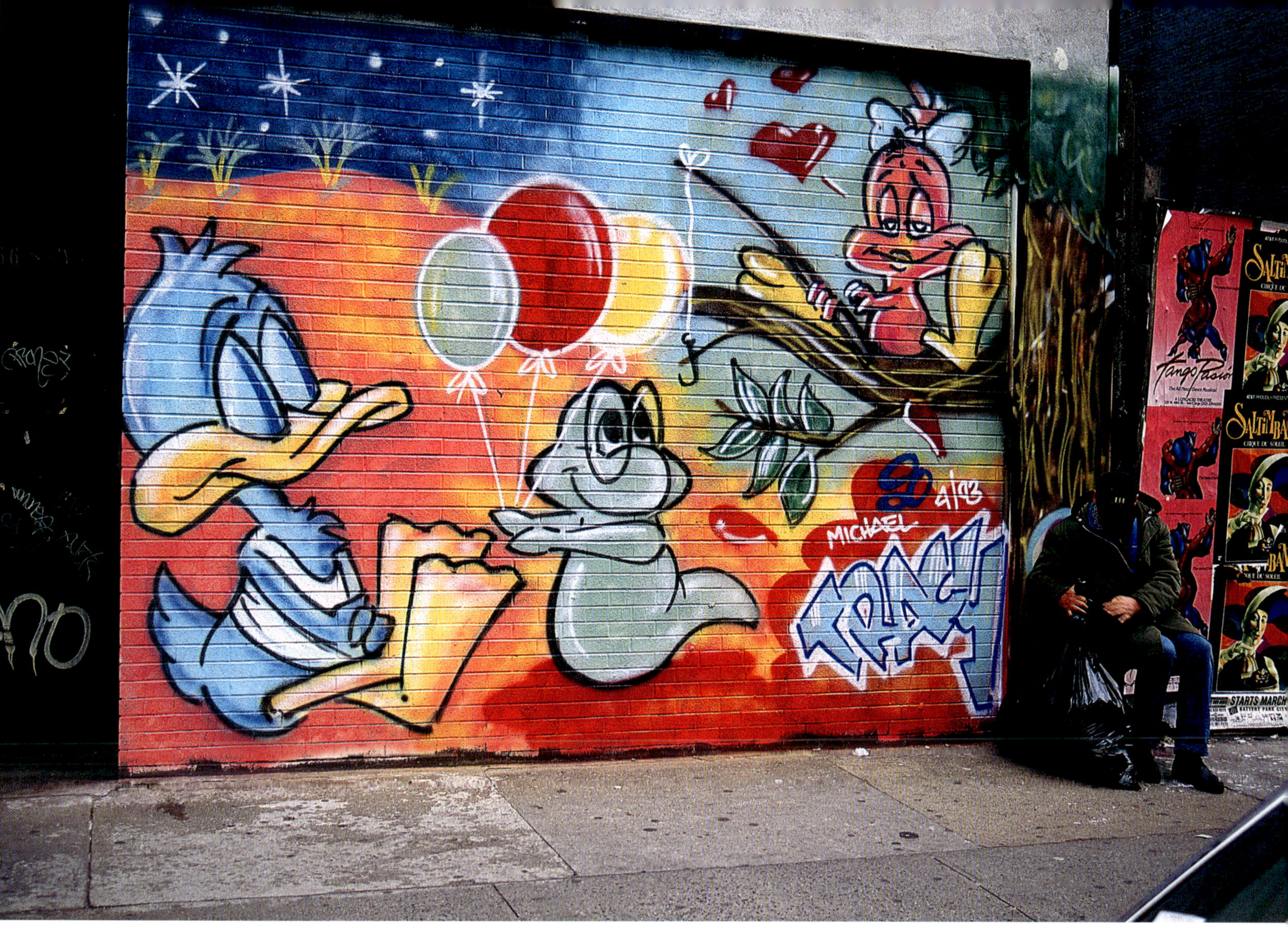
MICHAEL
4/93
Tango Pasión
The All New Dance Musical
LONGACRE THEATRE
CIRQUE DU SOLEIL
STARTS MARCH
BATTERY PARK CITY

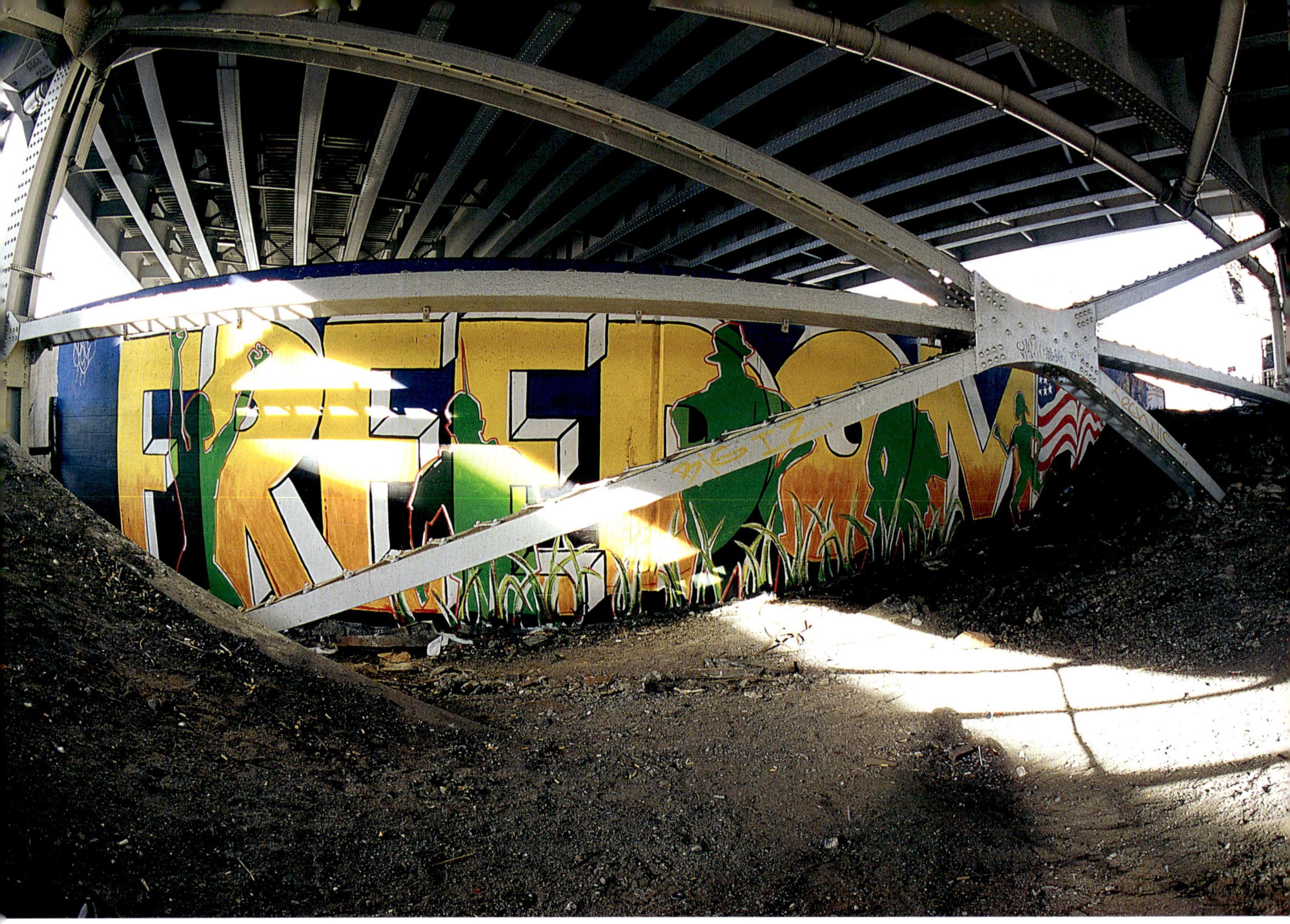

A walk under the Long Island Expressway shows eight-foot-high lettering that reads "Freedom." Local artists and homeless veterans from a nearby shelter painted it as a reminder of having survived Vietnam, a struggle that did not end for all of them when they came back home. One of the artists said, "We didn't want to do anything that glorified war."

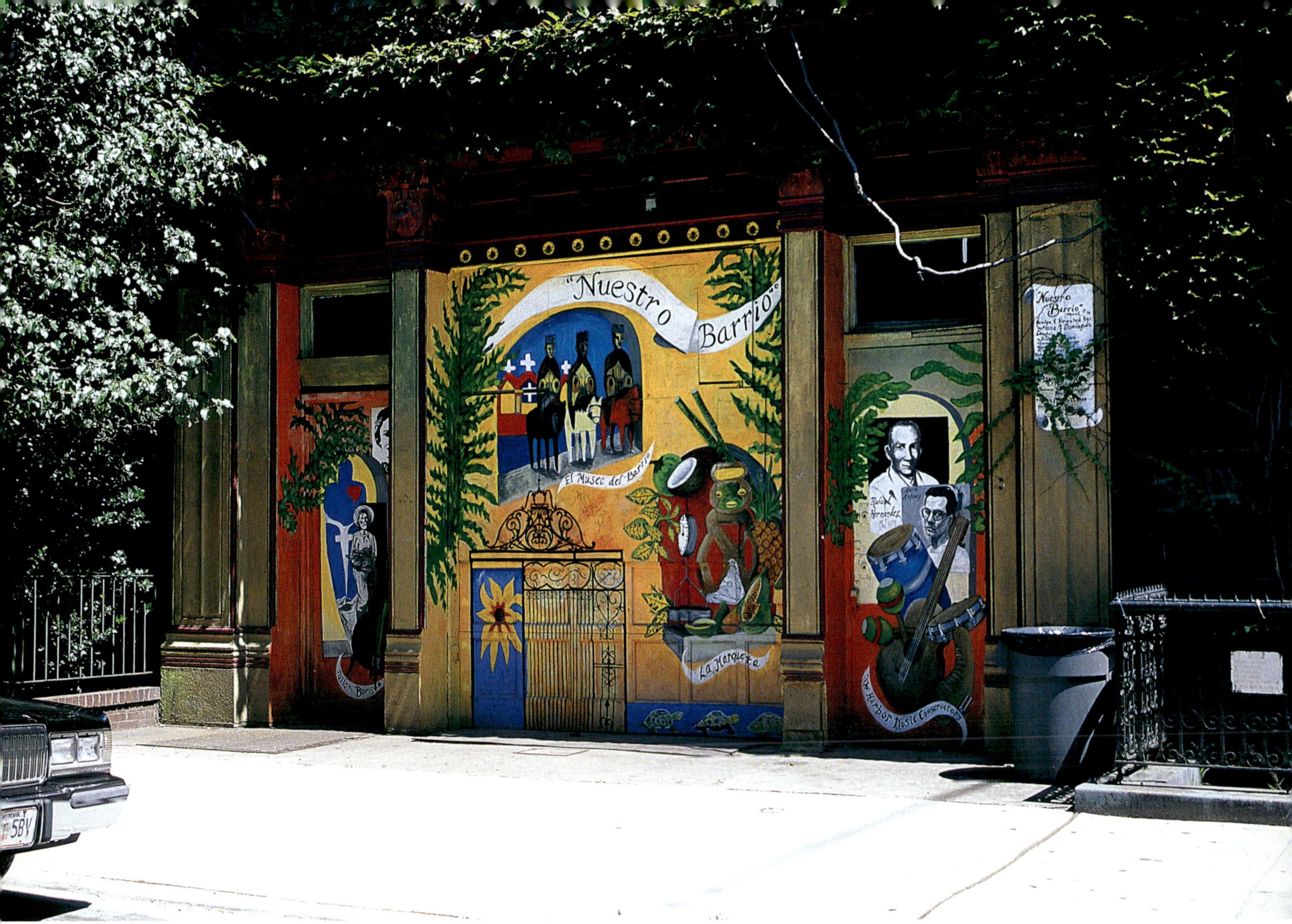

A local artist's decorative mural in Spanish Harlem that pays homage to everyday aspects of barrio life: migration, the home, canción (song), and the church.

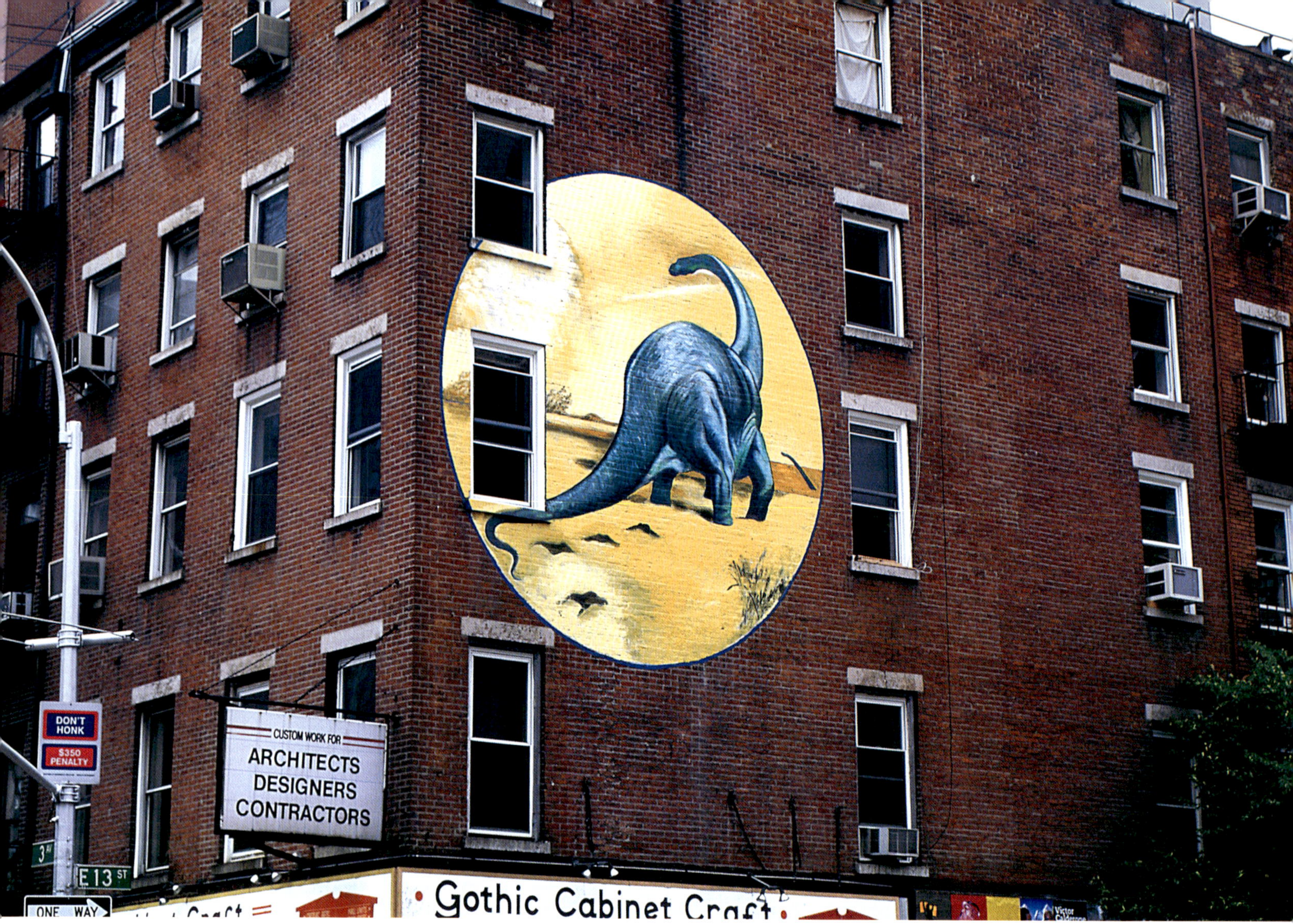

In New York's East Village, landlords Jerry Atkins and Stephen Breskin decided their tenements were ugly, so they had paintings of animals added to them. Atkins said, "We would never do this to a building with any architectural character, but these tenements have so little charm."

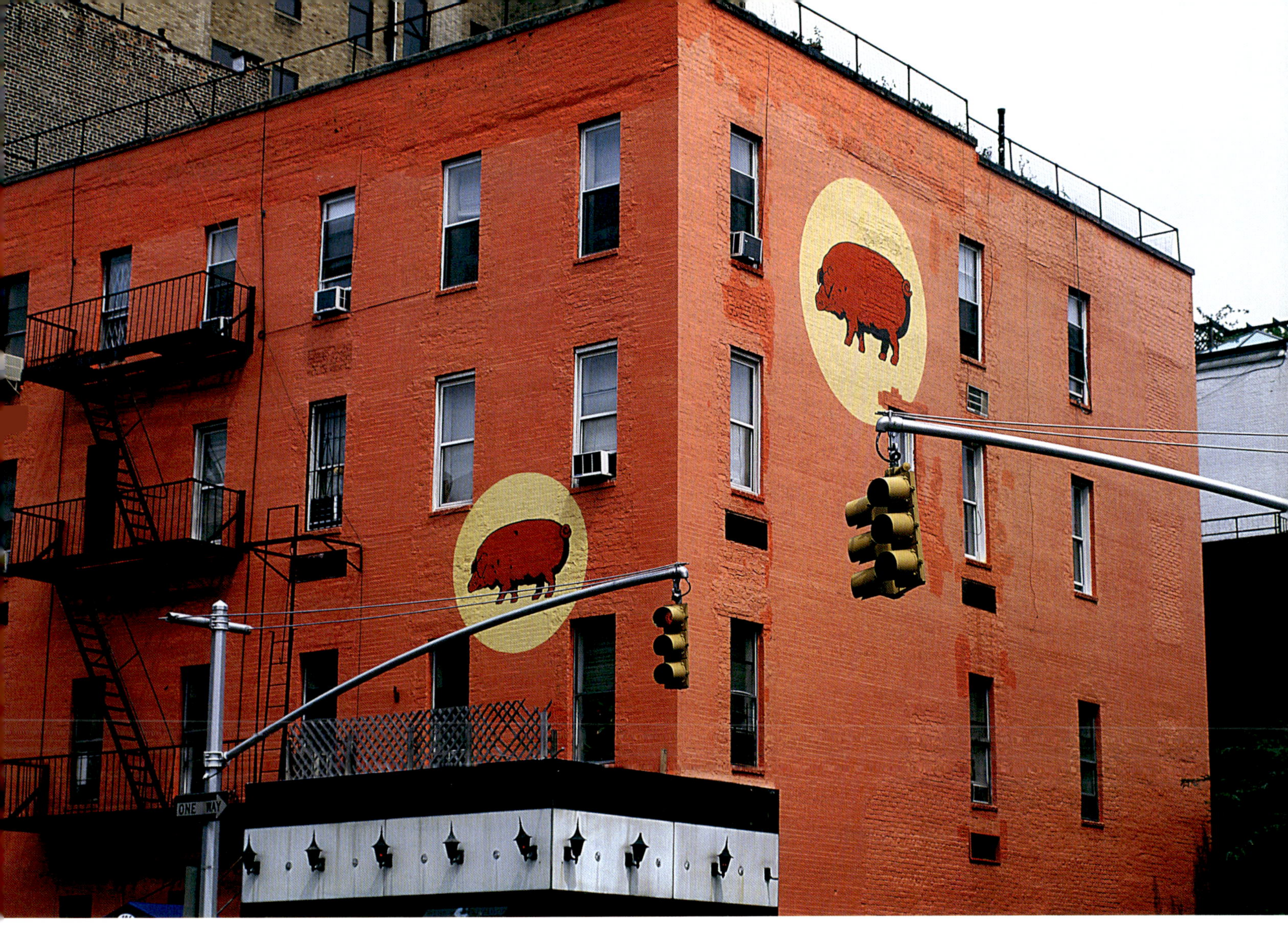
ONE WAY

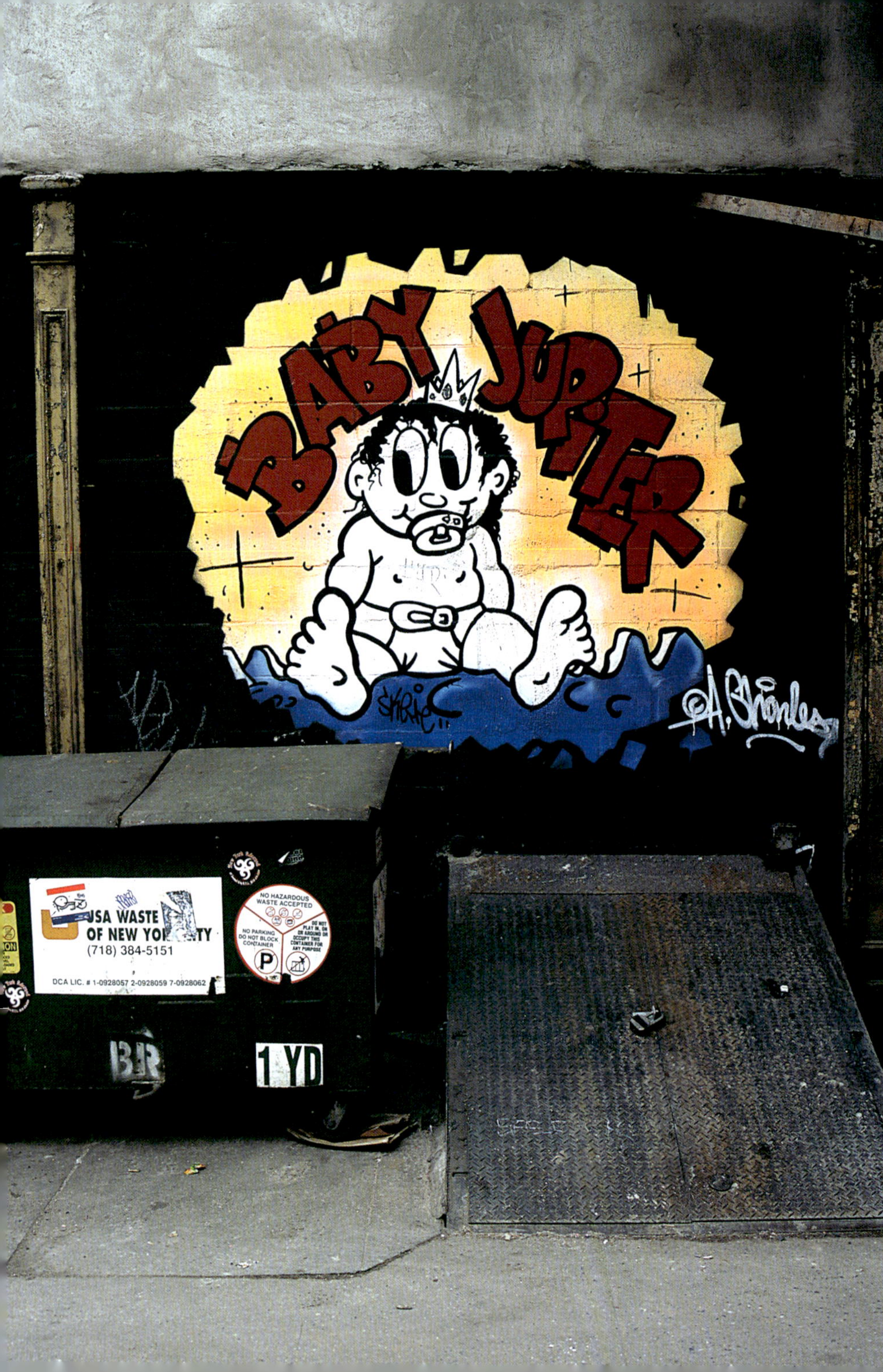

Andre Charles's trademark logo, Brandon, a cartoonist "urban ghetto baby," is a familiar face on East Village walls. Andre has dreamt of introducing Brandon in children's books and toys. His work continues to attract considerable attention from the media and art patrons. In 1997, a vice president of the prestigious magazine the *New Yorker* commissioned Andre to make a four-paneled mural for his office. A student of Keith Haring and Jean-Michel Basquiat, he strives to achieve their status.

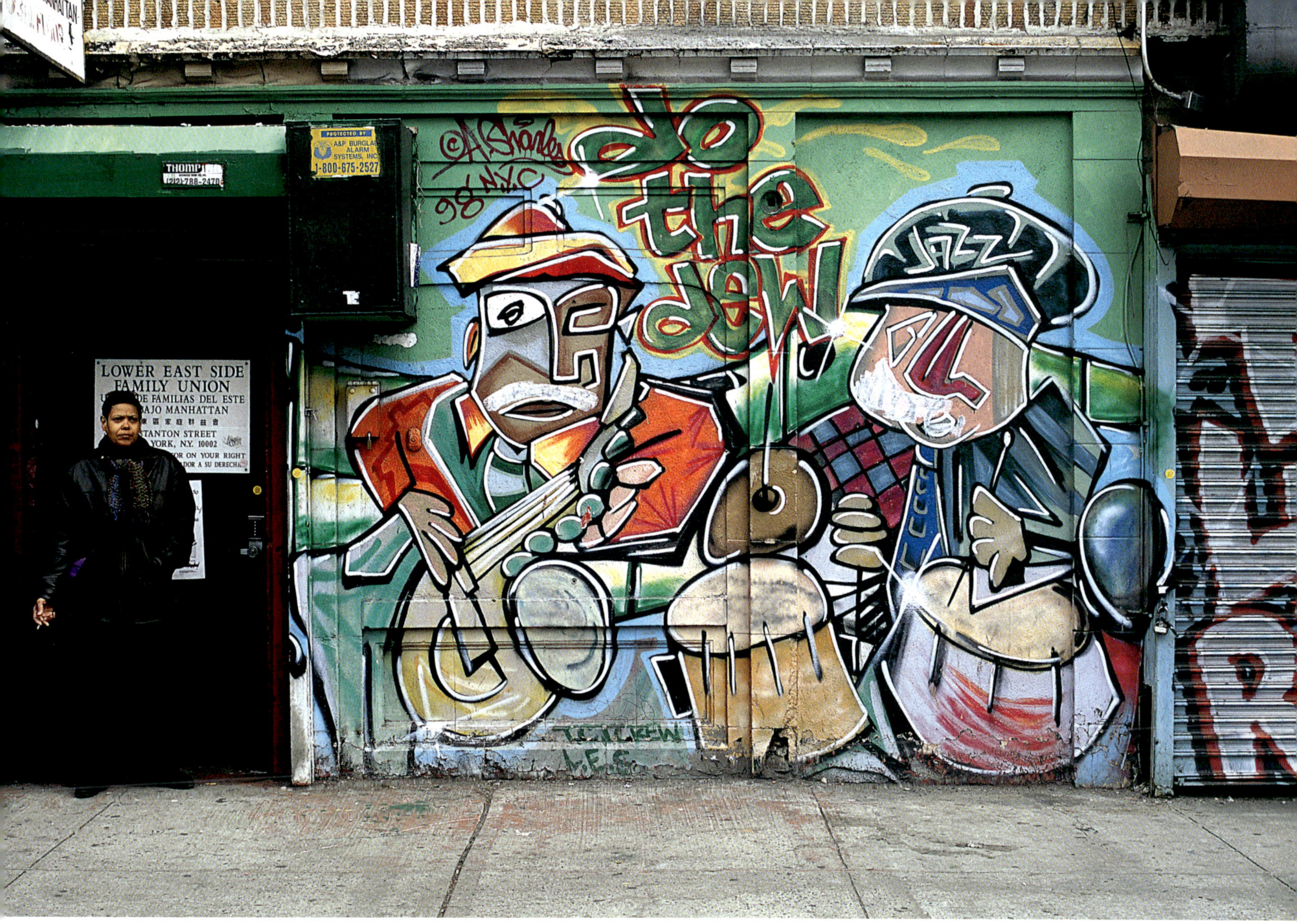

Andre Charles's colorful Caribbean characters playing congas and bongos.

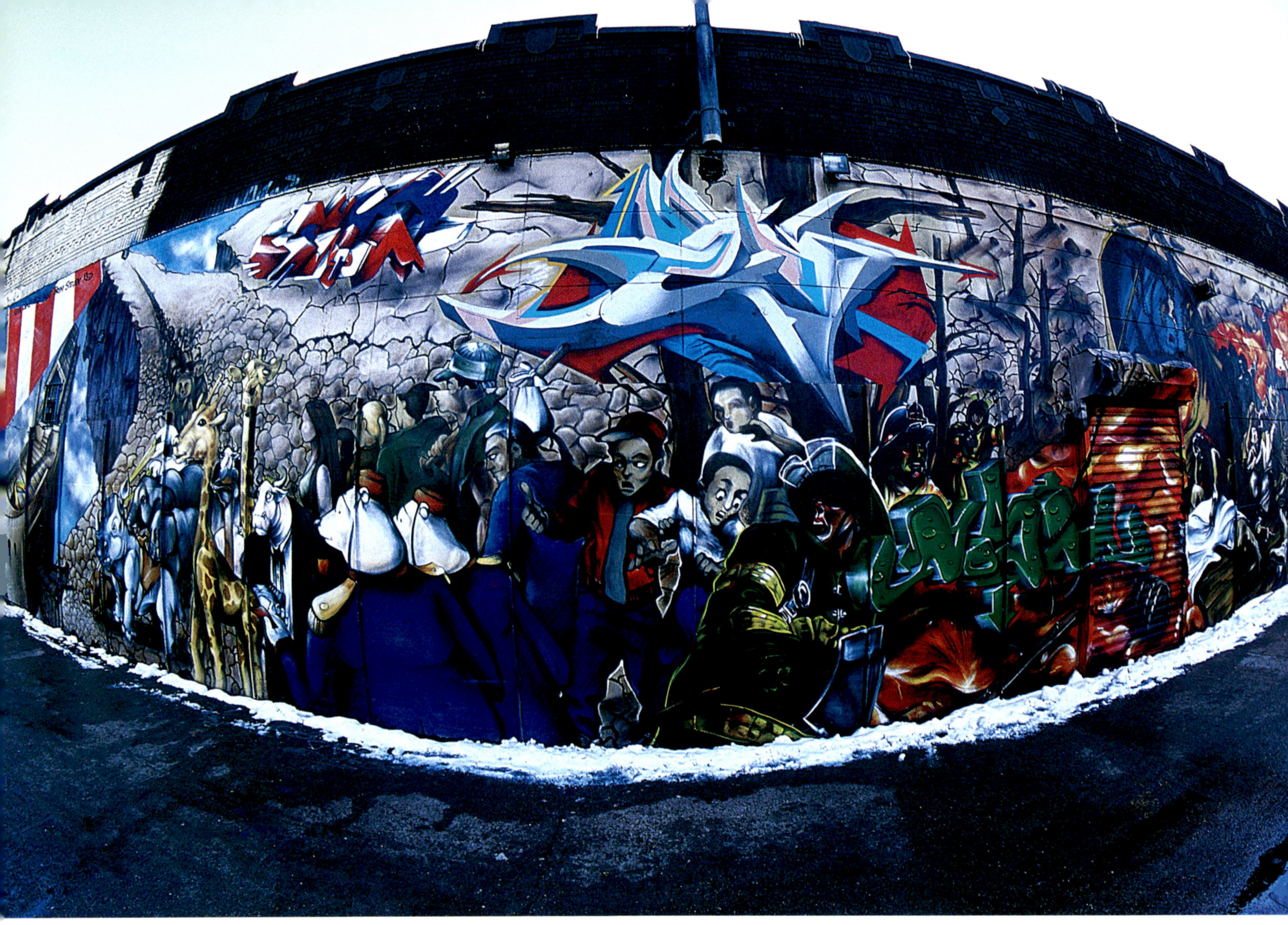

TATS CRU's mural in the Bronx, to be considered a 9/11 mural.

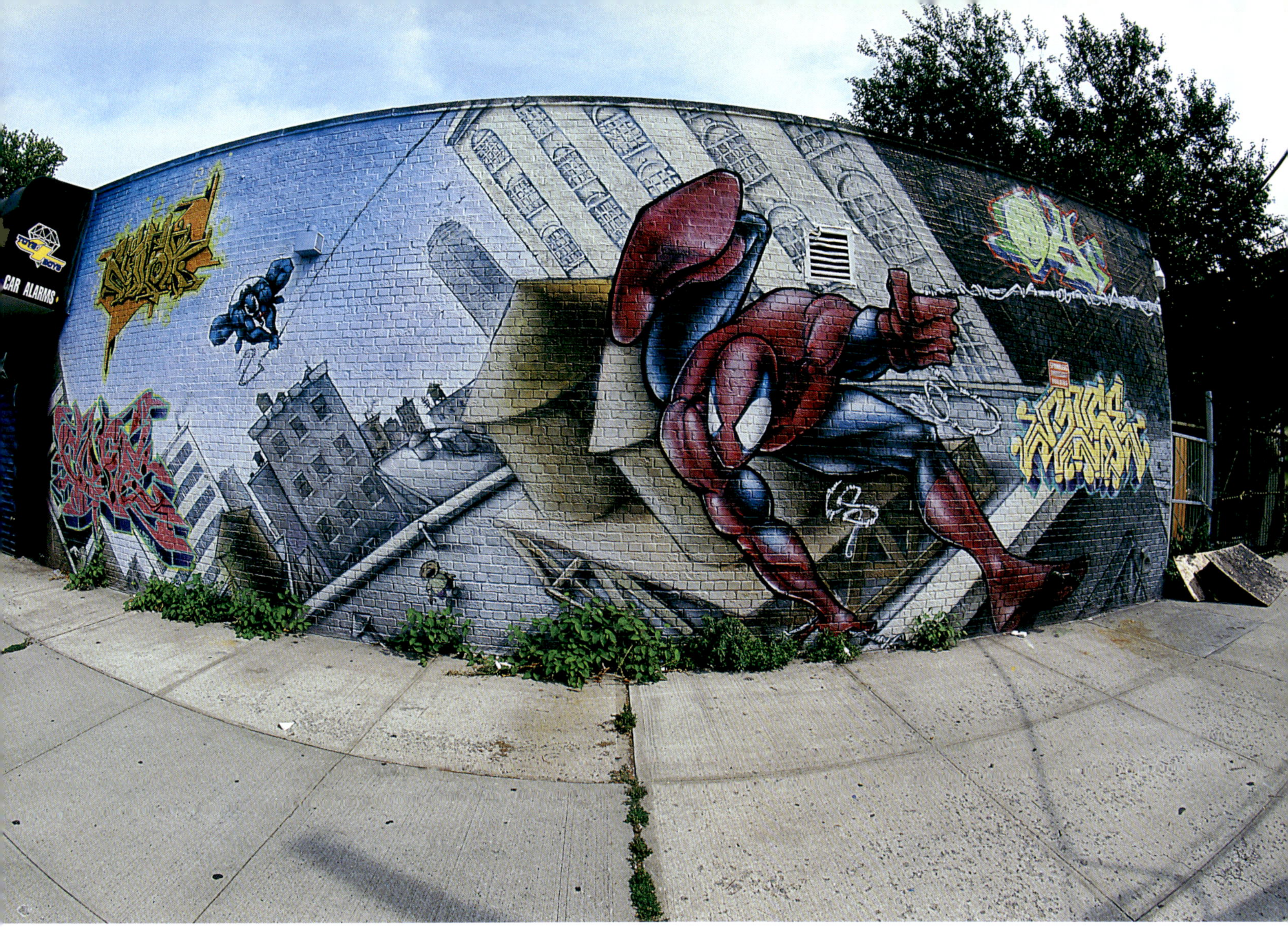

Spiderman battles Venom in an Astoria, Queens, mural by MUZE, OH, COPE, and EWOK.

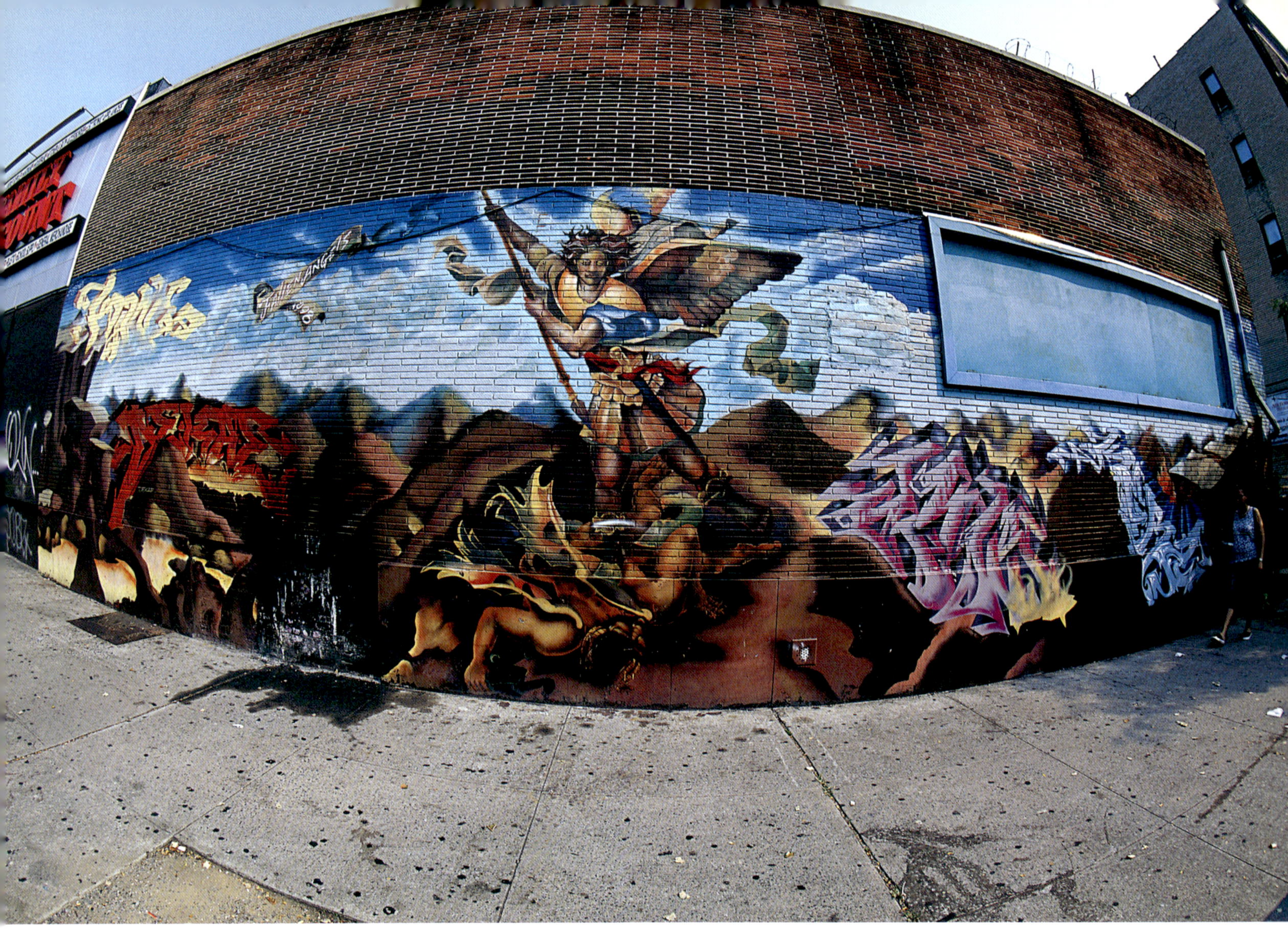

Archangel Michael in a struggle of good vs. evil on a Queens wall.

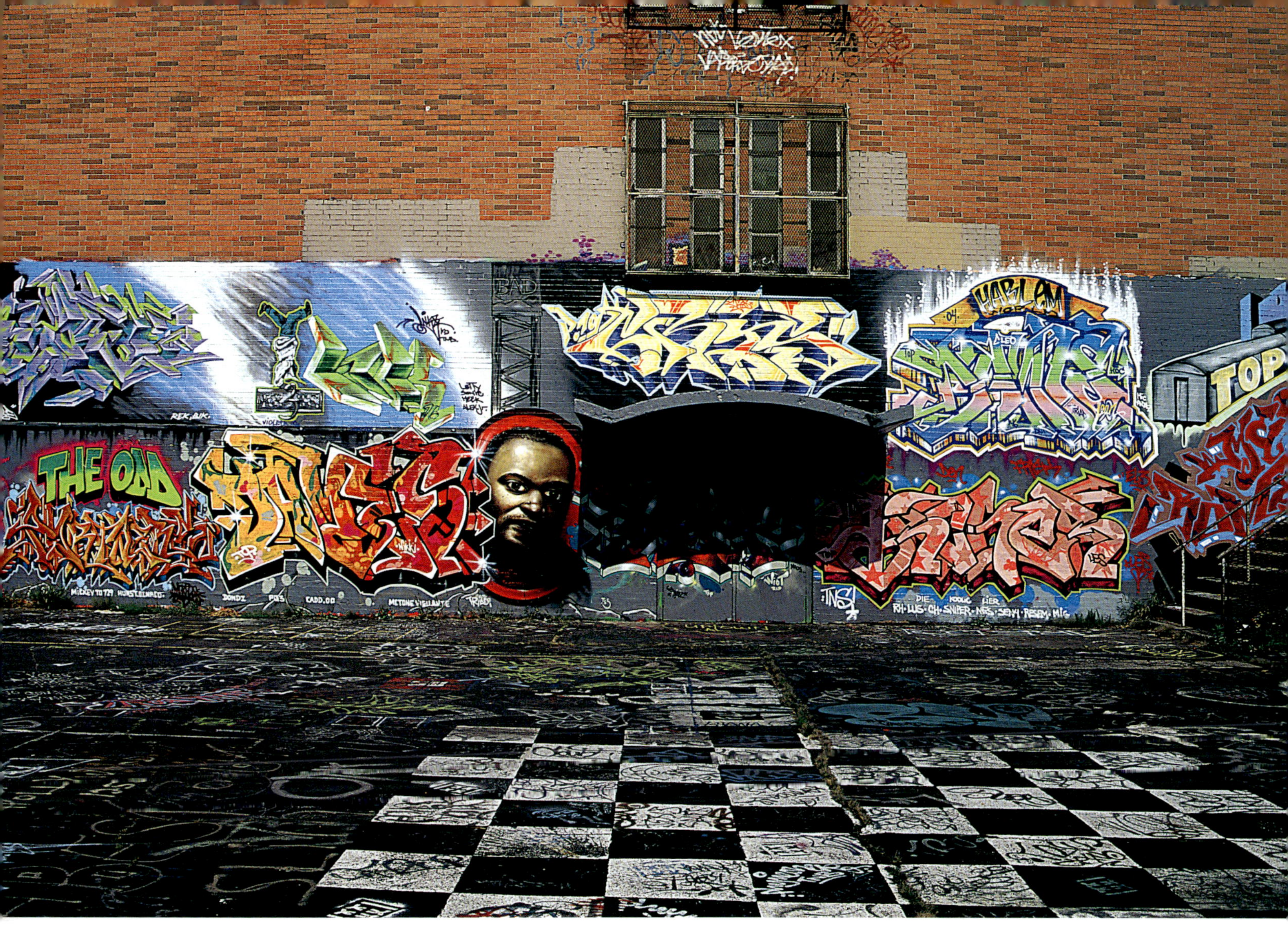

In 2005, multiple tags tattooed onto the historic Manhattan Graffiti Hall of Fame on Park Avenue and 107th Street are a forceful reminder of the origins of New York City street art and writing.

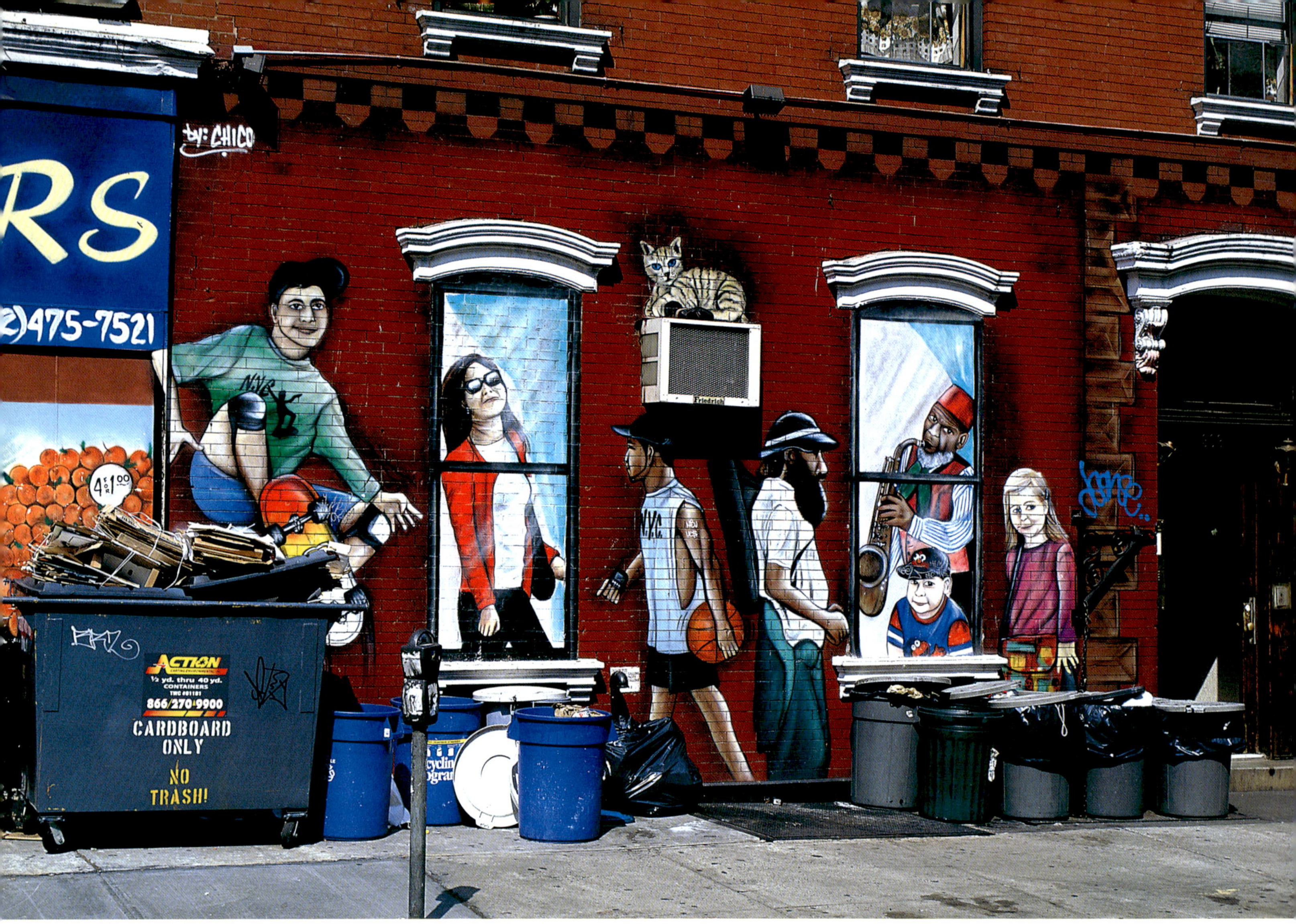

CHICO's trompe l'oeil on the corner of 8th Street and 2nd Avenue was commissioned by the building's owner to discourage graffiti tagging.

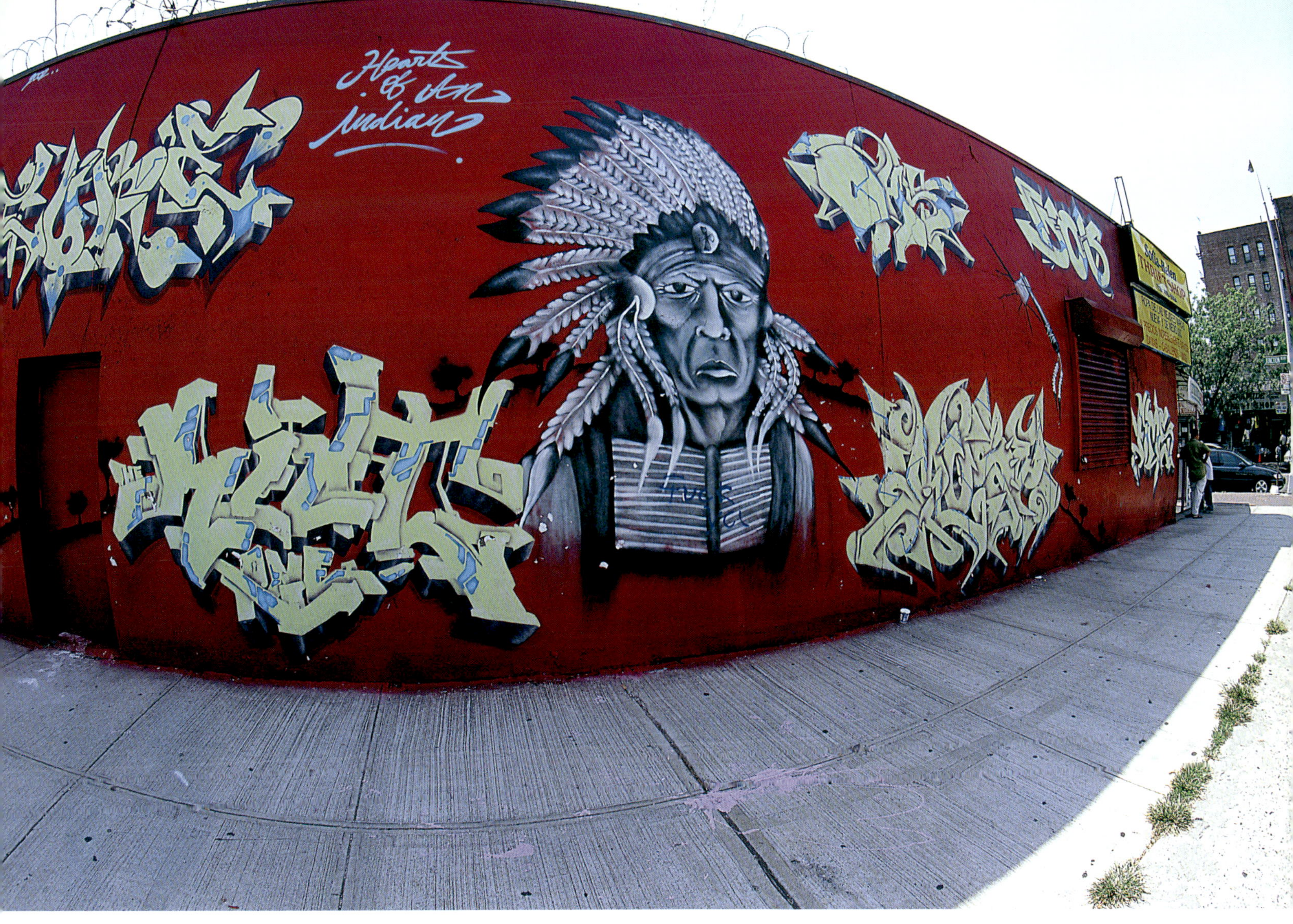

The spirit of an Indian warrior by RIOT, COPE, MUZE, and OH decorates a Queens wall.

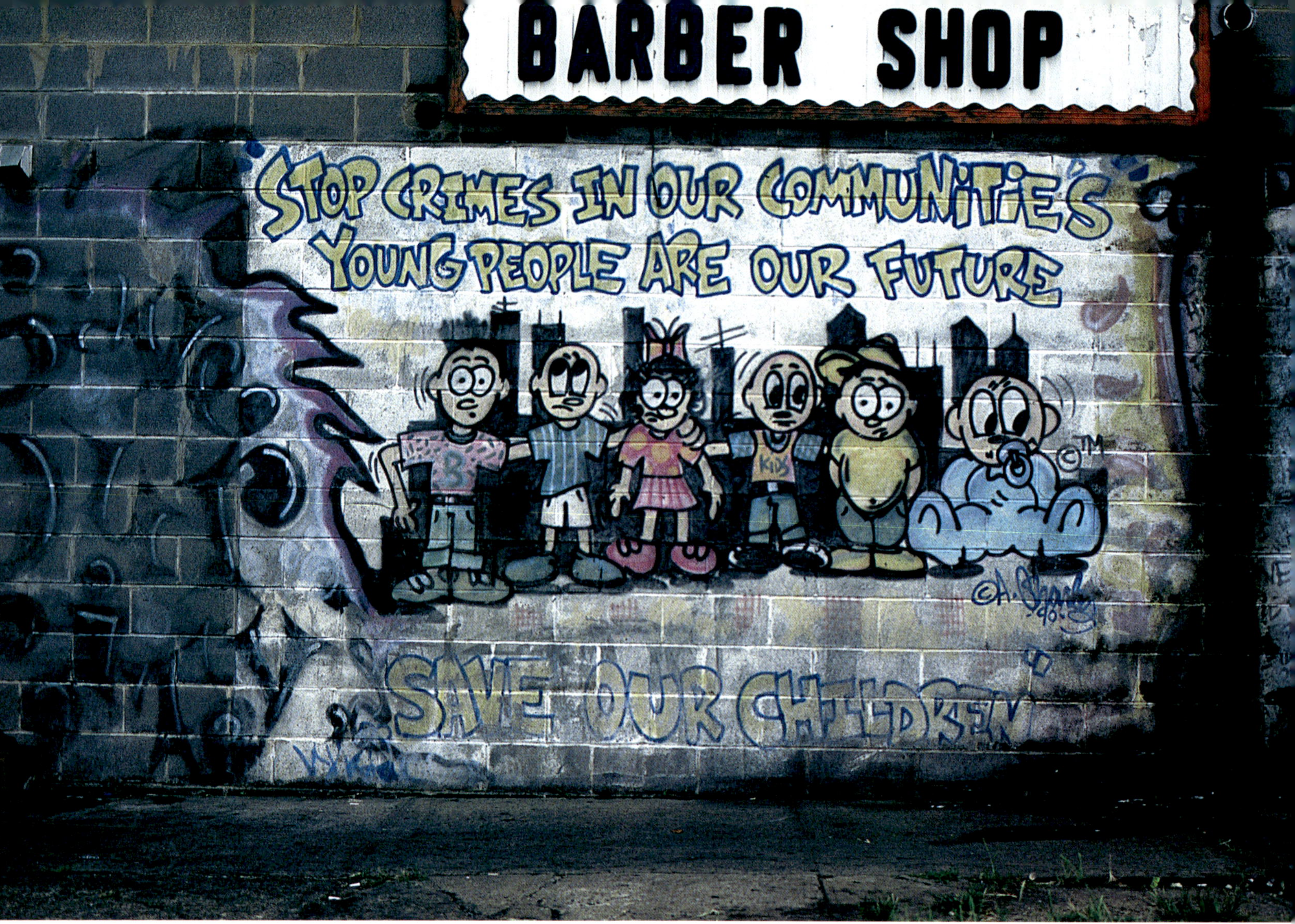

Andre Charles's pitch to stop crime features the charming "urban ghetto baby" Brandon in the company of other community children.

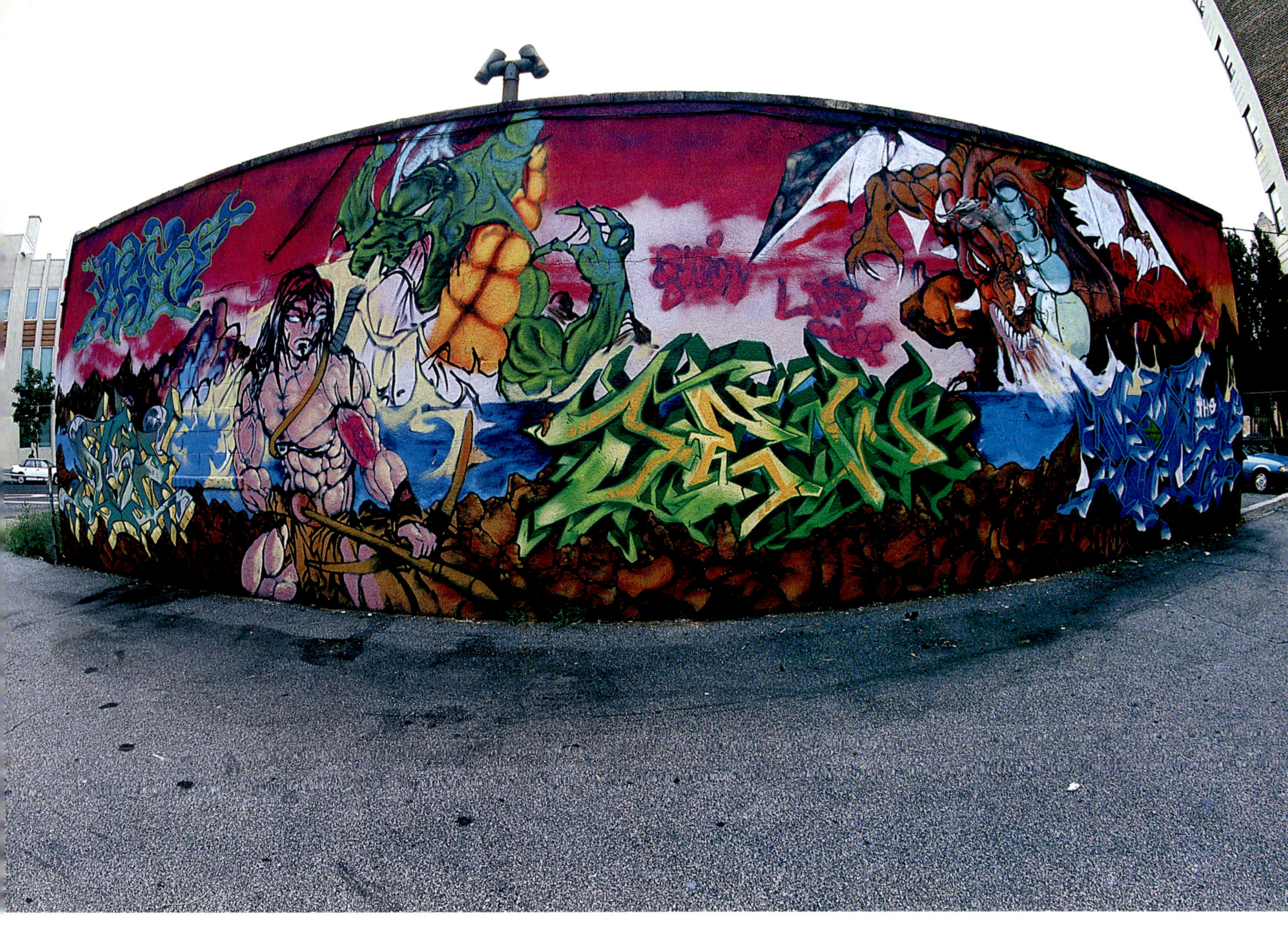

Signed by JEW (also known as WEST 1), a takeoff on comic book characters.

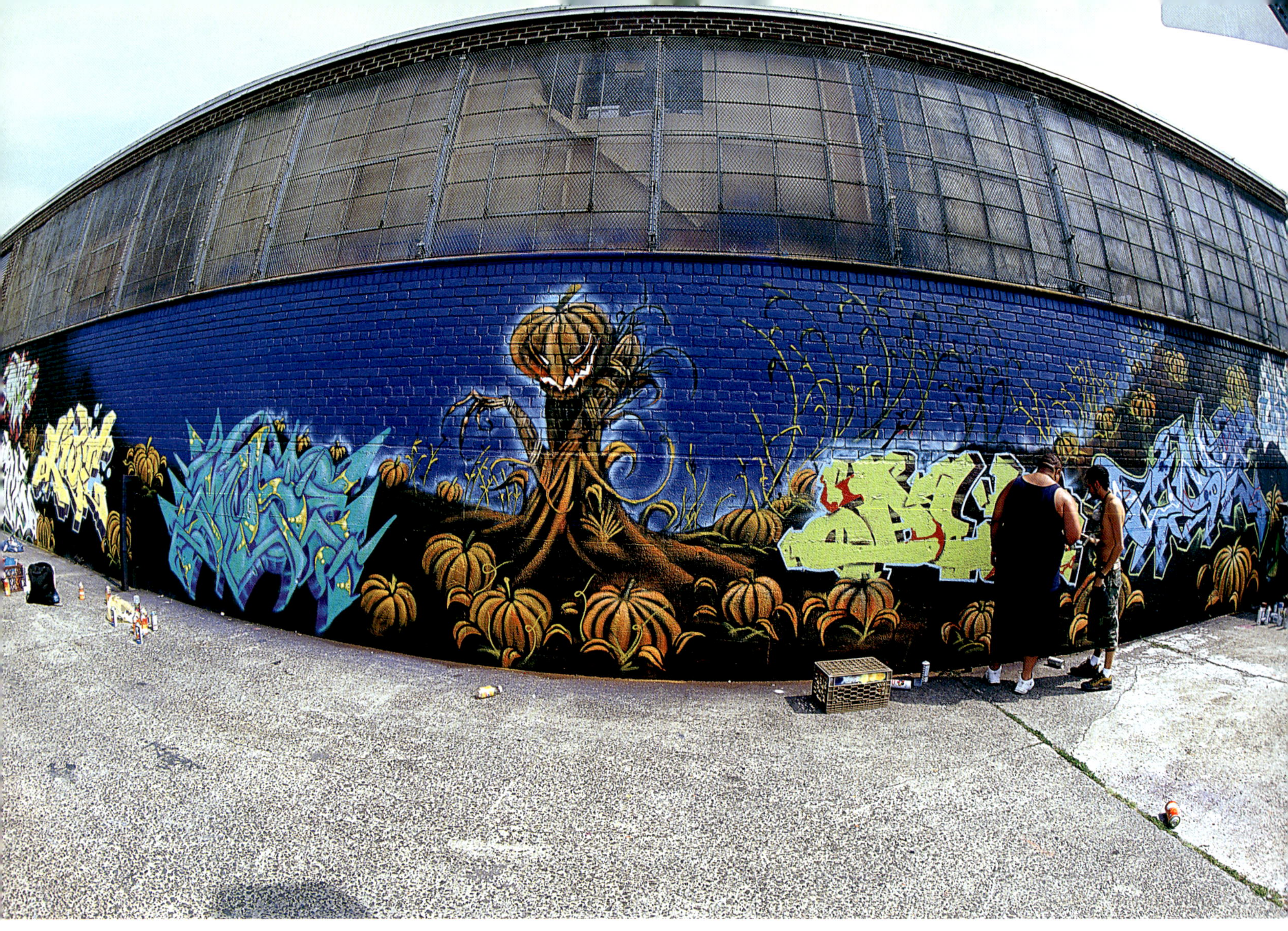

A Halloween mural in progress in Astoria, Queens, by MUZE, COPE, and OH.

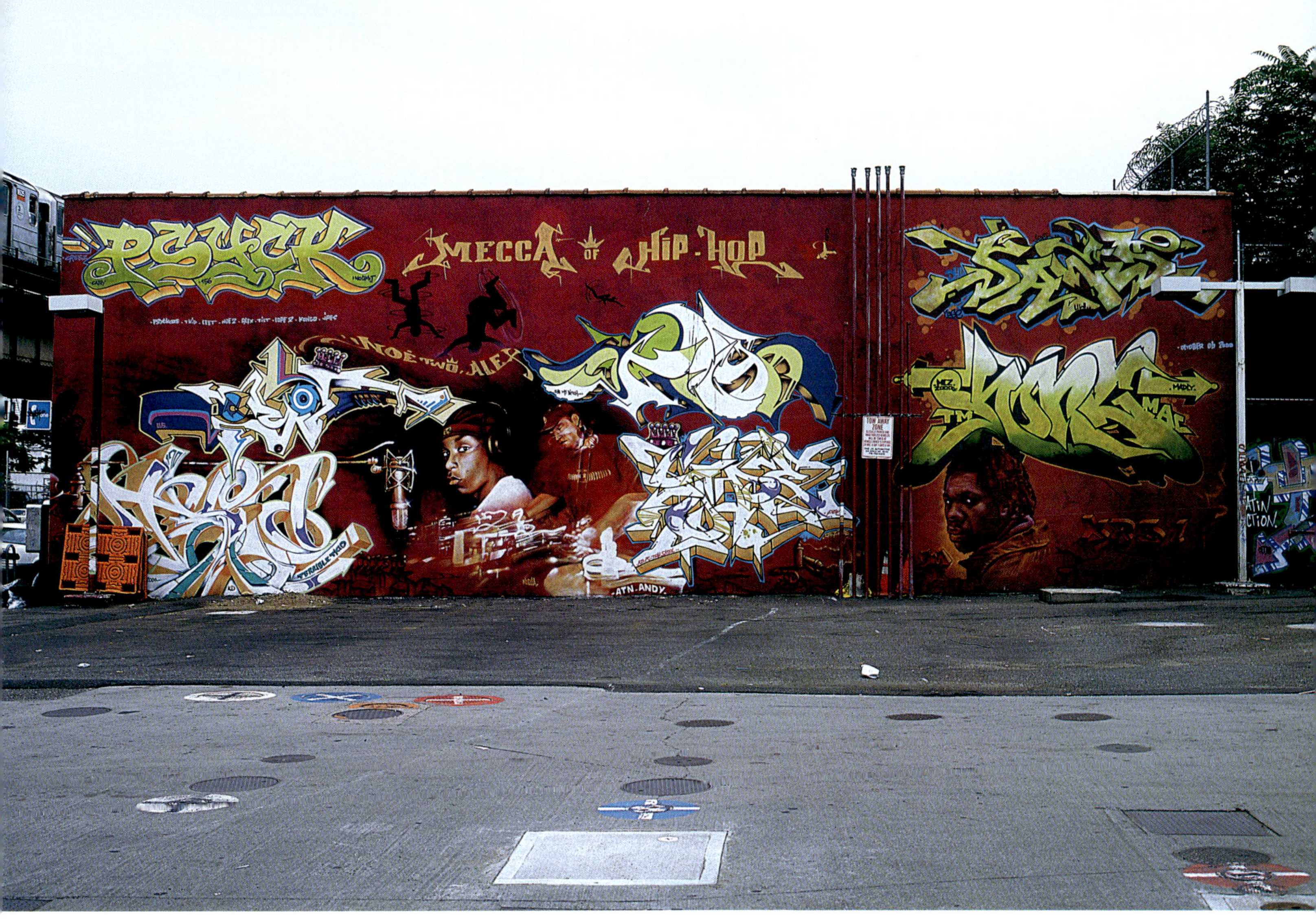

An attention-grabbing monumental mural in the Bronx by PSYCHO, SANE, and AD is a billboard for a hip-hop artist.

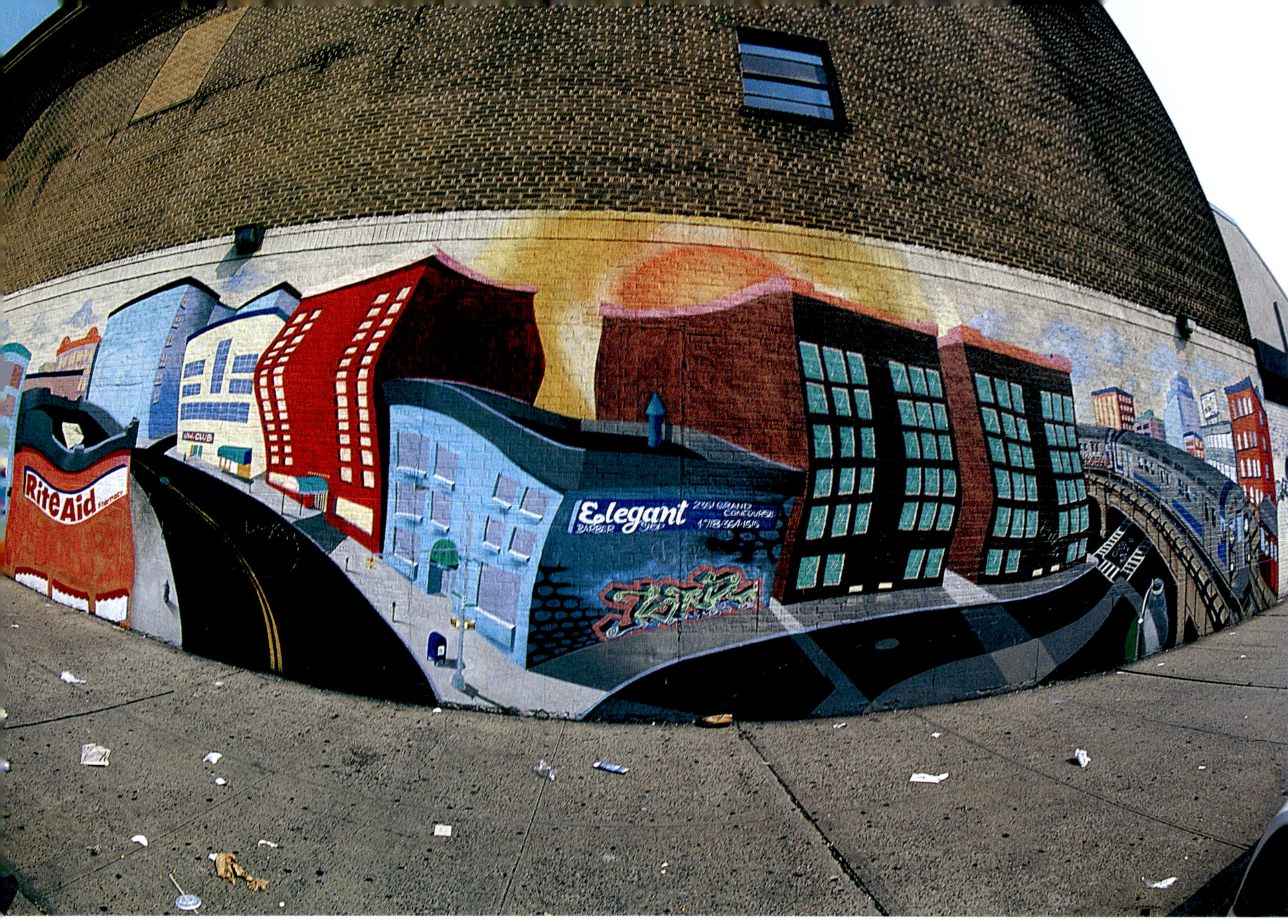

A commissioned mural by a local artist in the Bronx.